You Just Don't Understand

YOU JUST DON'T UNDERSTAND

Women and Men in Conversation

Deborah Tannen, Ph.D.

William Morrow and Company, Inc.

NEW YORK

Ann Landers's column reprinted with permission of Ann Landers, Creators and Los Angeles Times Syndicates.

"In the Crook of His Neck" from *Circling Home,* copyright © 1989 by Cheryl Romney-Brown. Reprinted by permission.

Excerpts from "The Whistle Blower's Morning After," copyright © 1986 by The New York Times Company. Reprinted by permission.

Excerpts from *Fear of Flying* by Erica Jong, copyright © 1973 by Erica Mann Jong. Reprinted by permission of Henry Holt and Company, Inc.

Excerpt from *The Accidental Tourist* by Anne Tyler, copyright © 1985 by Anne Tyler Modarressi. Reprinted by permission of Alfred A. Knopf, Inc.

Excerpts from *Scenes from a Marriage* by Ingmar Bergman, translated by Alan Blair. English translation copyright © 1974 by Alan Blair. Reprinted by permission of Pantheon Books, a division of Random House, Inc.

Excerpts from *In a Different Voice* by Carol Gilligan, copyright © by Carol Gilligan. Reprinted by permission of the author and Harvard University Press. All rights reserved.

Excerpts from "You're Ugly Too" by Lorrie Moore, copyright © 1989 by Lorrie Moore. Reprinted by permission. Originally published in *The New Yorker.*

Excerpts from "Volpone" by Jane Shapiro, copyright © 1987 by Jane Shapiro. Reprinted by permission. Originally published in *The New Yorker.*

Excerpts from *Grown Ups,* copyright by Jules Feiffer. Used by permission of The Lantz Company.

Recognizing the importance of preserving what has been written, it is the policy of William Morrow and Company, Inc., and its imprints and affiliates to have the books it publishes printed on acid-free paper, and we exert our best efforts to that end.

Library of Congress Cataloging-in-Publication Data

Tannen, Deborah.
You just don't understand : women and men in conversation / Deborah Tannen.
p.   cm.
ISBN 0-688-07822-2
1. Communication in marriage.   2. Interpersonal communication.
3. Sex differences (Psychology)   I. Title.
HQ734.T24   1990
302—dc20   89-49000
                                                            CIP

Printed in the United States of America

First Edition

1 2 3 4 5 6 7 8 9 10

BOOK DESIGN BY RICHARD ORIOLO

TO MY FATHER AND MOTHER
SOURCE AND SUSTENANCE

CONTENTS

ACKNOWLEDGMENTS

No usual thanks are sufficient to acknowledge my debt to the generous colleagues who read drafts of this book and improved it with their comments. For these gifts of time and attention, I am grateful to A. L. Becker, Penelope Eckert, Ralph Fasold, Michael Geis, Karl Goldstein, Robin Lakoff, Neal Norrick, Susan Philips, Naomi Tannen, Barrie Thorne, and David Wise.

My debt to Robin Lakoff goes further back. The pioneer in linguistic research on language and gender, she provided a starting point for me, and for a generation of scholars, by blazing a trail that has since branched into many diverging paths of inquiry. Her course at the 1973 Linguistic Institute largely inspired me to become a linguist and to choose as my training ground the University of California, Berkeley, where she was one of my teachers. She has remained a friend, a generous supporter, and a model of a scholar who pursues theoretical research without losing sight of its practical implications.

My gratitude to Ralph Fasold is also far ranging. He has been a continuing and cherished source of intellectual support and challenge, engaging me in dialogue on my research and offering illuminating perspectives, examples, and sources from his own—as well as invaluable computer consulting. I am grateful to Georgetown University for providing me with this perfect colleague and friend.

Also at Georgetown, I thank James Alatis, dean of the School of Languages and Linguistics; my colleagues in the sociolinguistics program; and the students who have listened and contributed to my developing ideas.

Many others were helpful in vital ways, including reading and commenting on parts of drafts, giving examples from their own experience, or discussing ideas with me. Although I list them together, each person's contribution is individually appreciated: Katherine Abramovitz, Steve Barish, Niko Besnier, Tom Brazaitis, Bruce Brigham, Marjorie Brigham, Penelope Brown, Jocelyn Burton, Caroline Celce-Murcia, Andrew Cohen, Bronwyn Davies, Bambi Evans-Murray, Paul Friedrich, Allen Furbeck, Jim Garofallou, John Goldsmith, Paul Goldstein, Marjorie Harness Goodwin, John Guarnaschelli, Annie Hawkinson, Ray Hays, Paul Hopper, Deborah James, Christina Kakava, Judith Katz-Schwartz, Carolyn Kinney, Mark Kohut, Helen Kotsonis, Addie Macovski, Joseph Mahay, Alan Marx, Rachel Myerowitz, Susie Napper, Myriam Nastase, Mandana Navid-Tabrizi, Rebekah Perks, Molly Peterson, PuaPua Ponafala, Dennis Preston, Lucy Ray, Dan Read, Chuck Richardson, Celia Roberts, Joanna Robin, Elif Rosenfeld, Cynthia Roy, Pamela Saunders, Deborah Schiffrin, Gail Schricker, Tom Schricker, Amy Sheldon, Wendy Smith, Kyong Sook Song, Carola Sprengel, Jana Staton, Dorothy Tannen, Eli Tannen, Gary Weaver, Bob Webb, Etsuko Yamada, and Haru Yamada.

I thank Bruce Dorval for the opportunity to analyze his videotapes and transcripts of friends talking and for permission to use excerpts from them. I also thank Suzanne Gluck, who is everything anyone could wish for in an agent and more, and the entire staff of William Morrow and Company, but especially my editor, Maria Guarnaschelli, who has believed passionately in the book from its inception and has lavished on it her boundless enthusiasm and energy.

To my husband, thank you for everything.

E ach person's life is lived as a series of conversations. Analyzing everyday conversations, and their effects on relationships, has been the focus of my career as a sociolinguist. In this book I listen to the voices of women and men. I make sense of seemingly senseless misunderstandings that haunt our relationships, and show that a man and a woman can interpret the same conversation differently, even when there is no apparent misunderstanding. I explain why sincere attempts to communicate are so often confounded, and how we can prevent or relieve some of the frustration.

My book *That's Not What I Meant!* showed that people have different conversational styles. So when speakers from different parts of the country, or of different ethnic or class backgrounds, talk to each other, it is likely that their words will not be understood exactly as they were meant. But we are not required to pair off for life with people from different parts of the country or members of different ethnic groups, though many choose to. We *are* expected to pair off with people of the other gender, and many do, for long periods of time if not for life. And whereas many of us (though fewer and fewer) can spend large portions of our lives without coming into close contact with people of vastly different cultural backgrounds, few people—not even those who have no partners in life or whose primary relationships are with same-sex partners—can avoid close contact with people of the other gender, as relatives and co-workers if not as friends.

That's Not What I Meant! had ten chapters, of which one dealt with gender differences in conversational style. But when I received requests for interviews, articles, and lectures, 90 percent wanted me to focus on 10 percent of the book—the chapter on male-female differences. Everyone wanted to know more about gender and conversational style.

I too wanted to find out more. Indeed, I had decided to become a linguist largely because of a course taught by Robin Lakoff that included her research on gender and language. My first major linguistic study was of gender and cultural differences in indirectness, and I was fairly familiar with others' research on the topic. But although I had always inhabited the outskirts of gender research, I had not leaped into its inner circle, partly because the field is so controversial.

Whenever I write or speak about conversational style differences between women and men, sparks fly. Most people exclaim that what I say is true, that it explains their own experience. They are relieved to learn that what has caused them trouble is a common condition, and there is nothing terribly wrong with them, their partners, or their relationships. Their partners' ways of talking, which they had ascribed to personal failings, could be reframed as reflecting a different system. And their own ways of talking, which their partners had been hounding them about for years, could be defended as logical and reasonable.

But although most people find that my explanation of gender differences in ways of talking accounts for their own experience—and they are eager to offer their own examples to prove it—some people become agitated as soon as they hear a reference to gender. A few become angry at the mere suggestion that women and men are different. And this reaction can come from either women or men.

Some men hear any statement about women and men, coming from a woman, as an accusation—a fancy way of throwing up her hands, as if to say, "You men!" They feel they are being objectified, if not slandered, by being talked about at all.

But it is not only men who bridle at statements about women and men. Some women fear, with justification, that any observation of gender differences will be heard as implying that it is women who are different—different from the standard, which is

14

whatever men are. The male is seen as normative, the female as departing from the norm. And it is only a short step—maybe an inevitable one—from "different" to "worse."

Furthermore, if women's and men's styles are shown to be different, it is usually women who are told to change. I have seen this happen in response to my own work. In an article I wrote for *The Washington Post,* I presented a conversation that had taken place between a couple in their car. The woman had asked, "Would you like to stop for a drink?" Her husband had answered, truthfully, "No," and they hadn't stopped. He was later frustrated to learn that his wife was annoyed because she had wanted to stop for a drink. He wondered, "Why didn't she just say what she wanted? Why did she play games with me?" The wife, I explained, was annoyed not because she had not gotten her way, but because her preference had not been considered. From her point of view, she had shown concern for her husband's wishes, but he had shown no concern for hers.

My analysis emphasized that the husband and wife in this example had different *but equally valid* styles. This point was lost in a heavily edited version of my article that appeared in the *The Toronto Star,* which had me advising: "The woman must realize that when he answers 'yes' or 'no' he is not making a non-negotiable demand." The *Star* editor had deleted the immediately preceding text, which read: "In understanding what went wrong, the man must realize that when she asks what he would like, she is not asking an information question but rather starting a negotiation about what both would like. For her part, however, the woman must realize that . . ." Deft wielding of the editorial knife had transformed my claim that women and men should *both* make adjustments into a claim that women must make a unilateral effort to understand men. Informing women of what they alone must "realize" implies that the man's way is right and the woman's wrong. This edited version was reprinted in a textbook, and the error proliferated.

We all know we are unique individuals, but we tend to see others as representatives of groups. It's a natural tendency, since we must see the world in patterns in order to make sense of it; we wouldn't be able to deal with the daily onslaught of people and objects if we couldn't predict a lot about them and feel that we know who and what they are. But this natural and useful ability to see patterns of similarity has unfortunate consequences. It is offensive to reduce an individual to a category, and it is also misleading. Dividing women and men into categories risks reinforcing this reductionism.

Generalizations, while capturing similarities, obscure differences. Everyone is shaped by innumerable influences such as ethnicity, religion, class, race, age, profession, the geographical regions they and their relatives have lived in, and many other group identities—all mingled with individual personality and predilection. People are apt to sum up others by reference to one category or a few, such as "southern belle," "New York Jewish intellectual," "Boston Brahmin," or "hot-tempered Italian." Although these categories might predict some of the behaviors of the people so described, they miss far more about them than they capture. In innumerable ways, every person is utterly unlike anyone else—including anyone else from many of the same categories.

Despite these dangers, I am joining the growing dialogue on gender and language because the risk of ignoring differences is greater than the danger of naming them. Sweeping something big under the rug doesn't make it go away; it trips you up and sends you sprawling when you venture across the room. Denying real differences can only compound the confusion that is already widespread in this era of shifting and re-forming relationships between women and men.

Pretending that women and men are the same hurts women, because the ways they are treated are based on the norms for men. It also hurts men who, with good intentions, speak to women as they would to men, and are nonplussed when their words don't work as they expected, or even spark resentment and anger.

This paradox is expressed by an American Indian woman, Abby Abinanti, describing why she found law school a difficult and alienating experience:

People did not like or accept the idea of Indians or women being lawyers. Some people could not decide which idea they hated more. Some pretended that it didn't make any difference, that we were all the same. I, too, could be "one of the boys," "one of the white boys." Not likely. Both of these approaches created problems for me.

It is easy to see how people who hate the idea of women or Indians being lawyers would create problems for an Indian woman in law school. It is harder to see how those who wanted to accept her as an equal also created problems for her. Assuming she was the same was destructive, because she was not the same; the assumptions, values, and styles that reflected and validated their identities undercut hers.

The desire to affirm that women are equal has made some scholars reluctant to show they are different, because differences can be used to justify unequal treatment and opportunity. Much as I understand and am in sympathy with those who wish there were no differences between women and men—only reparable social injustice—my research, others' research, and my own and others' experience tell me it simply isn't so. There *are* gender differences in ways of speaking, and we need to identify and understand them. Without such understanding, we are doomed to blame others or ourselves—or the relationship—for the otherwise mystifying and damaging effects of our contrasting conversational styles.

Recognizing gender differences frees individuals from the burden of individual pathology. Many women and men feel dissatisfied with their close relationships and become even more frustrated when they try to talk things out. Taking a *sociolinguistic* approach to relationships makes it possible to explain these dissatisfactions without accusing anyone of being crazy or wrong, and without blaming—or discarding—the relationship. If we recognize and understand the differences beween us, we can take them into account, adjust to, and learn from each other's styles.

The sociolinguistic approach I take in this book shows that

many frictions arise because boys and girls grow up in what are essentially different cultures, so talk between women and men is cross-cultural communication. A cross-cultural approach to gender differences in conversational style differs from the work on gender and language which claims that conversations between men and women break down because men seek to dominate women. No one could deny that men as a class are dominant in our society, and that many individual men seek to dominate women in their lives. And yet male dominance is not the whole story. It is not sufficient to account for everything that happens to women and men in conversations—especially conversations in which both are genuinely trying to relate to each other with attention and respect. The effect of dominance is not always the result of an intention to dominate. That is the news that this book brings.

In this era of opening opportunity, women are beginning to move into positions of authority. At first we assumed they could simply talk the way they always had, but this often doesn't work. Another logical step is that they should change their styles and talk like men. Apart from the repugnance of women's having to do all the changing, this doesn't work either, because women who talk like men are judged differently—and harshly. We have no choice but to examine our choices and their effects. Only by understanding each other's styles and our own options can we begin to realize our opportunities and escape the prison of a monolithic conversational style.

Conversational style differences do not explain all the problems that arise in relationships between women and men. Relationships are sometimes threatened by psychological problems, true failures of love and caring, genuine selfishness—and real effects of political and economic inequity. But there are also innumerable situations in which groundless allegations of these failings are made, simply because partners are expressing their thoughts and feelings, and their assumptions about how to communicate, in different ways. If we can sort out differences based on conversational style, we will be in a better position to confront real conflicts of interest—and to find a shared language in which to negotiate them.

PREFACE

In opening the preface to *That's Not What I Meant!*, I told of a student who said that taking a course I taught at Georgetown University had saved her marriage. Not long ago, the same woman—now a professor, and still married—wrote me a letter. She said that she and her husband had been talking, and somehow the conversation had turned into an argument. In the middle of it he said in exasperation, "Dr. Tannen had better hurry up and write that new book, because this business of men and women talking has got to be the biggest problem around!" In closing this preface, I offer this book to him, and to women and men everywhere who are trying their best to talk to each other.

You Just Don't Understand

ONE

Different Words, Different Worlds

Many years ago I was married to a man who shouted at me, "I do not give you the right to raise your voice to me, because you are a woman and I am a man." This was frustrating, because I knew it was unfair. But I also knew just what was going on. I ascribed his unfairness to his having grown up in a country where few people thought women and men might have equal rights.

Now I am married to a man who is a partner and friend. We come from similar backgrounds and share values and interests. It is a continual source of pleasure to talk to him. It is wonderful to have someone I can tell everything to, someone who understands. But he doesn't always see things as I do, doesn't always react to things as I expect him to. And I often don't understand why he says what he does.

At the time I began working on this book, we had jobs in different cities. People frequently expressed sympathy by making comments like "That must be rough," and "How do you stand it?" I was inclined to accept their sympathy and say things like "We fly a lot." Sometimes I would reinforce their concern: "The worst part is having to pack and unpack all the time." But my husband reacted differently, often with irritation. He might respond by de-emphasizing the inconvenience: As academics, we had four-day weekends together, as well as long vacations throughout the year and four months in the summer. We even benefited from the intervening days of uninterrupted time for work. I once overheard him telling a dubious man that we were lucky, since studies have shown that married couples who live together spend less than half an hour a week talking to each other; he was implying that our situation had advantages.

I didn't object to the way my husband responded—everything he said was true—but I was surprised by it. I didn't understand why he reacted as he did. He explained that he sensed condescension in some expressions of concern, as if the questioner were implying, "Yours is not a real marriage; your ill-chosen profession has resulted in an unfortunate arrangement. I pity you, and look down at you from the height of complacence, since my wife and I have avoided your misfortune." It had not occurred to me that there might be an element of one-upmanship in these expressions of concern, though I could recognize it when it was pointed out. Even after I saw the point, though, I was inclined to regard my husband's response as slightly odd, a personal quirk. He frequently seemed to see others as adversaries when I didn't.

Having done the research that led to this book, I now see that my husband was simply engaging the world in a way that many men do: as an individual in a hierarchical social order in which he was either one-up or one-down. In this world, conversations are negotiations in which people try to achieve and maintain the upper hand if they can, and protect themselves from others' attempts to put them down and push them around. Life, then, is a contest, a struggle to preserve independence and avoid failure.

I, on the other hand, was approaching the world as many women do: as an individual in a network of connections. In this world, conversations are negotiations for closeness in which people try to seek and give confirmation and support, and to reach consensus. They try to protect themselves from others' attempts to push them away. Life, then, is a community, a struggle to preserve intimacy and avoid isolation. Though there are hierarchies in this world too, they are hierarchies more of friendship than of power and accomplishment.

Women are also concerned with achieving status and avoiding failure, but these are not the goals they are *focused* on all the time, and they tend to pursue them in the guise of connection. And men are also concerned with achieving involvement and avoiding isolation, but they are not *focused* on these goals, and they tend to pursue them in the guise of opposition.

Discussing our differences from this point of view, my husband pointed out to me a distinction I had missed: He reacted the way I just described only if expressions of concern came from men in whom he sensed an awareness of hierarchy. And there were times when I too disliked people's expressing sympathy about our commuting marriage. I recall being offended by one man who seemed to have a leering look in his eye when he asked, "How do you manage this long-distance romance?" Another time I was annoyed when a woman who knew me only by reputation approached us during the intermission of a play, discovered our situation by asking my husband where he worked, and kept the conversation going by asking us all about it. In these cases, I didn't feel put down; I felt intruded upon. If my husband was offended by what he perceived as claims to superior status, I felt these sympathizers were claiming inappropriate intimacy.

INTIMACY
AND INDEPENDENCE

Intimacy is key in a world of connection where individuals negotiate complex networks of friendship, minimize differences, try to reach consensus, and avoid the appearance of superiority, which would highlight differences. In a world of status, *independence* is key, because a primary means of establishing status is to tell others what to do, and taking orders is a marker of low status. Though all humans need both intimacy and independence, women tend to focus on the first and men on the second. It is as if their lifeblood ran in different directions.

These differences can give women and men differing views of the same situation, as they did in the case of a couple I will call Linda and Josh. When Josh's old high-school chum called him at work and announced he'd be in town on business the following month, Josh invited him to stay for the weekend. That evening he informed Linda that they were going to have a houseguest, and that he and his chum would go out together the first night to shoot the breeze like old times. Linda was upset. She was going to be away on business the week before, and the Friday night when Josh would be out with his chum would be her first night home. But what upset her the most was that Josh had made these plans on his own and informed her of them, rather than discussing them with her before extending the invitation.

Linda would never make plans, for a weekend or an evening, without first checking with Josh. She can't understand why he doesn't show her the same courtesy and consideration that she shows him. But when she protests, Josh says, "I can't say to my friend, 'I have to ask my wife for permission'!"

To Josh, checking with his wife means seeking permission, which implies that he is not independent, not free to act on his own. It would make him feel like a child or an underling. To

Linda, checking with her husband has nothing to do with permission. She assumes that spouses discuss their plans with each other because their lives are intertwined, so the actions of one have consequences for the other. Not only does Linda not mind telling someone, "I have to check with Josh"; quite the contrary—she likes it. It makes her feel good to know and show that she is involved with someone, that her life is bound up with someone else's.

Linda and Josh both felt more upset by this incident, and others like it, than seemed warranted, because it cut to the core of their primary concerns. Linda was hurt because she sensed a failure of closeness in their relationship: He didn't care about her as much as she cared about him. And he was hurt because he felt she was trying to control him and limit his freedom.

A similar conflict exists between Louise and Howie, another couple, about spending money. Louise would never buy anything costing more than a hundred dollars without discussing it with Howie, but he goes out and buys whatever he wants and feels they can afford, like a table saw or a new power mower. Louise is disturbed, not because she disapproves of the purchases, but because she feels he is acting as if she were not in the picture.

Many women feel it is natural to consult with their partners at every turn, while many men automatically make more decisions without consulting their partners. This may reflect a broad difference in conceptions of decision making. Women expect decisions to be discussed first and made by consensus. They appreciate the discussion itself as evidence of involvement and communication. But many men feel oppressed by lengthy discussions about what they see as minor decisions, and they feel hemmed in if they can't just act without talking first. When women try to initiate a freewheeling discussion by asking, "What do you think?" men often think they are being asked to decide.

Communication is a continual balancing act, juggling the conflicting needs for intimacy and independence. To survive in the world, we have to act in concert with others, but to survive as ourselves, rather than simply as cogs in a wheel, we have to act alone. In some ways, all people are the same: We all eat and sleep and drink and laugh and cough, and often we eat, and laugh at, the same things. But in some ways, each person is different, and individuals' differing wants and preferences may conflict with each other. Offered the same menu, people make different choices. And if there is cake for dessert, there is a chance one person may get a larger piece than another—and an even greater chance that one will *think* the other's piece is larger, whether it is or not.

ASYMMETRIES

If intimacy says, "We're close and the same," and independence says, "We're separate and different," it is easy to see that intimacy and independence dovetail with connection and status. The essential element of connection is symmetry: People are the same, feeling equally close to each other. The essential element of status is asymmetry: People are not the same; they are differently placed in a hierarchy.

This duality is particularly clear in expressions of sympathy or concern, which are all potentially ambiguous. They can be interpreted either symmetrically, as evidence of fellow feeling among equals, or asymmetrically, offered by someone one-up to someone one-down. Asking if an unemployed person has found a job, if a couple have succeeded in conceiving the child they crave, or whether an untenured professor expects to get tenure can be meant—and interpreted, regardless of how it is meant—as an expression of human connection by a person who understands and cares, or as a reminder of weakness from someone who is better off and knows it, and hence as condescending. The latter view of sympathy seems self-evident to many men. For example, a handicapped mountain climber named Tom Whittaker, who leads groups of disabled people on outdoor expeditions, remarked, "You can't feel sympathetic for someone you admire"— a statement that struck me as not true at all.

The symmetry of connection is what creates community: If two people are struggling for closeness, they are both struggling for the same thing. And the asymmetry of status is what creates contest: Two people can't both have the upper hand, so negotiation for status is inherently adversarial. In my earlier work, I explored in detail the dynamics of intimacy (which I referred to as involvement) and independence, but I tended to ignore the force of status and its adversarial nature. Once I identified these dynamics, however, I saw them all around me. The puzzling behavior of friends and co-workers finally became comprehensible.

Differences in how my husband and I approached the same situation, which previously would have been mystifying, suddenly made sense. For example, in a jazz club the waitress recommended the crab cakes to me, and they turned out to be terrible. I was uncertain about whether or not to send them back. When the waitress came by and asked how the food was, I said that I didn't really like the crab cakes. She asked, "What's wrong with them?" While staring at the table, my husband answered, "They don't taste fresh." The waitress snapped, "They're frozen! What do you expect?" I looked directly up at her and said, "We just don't like them." She said, "Well, if you don't like them, I could take them back and bring you something else."

After she left with the crab cakes, my husband and I laughed because we realized we had just automatically played out the scripts I had been writing about. He had heard her question "What's wrong with them?" as a challenge that he had to match. He doesn't like to fight, so he looked away, to soften what he felt was an obligatory counterchallenge: He felt instinctively that he had to come up with something wrong with the crab cakes to justify my complaint. (He was fighting for me.) I had taken the question "What's wrong with them?" as a request for information. I instinctively sought a way to be right without making her wrong. Perhaps it was because she was a woman that she responded more favorably to my approach.

When I have spoken to friends and to groups about these

differences, they too say that now they can make sense of previously perplexing behavior. For example, a woman said she finally understood why her husband refused to talk to his boss about whether or not he stood a chance of getting promoted. He wanted to know because if the answer was no, he would start looking for another job. But instead of just asking, he stewed and fretted, lost sleep, and worried. Having no others at her disposal, this wife had fallen back on psychological explanations: Her husband must be insecure, afraid of rejection. But then, everyone is insecure, to an extent. Her husband was actually quite a confident person. And she, who believed herself to be at least as insecure as he, had not hesitated to go to her boss to ask whether he intended to make her temporary job permanent.

Understanding the key role played by status in men's relations made it all come clear. Asking a boss about chances for promotion highlights the hierarchy in the relationship, reminding them both that the employee's future is in the boss's hands. Taking the low-status position made this man intensely uncomfortable. Although his wife didn't especially relish taking the role of supplicant with respect to her boss, it didn't set off alarms in her head, as it did in his.

In a similar flash of insight, a woman who works in sales exclaimed that now she understood the puzzling transformation that the leader of her sales team had undergone when he was promoted to district manager. She had been sure he would make a perfect boss because he had a healthy disregard for authority. As team leader, he had rarely bothered to go to meetings called by management and had encouraged team members to exercise their own judgment, eagerly using his power to waive regulations on their behalf. But after he became district manager, this man was unrecognizable. He instituted more regulations than anyone had dreamed of, and insisted that exceptions could be made only on the basis of written requests to him.

This man behaved differently because he was now differently placed in the hierarchy. When he had been subject to the authority of management, he'd done all he could to limit it. But when the authority of management was vested in him, he did all he could to enlarge it. By avoiding meetings and flouting regulations, he had evidenced not disregard for hierarchy but rather discomfort at being in the subordinate position within it.

Yet another woman said she finally understood why her fiancé, who very much believes in equality, once whispered to her that she should keep her voice down. "My friends are downstairs," he said. "I don't want them to get the impression that you order me around."

That women have been labeled "nags" may result from the interplay of men's and women's styles, whereby many women are inclined to do what is asked of them and many men are inclined to resist even the slightest hint that anyone, especially a woman, is telling them what to do. A women will be inclined to repeat a request that doesn't get a response because she is convinced that her husband would do what she asks, if he only understood that she *really* wants him to do it. But a man who wants to avoid feeling that he is following orders may instinctively wait before doing what she asked, in order to imagine that he is doing it of his own free will. Nagging is the result, because each time she repeats the request, he again puts off fulfilling it.

THE MIXED METAMESSAGES OF HELP

Emily and Jacob were planning their wedding themselves, but Emily's parents were footing a large part of the bill. Concerned that things come out right, her parents frequently called and asked detailed questions about the prices they were paying and the service they were getting: What hors d'oeuvres would be served? How many pieces would be provided per guest? What did dinner include? Would celery and olives be placed on each table? What flowers would be on the tables? Had all this been put in writing? Emily and Jacob heard the detailed questions as implying that the wedding was poised on the brink of disaster because they were not competent to arrange it. In response to Emily's protests, her mother explained, "We want to be part of the planning; we want to help."

As with offers of sympathy, there is always a paradox entailed in offering or giving help. Insofar as it serves the needs of the one helped, it is a generous move that shows caring and builds rapport. But insofar as it is asymmetrical, giving help puts one person in a superior position with respect to the other. Borrowing the terminology of Gregory Bateson, we may regard the help as the *message*—the obvious meaning of the act. But at the same time, the act of helping sends *metamessages*—that is, information about the relations among the people involved, and their attitudes toward what they are saying or doing and the people they are saying or doing it to. In other words, the message of helping says, "This is good for you." But the fact of giving help may seem to send the metamessage "I am more competent than you," and in that sense it is good for the helper.

In interpreting the metamessages of status and connection in a particular instance of giving help, or any communication act, much depends on how things are done and said. For example, in an expression of sympathy, how comments are worded, in what tone of voice they are spoken, accompanied by what facial expressions and gestures all determine the impression made. All these signals send metamessages about how the communication is meant. A "soothing" pat might reinforce the impression of condescension; a look of great concern might intensify the impression that the other person is in deep trouble; an offhand smile might suggest instead that a question is intended as concern between equals.

The conflicting metamessages inherent in giving help become especially apparent when people are in a hierarchical relationship to each other by virtue of their jobs. Just as parents are often frustrated in attempts to be their children's "friends," so bosses who try to give friendly advice to subordinates may find that their words, intended symmetrically, are interpreted through an asymmetrical filter. For example, the director of a residential facility for retarded people was sympathetic to complaints by staff members about their low wages, so he spoke at a meeting with what he thought was forthrightness and concern. He leveled with them by admitting that their jobs would never pay enough to support a family. He also told them they would not be able to advance to higher-paying jobs if they did not have graduate degrees. As their friend, he advised that if they wanted jobs that could lead to more lucrative careers, they would have to find different jobs. The staff did not appreciate their director's candor, because they did not receive his communication as an expression of concern for their welfare coming from a peer. Rather, they heard it as a threat from a boss: "If you don't like it here, you can jolly well leave."

FRAMING

Another way to think about metamessages is that they *frame* a conversation, much as a picture frame provides a context for the images in the picture. Metamessages let you know how to interpret what someone is saying by identifying the activity that is going on: Is this an argument or a chat? Is it helping, advising, or scolding? At the same time, they let you know what position the speaker is assuming in the activity, and what position you are being assigned.

Sociologist Erving Goffman uses the term *alignment* to express this aspect of framing. If you put me down, you are taking a superior alignment with respect to me. Furthermore, by showing the alignment that you take with regard to others, what you say frames you, just as you are framing what you say. For example, if you talk to others as if you were a teacher and they were your students, they may perceive that your way of talking frames you as condescending or pedantic. If you talk to others as if you were a student seeking help and explanations, they may perceive you as insecure, incompetent, or naïve. Our reactions to what others say or do are often sparked by how we feel we are being framed.

THE MODERN FACE
OF CHIVALRY

Framing is key in the following commonplace scene. A car is moving slowly down the street while another is edging out of a parking spot. The driver of the parked car hesitates, but the driver of the other car stops and signals, with a hand wave, that he is yielding the right-of-way. If the driver of the parked car is a woman, chances are she will smile her thanks and proceed while the gallant man waits. But if the driver of the parked car is a man, he may well return wave for wave and insist on waiting himself, even if, under other circumstances, he might try to move out quickly before an advancing car got in his way.

The chivalrous man who holds a door open or signals a woman to go ahead of him when he's driving is negotiating both status and connection. The status difference is implied by a me-tamessage of control: The woman gets to proceed not because it is her right but because he has granted her permission, so she is being framed as subordinate. Furthermore, those in a position to grant privileges are also in a position to change their minds and take them away. This is the dimension to which some women respond when they protest gallant gestures as "chauvinist." Those who appreciate such gestures as "polite" see only the connection: He's being nice. And it is also the dimension the man performing the generous gesture is likely to see, and the reason he may be understandably incensed if his polite gesture sparks protest rather than thanks.

But if being allowed to proceed in traffic is simply a polite gesture that gives one an advantage, why do so many men decline the gift of the right-of-way and gesture the other car, or a pedestrian, to proceed ahead of them instead? Because waving another person on in traffic also preserves independence: The driver is deciding on his own course of action, rather than being told what to do by someone else.

THE PROTECTIVE FRAME

A protective gesture from a man reinforces the traditional alignment by which men protect women. But a protective gesture from a woman suggests a different scenario: one in which women protect children. That's why many men resist women's efforts to reciprocate protectiveness—it can make them feel that they are being framed as children. These underlying dynamics create sense out of what otherwise seem to be senseless arguments between women and men.

Here is an example of a momentary gesture that led to momentous frustration. Sandra was driving, and Maurice was sitting in the seat beside her. When she had to brake suddenly, she did what her father had always done if he had to stop suddenly when Sandra was sitting beside him: At the moment she braked, she extended her right arm to protect the person beside her from falling forward.

This gesture was mostly symbolic. Sandra's right arm was not strong enough to restrain Maurice. Perhaps its main function was simply to alert him that she was stopping unexpectedly. In any case, the gesture had become for her, as it was for her father, automatic, and it made her feel competent and considerate. But it infuriated Maurice. The explanation he gave was that she should keep both hands on the wheel for reasons of safety. She knew she did not lose control of the car when she extended her arm, so they never could settle this difference. Eventually she trained herself to resist this impulse with Maurice to avoid a fight, but she felt sadly constrained by what she saw as his irrational reaction.

Though Maurice explained his reaction in terms of safety,

he was actually responding to the framing implied by the gesture. He felt belittled, treated like a child, because by extending her arm to break his fall, Sandra was protecting him. In fact, Maurice was already feeling uncomfortable about sitting passively while Sandra was driving, even though it was her car. Many men and women who feel they have achieved equality in their relationship find that whenever they get into a car together, she automatically heads for the passenger seat and he for the driver's; she drives only when he is not there.

The act of protecting frames the protector as dominant and the protected as subordinate. But the status difference signaled by this alignment may be more immediately apparent to men. As a result, women who are thinking in terms of connection may talk and behave in ways that accept protection, unaware that others may see them as taking a subordinate position.

DIFFERENT MEANS TO THE SAME END

Both status and connection can be used as means to get things done by talking. Suppose you want to get an appointment with a plumber who is fully booked for a month. You may use strategies that manipulate your connections or your differences in status. If you opt for status, you may operate either as one-down or one-up. For example, one-up: You let it be known that you are an important person, a city official who has influence in matters such as licensing and permits that the plumber has need of. Or one-down: You plaintively inform the receptionist that you are new in town, and you have no neighbors or relatives to whom you could turn to take a shower or use the facilities. You hope she will feel sorry for you and give you special consideration. Whether you take a one-up or one-down stance, both these approaches play on differences in status by acknowledging that the two people involved are in asymmetrical relation to each other.

On the other hand, you could try reinforcing your sameness.

If you are from the same town as the plumber's receptionist, or if you are both from the same country or cultural group, you may engage her in talk about your hometown, or speak in your home dialect or language, hoping that this will remind her that you come from the same community so she will give you special consideration. If you know someone she knows, you may mention that person and hope this will create a feeling of closeness that will make her want to do something special for you. This is why it is useful to have a personal introduction to someone you want to meet, to transform you from a stranger into someone with whom there is a personal connection.

The example of talking to a plumber's receptionist illustrates options that are available whenever anyone tries to get something done. Ways of talking are rarely if ever composed entirely of one approach or the other, but rather are composed of both and interpretable as either. For example, many people consider name-dropping to be a matter of status: "Look how important I am, because I know important people." But it is also a play on intimacy and close connections. Claiming to know someone famous is a bit like claiming to know someone's mother or cousin or childhood friend—an attempt to gain approval by showing that you know someone whom others also know. In name-dropping they don't actually know the people named, but they know *of* them. You are playing on connections, in the sense that you bring yourself closer to the people you are talking to by showing you know someone they know of; but to the extent that you make yourself more important by showing you *know* someone they have *only heard* of, you are playing on status.

Much—even most—meaning in conversation does not reside in the words spoken at all, but is filled in by the person listening. Each of us decides whether we think others are speaking in the spirit of differing status or symmetrical connection. The likelihood that individuals will tend to interpret someone else's words as one or the other depends more on the hearer's own focus, concerns, and habits than on the spirit in which the words were intended.

WHO'S DECEPTIVE?

In regarding these varying but related approaches to human relationships, people tend to sense that one or the other is the real dynamic. One man, on hearing my analysis of ways of talking to the plumber, commented, "Wouldn't using solidarity be deceptive?" If, like many men, one believes that human relations are fundamentally hierarchical, then playing on connection rather than status amounts to "pretending" there is no status—in other words, being deceptive. But those who tend to regard connection as the basic dynamic operating between people see attempts to use status differences as manipulative and unfair.

Both status and connection are ways of being involved with others and showing involvement with others, although those who are focused on one may not see the other as a means of involvement. Men are more often inclined to focus on the jockeying for status in a conversation: Is the other person trying to be one-up or put me down? Is he trying to establish a dominant position by getting me to do his bidding? Women are more often attuned to the negotiation of connections: Is the other person trying to get closer or pull away? Since both elements are always present, it is easy for women and men to focus on different elements in the same conversation.

MIXED JUDGMENTS AND MISJUDGMENTS

Because men and women are regarding the landscape from contrasting vantage points, the same scene can appear very different to them, and they often have opposite interpretations of the same action.

A colleague mentioned that he got a letter from a production editor working on his new book, instructing him to let her know if he planned to be away from his permanent address at any time in the next six months, when his book would be in production. He commented that he hadn't realized how like a parole officer a production editor could be. His response to this letter surprised me, because I have received similar letters from publishers, and my response is totally different: I like them, because it makes me feel important to know that my whereabouts matter. When I mentioned this difference to my colleague, he was puzzled and amused, as I was by his reaction. Though he could understand my point of view intellectually, emotionally he could not imagine how one could not feel framed as both controlled and inferior in rank by being told to report one's movements to someone. And though I could understand his perspective intellectually, it simply held no emotional resonance for me.

In a similar spirit, my colleague remarked that he had read a journal article written by a woman who thanked her husband in the acknowledgments section of her paper for helpful discussion of the topic. When my colleague first read this acknowledgment, he thought the author must be incompetent, or at least insecure: Why did she have to consult her husband about her own work? Why couldn't she stand on her own two feet? After hearing my explanation that women value evidence of connection, he reframed the acknowledgment and concluded that the author probably valued her husband's involvement in her work and made reference to it with the pride that comes of believing one has evidence of a balanced relationship.

If my colleague's reaction is typical, imagine how often women who think they are displaying a positive quality—connection— are misjudged by men who perceive them as revealing a lack of independence, which the men regard as synonymous with incompetence and insecurity.

IN PURSUIT OF FREEDOM

A woman was telling me why a long-term relationship had ended. She recounted a recurrent and pivotal conversation. She and the man she lived with had agreed that they would both be free, but they would not do anything to hurt each other. When the man began to sleep with other women, she protested, and he was incensed at her protest. Their conversation went like this:

SHE: How can you do this when you know it's hurting me?
HE: How can you try to limit my freedom?
SHE: But it makes me feel awful.
HE: You are trying to manipulate me.

On one level, this is simply an example of a clash of wills: What he wanted conflicted with what she wanted. But in a fundamental way, it reflects the difference in focus I have been describing. In arguing for his point of view, the key issue for this man was his independence, his freedom of action. The key issue for the woman was their interdependence—how what he did made her feel. He interpreted her insistence on their interdependence as "manipulation": She was using her feelings to control his behavior.

The point is not that women do not value freedom or that men do not value their connection to others. It is rather that the desire for freedom and independence becomes more of an issue for many men in relationships, whereas interdependence and connection become more of an issue for many women. The difference is one of focus and degree.

In a study of how women and men talk about their divorces, Catherine Kohler Riessman found that both men and women mentioned increased freedom as a benefit of divorce. But the word *freedom* meant different things to them. When women told her they had gained freedom by divorce, they meant that they had gained "independence and autonomy." It was a relief for them

40

not to have to worry about how their husbands would react to what they did, and not have to be "responsive to a disgruntled spouse." When men mentioned freedom as a benefit of divorce, they meant freedom from obligation—the relief of feeling "less confined," less "claustrophobic," and having "fewer responsibilities."

Riessman's findings illuminate the differing burdens that are placed on women and men by their characteristic approaches to relationships. The burden from which divorce delivered the women was perceived as internally motivated: the continual preoccupation with how their husbands would respond to them and how they should respond to their husbands. The burden from which it delivered the men was perceived as externally imposed: the obligations of the provider role and a feeling of confinement from having their behavior constrained by others. Independence was not a gift of divorce for the men Riessman interviewed, because, as one man put it, "I always felt independent and I guess it's just more so now."

The Chronicle of Higher Education conducted a small survey, asking six university professors why they had chosen the teaching profession. Among the six were four men and two women. In answering the question, the two women referred to teaching. One said, "I've always wanted to teach." The other said, "I knew as an undergraduate that I wanted to join a faculty. . . . I realized that teaching was the thing I wanted to do." The four men's answers had much in common with each other and little in common with the women's. All four men referred to independence as their main motive. Here are excerpts from each of their responses:

I decided it was academe over industry because I would have my choice of research. There's more independence.

I wanted to teach, and I like the freedom to set your own research goals.

I chose an academic job because the freedoms of academia

outweighed the money disadvantages—and to pursue the research interest I'd like to, as opposed to having it dictated.

> I have a problem that interests me. . . . I'd rather make $30,000 for the rest of my life and be allowed to do basic research than to make $100,000 and work in computer graphics.

Though one man also mentioned teaching, neither of the women mentioned freedom to pursue their own research interests as a main consideration. I do not believe this means that women are not interested in research, but rather that independence, freedom from being told what to do, is not as significant a preoccupation for them.

In describing what appealed to them about teaching, these two women focused on the ability to influence students in a positive way. Of course, influencing students reflects a kind of power over them, and teaching entails an asymmetrical relationship, with the teacher in the higher-status position. But in talking about their profession, the women focused on connection to students, whereas the men focused on their freedom from others' control.

MALE-FEMALE CONVERSATION IS CROSS-CULTURAL COMMUNICATION

If women speak and hear a language of connection and intimacy, while men speak and hear a language of status and independence, then communication between men and women can be like cross-cultural communication, prey to a clash of conversational styles. Instead of different dialects, it has been said they speak different genderlects.

The claim that men and women grow up in different worlds may at first seem patently absurd. Brothers and sisters grow up in the same families, children to parents of both genders. Where, then, do women and men learn different ways of speaking and hearing?

IT BEGINS AT THE BEGINNING

Even if they grow up in the same neighborhood, on the same block, or in the same house, girls and boys grow up in different worlds of words. Others talk to them differently and expect and accept different ways of talking from them. Most important, children learn how to talk, how to have conversations, not only from their parents but from their peers. After all, if their parents have a foreign or regional accent, children do not emulate it; they learn to speak with the pronunciation of the region where they grow up. Anthropologists Daniel Maltz and Ruth Borker summarize research showing that boys and girls have very different ways of talking to their friends. Although they often play together, boys and girls spend most of their time playing in same-sex groups. And, although some of the activities they play at are similar, their favorite games are different, and their ways of using language in their games are separated by a world of difference.

Boys tend to play outside, in large groups that are hierarchically structured. Their groups have a leader who tells others what to do and how to do it, and resists doing what other boys propose. It is by giving orders and making them stick that high status is negotiated. Another way boys achieve status is to take center stage by telling stories and jokes, and by sidetracking or challenging the stories and jokes of others. Boys' games have winners and losers and elaborate systems of rules that are frequently the subjects of arguments. Finally, boys are frequently heard to boast of their skill and argue about who is best at what.

Girls, on the other hand, play in small groups or in pairs; the center of a girl's social life is a best friend. Within the group, intimacy is key: Differentiation is measured by relative closeness. In their most frequent games, such as jump rope and hopscotch, everyone gets a turn. Many of their activities (such as playing house) do not have winners or losers. Though some girls are certainly more skilled than others, girls are expected not to boast about it, or show that they think they are better than the others. Girls don't give orders; they express their preferences as suggestions, and suggestions are likely to be accepted. Whereas boys say, "Gimme that!" and "Get outta here!" girls say, "Let's do this," and "How about doing that?" Anything else is put down as "bossy." They don't grab center stage—they don't want it—so they don't challenge each other directly. And much of the time, they simply sit together and talk. Girls are not accustomed to jockeying for status in an obvious way; they are more concerned that they be liked.

Gender differences in ways of talking have been described by researchers observing children as young as three. Amy Sheldon videotaped three- to four-year-old boys and girls playing in threesomes at a day-care center. She compared two groups of three—one of boys, one of girls—that got into fights about the same play item: a plastic pickle. Though both groups fought over the same thing, the dynamics by which they negotiated their conflicts were different. In addition to illustrating some of the patterns I have just described, Sheldon's study also demonstrates the complexity of these dynamics.

While playing in the kitchen area of the day-care center, a little girl named Sue wanted the pickle that Mary had, so she argued that Mary should give it up because Lisa, the third girl, wanted it. This led to a conflict about how to satisfy Lisa's (invented) need. Mary proposed a compromise, but Sue protested:

MARY: I cut it in half. One for Lisa, one for me, one for me.
SUE: But, Lisa wants a *whole* pickle!

Mary comes up with another creative compromise, which Sue also rejects:

MARY: Well, it's a whole *half* pickle.
SUE: No, it isn't.

MARY: Yes, it is, a whole *half* pickle.
  SUE: *I'll* give her a whole half. I'll give her a *whole whole*.
     I gave her a whole one.

At this point, Lisa withdraws from the alliance with Sue, who satisfies herself by saying, "I'm pretending I gave you one."

On another occasion, Sheldon videotaped three boys playing in the same kitchen play area, and they too got into a fight about the plastic pickle. When Nick saw that Kevin had the pickle, he demanded it for himself:

NICK: [Screams] Kevin, but the, oh, I *have* to cut! I want to cut it! It's mine!

Like Sue, Nick involved the third child in his effort to get the pickle:

NICK: [Whining to Joe] Kevin is not letting me cut the pickle.
  JOE: Oh, I know! I can pull it away from him and give it back to you. That's an idea!

The boys' conflict, which lasted two and a half times longer than the girls', then proceeded as a struggle between Nick and Joe on the one hand and Kevin on the other.

In comparing the boys' and girls' pickle fights, Sheldon points out that, for the most part, the girls mitigated the conflict and preserved harmony by compromise and evasion. Conflict was more prolonged among the boys, who used more insistence, appeals to rules, and threats of physical violence. However, to say that these little girls and boys used *more* of one strategy or another is not to say that they didn't use the other strategies at all. For example, the boys did attempt compromise, and the girls did attempt physical force. The girls, like the boys, were struggling for control of their play. When Sue says by mistake, "*I'll* give her a whole half," then quickly corrects herself to say, "I'll give her a *whole whole*," she reveals that it is not really the size of the portion that is important to her, but who gets to serve it.

While reading Sheldon's study, I noticed that whereas both

Nick and Sue tried to get what they wanted by involving a third child, the alignments they created with the third child, and the dynamics they set in motion, were fundamentally different. Sue appealed to Mary to fulfill someone else's desire; rather than saying that *she* wanted the pickle, she claimed that Lisa wanted it. Nick asserted his own desire for the pickle, and when he couldn't get it on his own, he appealed to Joe to get it for him. Joe then tried to get the pickle by force. In both these scenarios, the children were enacting complex lines of affiliation.

Joe's strong-arm tactics were undertaken not on his own behalf but, chivalrously, on behalf of Nick. By making an appeal in a whining voice, Nick positioned himself as one-down in a hierarchical structure, framing himself as someone in need of protection. When Sue appealed to Mary to relinquish her pickle, she wanted to take the one-up position of serving food. She was fighting not for the right to *have* the pickle, but for the right to *serve* it. (This reminded me of the women who said they'd become professors in order to teach.) But to accomplish her goal, Sue was depending on Mary's desire to fulfill others' needs.

This study suggests that boys and girls both want to get their way, but they tend to do so differently. Though social norms encourage boys to be openly competitive and girls to be openly cooperative, different situations and activities can result in different ways of behaving. Marjorie Harness Goodwin compared boys and girls engaged in two task-oriented activities: The boys were making slingshots in preparation for a fight, and the girls were making rings. She found that the boys' group was hierarchical: The leader told the others what to do and how to do it. The girls' group was egalitarian: Everyone made suggestions and tended to accept the suggestions of others. But observing the girls in a different activity—playing house—Goodwin found that they too adopted hierarchical structures: The girls who played mothers issued orders to the girls playing children, who in turn sought permission from their play-mothers. Moreover, a girl who was a play-mother was also a kind of manager of the game. This study shows that girls know how to issue orders and operate in a hierarchical structure, but they don't find that mode of behavior appropriate when they engage in task activities with their peers. They do find it appropriate in parent-child relationships, which they enjoy practicing in the form of play.

These worlds of play shed light on the world views of women and men in relationships. The boys' play illuminates why men would be on the lookout for signs they are being put down or told what to do. The chief commodity that is bartered in the boys' hierarchical world is status, and the way to achieve and maintain status is to give orders and get others to follow them. A boy in a low-status position finds himself being pushed around. So boys monitor their relations for subtle shifts in status by keeping track of who's giving orders and who's taking them.

These dynamics are not the ones that drive girls' play. The chief commodity that is bartered in the girls' community is intimacy. Girls monitor their friendships for subtle shifts in alliance, and they seek to be friends with popular girls. Popularity is a kind of status, but it is founded on connection. It also places popular girls in a bind. By doing field work in a junior high school, Donna Eder found that popular girls were paradoxically—and inevitably—disliked. Many girls want to befriend popular girls, but girls' friendships must necessarily be limited, since they entail intimacy rather than large group activities. So a popular girl must reject the overtures of most of the girls who seek her out—with the result that she is branded "stuck up."

THE KEY IS UNDERSTANDING

If adults learn their ways of speaking as children growing up in separate social worlds of peers, then conversation between women and men is cross-cultural communication. Although each style is valid on its own terms, misunderstandings arise because the styles are different. Taking a cross-cultural approach to male-female conversations makes it possible to explain why dissatisfactions are justified without accusing anyone of being wrong or crazy.

Learning about style differences won't make them go away,

but it can banish mutual mystification and blame. Being able to understand why our partners, friends, and even strangers behave the way they do is a comfort, even if we still don't see things the same way. It makes the world into more familiar territory. And having others understand why we talk and act as we do protects us from the pain of their puzzlement and criticism.

In discussing her novel *The Temple of My Familiar,* Alice Walker explained that a woman in the novel falls in love with a man because she sees in him "a giant ear." Walker went on to remark that although people may think they are falling in love because of sexual attraction or some other force, "really what we're looking for is someone to be able to hear us."

We all want, above all, to be heard—but not merely to be heard. We want to be understood—heard for what we think we are saying, for what we know we meant. With increased understanding of the ways women and men use language should come a decrease in frequency of the complaint "You just don't understand."

TWO

Asymmetries: Women and Men Talking at Cross-purposes

Eve had a lump removed from her breast. Shortly after the operation, talking to her sister, she said that she found it upsetting to have been cut into, and that looking at the stitches was distressing because they left a seam that had changed the contour of her breast. Her sister said, "I know. When I had my operation I felt the same way." Eve made the same observation to her friend Karen, who said, "I know. It's like your body has been violated." But when she told her husband, Mark, how she felt, he said, "You can have plastic surgery to cover up the scar and restore the shape of your breast."

Eve had been comforted by her sister and her friend, but she was not comforted by Mark's comment. Quite the contrary, it upset her more. Not only didn't she hear what she wanted, that he understood her feelings, but, far worse, she felt he was asking her to undergo more surgery just when she was telling him how much this operation had upset her. "I'm not having any more surgery!" she protested. "I'm sorry you don't like the way it looks." Mark was hurt and puzzled. "I don't care," he protested. "It doesn't bother me at all." She asked, "Then why are you telling me to have plastic surgery?" He answered, "Because you were saying *you* were upset about the way it looked."

Eve felt like a heel: Mark had been wonderfully supportive and concerned throughout her surgery. How could she snap at him because of what he said—"just words"—when what he had done was unassailable? And yet she had perceived in his words metamessages that cut to the core of their relationship. It was self-evident to him that his comment was a reaction to her complaint, but she heard it as an independent complaint of his. He thought he was reassuring her that she needn't feel bad about her scar because there was something she could *do* about it. She heard his suggestion that she do something about the scar as evidence that *he* was bothered by it. Furthermore, whereas she wanted reassurance that it was normal to feel bad in her situation, his telling her that the problem could easily be fixed implied she had no right to feel bad about it.

Eve wanted the gift of understanding, but Mark gave her the gift of advice. He was taking the role of problem solver, whereas she simply wanted confirmation for her feelings.

A similar misunderstanding arose between a husband and wife following a car accident in which she had been seriously injured. Because she hated being in the hospital, the wife asked to come home early. But once home, she suffered pain from having to move around more. Her husband said, "Why didn't you stay in the hospital where you would have been more comfortable?" This hurt her because it seemed to imply that he did not want her home. She didn't think of his suggestion that she should have stayed in the hospital as a response to her complaints about the pain she was suffering; she thought of it as an independent expression of his preference not to have her at home.

"THEY'RE MY TROUBLES—NOT YOURS"

If women are often frustrated because men do not respond to their troubles by offering matching troubles, men are often frustrated because women do. Some men not only take no comfort in such a response, they take offense. For example, a woman told me that when her companion talks about a personal concern—for example, his feelings about growing older—she responds, "I know how you feel; I feel the same way." To her surprise and chagrin, he gets annoyed; he feels she is trying to take something away from him by denying the uniqueness of his experience.

A similar miscommunication was responsible for the following interchange, which began as a conversation and ended as an argument:

> HE: I'm really tired. I didn't sleep well last night.
> SHE: I didn't sleep well either. I never do.
> HE: Why are you trying to belittle me?
> SHE: I'm not! I'm just trying to show that I understand!

This woman was not only hurt by her husband's reaction; she was mystified by it. How could he think she was belittling him? By "belittle me," he meant "belittle my experience." He was filtering her attempts to establish connection through his concern with preserving independence and avoiding being put down.

"I'LL FIX IT FOR YOU"

Women and men are both often frustrated by the other's way of responding to their expression of troubles. And they are further hurt by the other's frustration. If women resent men's tendency to offer solutions to problems, men complain about women's refusal to take action to solve the problems they complain about. Since many men see themselves as problem solvers, a complaint or a trouble is a challenge to their ability to think of a solution, just as a woman presenting a broken bicycle or stalling car poses a challenge to their ingenuity in fixing it. But whereas many women appreciate help in fixing mechanical equipment, few are inclined to appreciate help in "fixing" emotional troubles.

The idea that men are problem solvers was reinforced by the contrasting responses of a husband and wife to the same question on a radio talk show. The couple, Barbara and William Christopher, were discussing their life with an autistic child. The host asked if there weren't times when they felt sorry for themselves and wondered, "Why me?" Both said no, but they said it in different ways. The wife deflected attention from herself: She said that the real sufferer was her child. The husband said, "Life is problem solving. This is just one more problem to solve."

This explains why men are frustrated when their sincere attempts to help a woman solve her problems are met not with gratitude but with disapproval. One man reported being ready to tear his hair out over a girlfriend who continually told him about problems she was having at work but refused to take any of the advice he offered. Another man defended himself against his girlfriend's objection that he changed the subject as soon as she recounted something that was bothering her: "What's the point of talking about it any more?" he said. "You can't do anything about it." Yet another man commented that women seem to wallow in their problems, wanting to talk about them forever, whereas he and other men want to get them out and be done with them, either by finding a solution or by laughing them off.

Trying to solve a problem or fix a trouble focuses on the message level of talk. But for most women who habitually report problems at work or in friendships, the message is not the main point of complaining. It's the metamessage that counts: Telling about a problem is a bid for an expression of understanding ("I know how you feel") or a similar complaint ("I felt the same way when something similar happened to me"). In other words, troubles talk is intended to reinforce rapport by sending the metamessage "We're the same; you're not alone." Women are frustrated when they not only don't get this reinforcement but, quite the opposite, feel distanced by the advice, which seems to send the metamessage "We're not the same. You have the problems; I have the solutions."

Furthermore, mutual understanding is symmetrical, and this symmetry contributes to a sense of community. But giving advice is asymmetrical. It frames the advice giver as more knowledgeable, more reasonable, more in control—in a word, one-up. And this contributes to the distancing effect.

The assumption that giving advice can be oneupmanship underlies an observation that appeared in a book review. In commenting on Alice Adams's *After You've Gone,* reviewer Ron Carlson explained that the title story is a letter from a woman to a man who has left her for a younger woman. According to Carlson, the woman informs her former lover about her life "and then steps up and clobbers him with sage advice. Here is clearly a superior woman. . . ." Although we do not know the intention of the woman who wrote the story, we see clearly that the man who reviewed it regards giving advice as a form of attack and sees one who gives advice as taking a superior position.

PARALLEL TRACKS

These differences seem to go far back in our growing up. A sixteen-year-old girl told me she tends to hang around with boys rather than girls. To test my ideas, I asked her whether boys and girls both talk about problems. Yes, she assured me, they both do. Do they do it the same way? I asked. Oh, no, she said. The girls go on and on. The boys raise the issue, one of them comes up with a solution, and then they close the discussion.

Women's and men's frustrations with each other's ways of

dealing with troubles talk amount to applying interpretations based on one system to talk that is produced according to a different system. Boys and men do not respond to each other the way women respond to each other in troubles talk. The roots of the very different way that men respond to talk about troubles became clear to me when I compared the transcript of a pair of tenth-grade boys talking to each other to the transcripts of girls' conversations from videotapes of best friends talking, recorded as part of a research project by psychologist Bruce Dorval.

Examining the videotaped conversations, I found that the boys and girls, who expressed deep concerns to each other, did it in different ways—ways that explain the differences that come up in daily conversations between women and men. The pairs of girls at both the sixth grade and tenth grade talked at length about one girl's problems. The other girl pressed her to elaborate, said, "I know," and gave supporting evidence. The following brief excerpts from the transcripts show the dramatic difference between the girls and boys.

The tenth-grade girls are talking about Nancy's problems with her boyfriend and her mother. It emerges that Nancy and Sally were both part of a group excursion to another state. Nancy suddenly left the group and returned home early at her mother's insistence. Nancy was upset about having to leave early. Sally reinforces Nancy's feelings by letting her know that her sudden departure was also upsetting to her friends:

> NANCY: God, it was *bad*. I couldn't believe she made me go home.
> SALLY: I thought it was kind of weird though, I mean, one minute we were going out and the next minute Nancy's going, "Excuse me, gotta be going." [Both laugh] I didn't know what was going *on*, and Judy comes up to me and she whispers (the whole place knows), "Do you know that Nancy's going home?" And I go, "What?" [Both laugh] "Nancy's going home." I go, *"Why?"* She goes, "Her mom's mak-

> ing her." I go [makes a face], "Ah." She comes back
> and goes, "Nancy's left." Well, I said, "WELL, that
> was a fine thing TO DO, she didn't even come and
> say goodbye." And she starts boiling all over me. I
> go [mimicking yelling], *"All right!!"* She was upset,
> Judy. I was like "God"—

Sally's way of responding to her friend's troubles is to confirm
Nancy's feelings of distress that her mother made her leave the
trip early, by letting her know that her leaving upset her friends.
In contrast, examining the transcript of a conversation between
boys of the same age shows how differently they respond to each
other's expressions of troubles.

The tenth-grade boys also express deep feelings. Theirs too
is troubles talk, but it is troubles talk with a difference. They
don't concentrate on the troubles of one, pursuing, exploring,
and elaborating. Instead, each one talks about his own troubles
and dismisses the other's as insignificant.

In the first excerpt from these boys' conversation, Richard
says he feels bad because his friend Mary has no date for an
upcoming dance, and Todd dismisses his concern:

> RICHARD: God, I'm going to feel so bad for her if she stays
> home.
> TODD: She's not going to stay home, it's ridiculous. Why
> doesn't she just ask somebody?

Yet Todd himself is upset because he has no date for the same
dance. He explains that he doesn't want to ask Anita, and Richard, in turn, scoffs at his distress:

> TODD: I felt so bad when she came over and started talk-
> ing to me last night.
> RICHARD: Why?
> TODD: I don't know. I felt uncomfortable, I guess.
> RICHARD: **I'll never understand that.** [Laugh]

Far from trying to show that he understands, Richard states flatly
that he doesn't, as shown in boldface type.

Richard then tells Todd that he is afraid he has a drinking problem. Todd responds by changing the subject to something that is bothering him, his feelings of alienation:

RICHARD: When I took Anne home last night she told me off.

TODD: Really?

. . .

RICHARD: You see when she found out what happened last Thursday night between Sam and me?

TODD: Mhm.

RICHARD: She knew about that. And she just said— and then she started talking about drinking. You know? . . . And then she said, you know, "You, how you hurt everybody when you do it. You're always cranky." And she just said, "I don't like it. You hurt Sam. You hurt Todd. You hurt Mary. You hurt Lois."

. . .

I mean, when she told me, you know I guess I was kind of stunned. [Pause] I didn't really drink that much.

TODD: **Are you still talking to Mary, a lot, I mean?**

RICHARD: Am I still talking to Mary?

TODD: Yeah, 'cause that's why— that's why I was mad Friday.

RICHARD: Why?

TODD: Because.

RICHARD: 'Cause why?

TODD: 'Cause I didn't know why you all just wa- I mean I just went back upstairs for things, then y'all never came back. I was going, "Fine. I don't care." I said, "He's going to start this again."

As the lines printed in boldface show, when Richard says that he is upset because Anne told him he behaved badly when he was drunk, Todd responds by bringing up his own concern: He feels left out, and he was hurt when Richard disappeared from a party with his friend Mary.

Throughout the conversation, Todd expresses distress over feeling alienated and left out. Richard responds by trying to argue Todd out of the way he feels. When Todd says he felt out of place at a party the night before, Richard argues:

RICHARD: **How could you feel out of place? You knew Lois, and you knew Sam.**

TODD: I don't know. I just felt really out of place and then last night again at the party, I mean, Sam was just running around, he knew everyone from the sorority. There was about five.

RICHARD: **Oh, no, he didn't.**

TODD: He knew a lot of people. He was— I don't know.

RICHARD: **Just Lois. He didn't know everybody.**

. . .

TODD: I just felt really out of place that day, all over the place. I used to feel, I mean—

RICHARD: Why?

TODD: I don't know. I don't even feel right in school anymore.

RICHARD: I don't know, last night, I mean—

TODD: I think I know what Ron Cameron and them feels like now. [Laugh]

RICHARD: [Laugh] **No, I don't think you feel as bad as Ron Cameron feels.**

TODD: I'm kidding.

RICHARD: Mm-mm. **Why should you? You know more people—**

TODD: I can't talk to anyone anymore.

RICHARD: **You know more people than me.**

By telling Todd that his feelings are unjustified and incomprehensible, Richard is not implying that he doesn't care. He clearly means to comfort his friend, to make him feel better. He's implying, "You shouldn't feel bad because your problems aren't so bad."

MATCHING TROUBLES

The very different way that women respond to the telling of troubles is dramatized in a short story, "New Haven," by Alice Mattison. Eleanor tells Patsy that she has fallen in love with a married man. Patsy responds by first displaying understanding and then offering a matching revelation about a similar experience:

> "Well," says Patsy. "I know how you feel."
> "You do?"
> "In a way, I do. Well, I should tell you. I've been sleeping with a married man for two years."

Patsy then tells Eleanor about her affair and how she feels about it. After they discuss Patsy's affair, however, Patsy says:

> "But you were telling me about this man and I cut you off. I'm sorry. See? I'm getting self-centered."
> "It's OK." But she is pleased again.

The conversation then returns to Eleanor's incipient affair. Thus Patsy responds first by confirming Eleanor's feelings and matching her experience, reinforcing their similarity, and then by encouraging Eleanor to tell more. Within the frame of Patsy's similar predicament, the potential asymmetry inherent in revealing personal problems is avoided, and the friendship is brought into balance.

What made Eleanor's conversation with Patsy so pleasing to Eleanor was that they shared a sense of how to talk about troubles, and this reinforced their friendship. Though Eleanor raised the matter of her affair, she did not elaborate on it until Patsy pressed her to do so. In another story by the same author, "The Knitting," a woman named Beth is staying with her sister in order to visit her sister's daughter Stephanie in a psychiatric hospital. While there, Beth receives a disturbing telephone call from her boyfriend, Alec. Having been thus reminded of her troubles, she wants to talk about them, but she refrains, because her sister doesn't ask. She feels required, instead, to focus on her sister's problem, the reason for her visit:

> She'd like to talk about her muted half-quarrels with Alec of the last weeks, but her sister does not ask about the phone call. Then Beth thinks they should talk about Stephanie.

The women in these stories are balancing a delicate system by which troubles talk is used to confirm their feelings and create a sense of community.

When women confront men's ways of talking to them, they judge them by the standards of women's conversational styles. Women show concern by following up someone else's statement of trouble by questioning her about it. When men change the subject, women think they are showing a lack of sympathy—a failure of intimacy. But the failure to ask probing questions could just as well be a way of respecting the other's need for independence. When Eleanor tells Patsy that she is in love with Peter, Patsy asks, "Are you sleeping with him?" This exploration of Eleanor's topic could well strike many men—and some women— as intrusive, though Eleanor takes it as a show of interest that nourishes their friendship.

Women tend to show understanding of another woman's feelings. When men try to reassure women by telling them that their situation is not so bleak, the women hear their feelings being belittled or discounted. Again, they encounter a failure of intimacy just when they were bidding to reinforce it. Trying to trigger a symmetrical communication, they end up in an asymmetrical one.

A DIFFERENT SYMMETRY

The conversation between Richard and Todd shows that although the boys' responses are asymmetrical if looked at separately—each dismisses the other's concerns—they are symmetrical when looked at together: Todd responds to Richard's concern about his drinking in exactly the same way that Richard responds to Todd's feeling of alienation, by denying it is a problem:

RICHARD: Hey, man, I just don't feel— I mean, after what Anne said last night, I just don't feel like doing that.

TODD: **I don't think it was that way. You yourself knew it was no big problem.**

RICHARD: Oh, Anne— Sam told Anne that I fell down the levee.

TODD: **It's a lie.**

RICHARD: I didn't fall. I slipped, slid. I caught myself.

TODD: **Don't worry about it.**

RICHARD: But I do, kind of. I feel funny in front of Sam. I don't want to do it in front of you.

TODD: **It doesn't matter 'cause sometimes you're funny when you're off your butt.**

Todd denies that Richard was so drunk he was staggering ("It's a lie") and then says that even if he was out of control, it wasn't bad; it was funny.

In interpreting this conversation between tenth-grade boys, I initially saw their mutual reassurances and dismissals, and their mutual revelations of troubles, in terms of connection and sameness. But another perspective is possible. Their conversation may be touching precisely because it was based on asymmetries of status—or, more precisely, a deflecting of such asymmetries. When Todd tells his troubles, he puts himself in a potentially one-down position and invites Richard to take a one-up position by disclaiming troubles and asymmetrically offering advice or sympathy. By offering troubles of his own, Richard declines to take the superior position and restores their symmetrical footing, sending the metamessage "We're just a couple of guys trying to make it in a world that's tough on both of us, and both of us are about equally competent to deal with it."

From this perspective, responding as a woman might—for example by saying, "I can see how you feel; you must feel awful; so would I if it happened to me"—would have a totally different meaning for boys, since they would be inclined to interpret it through the lens of status. Such a response would send a meta-message like "Yes, I know, you incompetent jerk, I know how awful you must feel. If I were as incompetent as you, I'd feel the same way. But, lucky for you, I'm not, and I can help you out here, because I'm far too talented to be upset by a problem like that." In other words, refraining from expressing sympathy is generous, insofar as sympathy potentially condescends.

Women are often unhappy with the reactions they get from men when they try to start troubles talk, and men are often unhappy because they are accused of responding in the wrong way when they are trying to be helpful. But Richard and Todd seem satisfied with each other's ways of reacting to their troubles. And their ways make sense. When men and women talk to each other, the problem is that each expects a different kind of response. The men's approach seeks to assuage feelings indirectly by attacking their cause. Since women expect to have their feelings supported, the men's approach makes them feel that they themselves are being attacked.

"DON'T ASK"

Talking about troubles is just one of many conversational tasks that women and men view differently, and that consequently cause trouble in talk between them. Another is asking for information. And this difference too is traceable to the asymmetries of status and connection.

A man and a woman were standing beside the information booth at the Washington Folk Life Festival, a sprawling complex of booths and displays. "You ask," the man was saying to the woman. "I don't ask."

Sitting in the front seat of the car beside Harold, Sybil is fuming. They have been driving around for half an hour looking for a street he is sure is close by. Sybil is angry not because Harold does not know the way, but because he insists on trying to find it himself rather than stopping and asking someone. Her anger stems from viewing his behavior through the lens of her own: If she were driving, she would have asked directions as soon as she realized she didn't know which way to go, and they'd now be comfortably ensconced in their friends' living room instead of driving in circles, as the hour gets later and later. Since asking directions does not make Sybil uncomfortable, refusing to ask makes no sense to her. But in Harold's world, driving around until he finds his way is the reasonable thing to do, since asking for help makes him uncomfortable. He's avoiding that discomfort and trying to maintain his sense of himself as a self-sufficient person.

Why do many men resist asking for directions and other kinds of information? And, it is just as reasonable to ask, why is it that many women don't? By the paradox of independence and intimacy, there are two simultaneous and different metamessages implied in asking for and giving information. Many men tend to focus on one, many women on the other.

When you offer information, the information itself is the message. But the fact that you have the information, and the person you are speaking to doesn't, also sends a metamessage of superiority. If relations are inherently hierarchical, then the one who has more information is framed as higher up on the ladder, by virtue of being more knowledgeable and competent. From this perspective, finding one's own way is an essential part of the independence that men perceive to be a prerequisite for self-respect. If self-respect is bought at the cost of a few extra minutes of travel time, it is well worth the price.

Because they are implicit, metamessages are hard to talk about. When Sybil begs to know why Harold won't just ask someone for directions, he answers in terms of the message, the information: He says there's no point in asking, because anyone he asks may not know and may give him wrong directions. This is theoretically reasonable. There are many countries, such as, for example, Mexico, where it is standard procedure for people to make up directions rather than refuse to give requested information. But this explanation frustrates Sybil, because it doesn't make sense to her. Although she realizes that someone might give faulty directions, she believes this is relatively unlikely, and surely it cannot happen every time. Even if it did happen, they would be in no worse shape than they are in now anyway.

Part of the reason for their different approaches is that Sybil believes that a person who doesn't know the answer will say so, because it is easy to say, "I don't know." But Harold believes that saying "I don't know" is humiliating, so people might well take a wild guess. Because of their different assumptions, and the invisibility of framing, Harold and Sybil can never get to the bottom of this difference; they can only get more frustrated with each other. Keeping talk on the message level is common, because it is the level we are most clearly aware of. But it is unlikely to resolve confusion since our true motivations lie elsewhere.

To the extent that giving information, directions, or help is of use to another, it reinforces bonds between people. But to the extent that it is asymmetrical, it creates hierarchy: Insofar as giving information frames one as the expert, superior in knowledge, and the other as uninformed, inferior in knowledge, it is a move in the negotiation of status.

It is easy to see that there are many situations where those who give information are higher in status. For example, parents explain things to children and answer their questions, just as teachers give information to students. An awareness of this dynamic underlies one requirement for proper behavior at Japanese dinner entertainment, according to anthropologist Harumi Befu. In order to help the highest-status member of the party to dominate the conversation, others at the dinner are expected to ask him questions that they know he can answer with authority.

Because of this potential for asymmetry, some men resist receiving information from others, especially women, and some women are cautious about stating information that they know, especially to men. For example, a man with whom I discussed these dynamics later told me that my perspective clarified a comment made by his wife. They had gotten into their car and were about to go to a destination that she knew well but he did not know at all. Consciously resisting an impulse to just drive off and find his own way, he began by asking his wife if she had any advice about the best way to get there. She told him the way, then added, "But I don't know. That's how I would go, but there might be a better way." Her comment was a move to redress the imbalance of power created by her knowing something he didn't know. She was also saving face in advance, in case he decided not to take her advice. Furthermore, she was reframing her directions as "just a suggestion" rather than "giving instructions."

"I'LL FIX IT IF IT KILLS ME"

The asymmetry implied in having and giving information is also found in having and demonstrating the skill to fix things—an orientation that we saw in men's approaches to troubles talk. To further explore the framing involved in fixing things, I will present a small encounter of my own.

Unable to remove the tiny lid that covers the battery compartment for the light meter on my camera, I took the camera to a photography store and asked for help. The camera salesman tried to unscrew the lid, first with a dime and then with a special instrument. When this failed, he declared the lid hopelessly stuck. He explained the reason (it was screwed in with the threads out of alignment) and then explained in detail how I could take pictures without a light meter by matching the light conditions to shutter settings in accordance with the chart included in rolls of film. Even though I knew there wasn't a chance in the world I would adopt his system, I listened politely, feigning interest, and assiduously wrote down his examples, based on an ASA of 100, since he got confused trying to give examples based on an ASA of 64. He further explained that this method was actually superior to using a light meter. In this way, he minimized the significance of not being able to help by freeing the battery lid; he framed himself as possessing useful knowledge and having solved my problem even though he couldn't fix my camera. This man wanted to help me—which I sincerely appreciated—but he also wanted to demonstrate that he had the information and skill required to help, even though he didn't.

There is a kind of social contract operating here. Many women not only feel comfortable seeking help, but feel honor-bound to seek it, accept it, and display gratitude in exchange. For their part, many men feel honor-bound to fulfill the request for help whether or not it is convenient for them to do so. A man told me about a time when a neighbor asked him if he could fix her car, which was intermittently stalling out. He spent more time than he could spare looking at her car, and concluded that he did not have the equipment needed to do the repair. He felt bad about not having succeeded in solving her problem. As if sensing this, she told him the next day, and the next, that her car was much better now, even though he knew he had done nothing to improve its performance. There is a balance between seeking help and showing appreciation. Women and men seem equally bound by the requirements of this arrangement: She was bound to show appreciation even though he hadn't helped, and he was bound to invest time and effort that he really couldn't spare, in trying to help.

Another example of the social contract of asking for help and showing appreciation occurred on a street corner in New York City. A woman emerged from the subway at Twenty-third Street and Park Avenue South, and was temporarily confused about which direction to walk in to reach Madison Avenue. She knew that Madison was west of Park, so with a little effort she could have figured out which way to go. But without planning or thinking, she asked the first person to appear before her. He replied that Madison did not come down that far south. Now, she knew this to be false. Furthermore, by this time she had oriented herself. But instead of saying, "Yes, it does," or "Never mind, I don't need your help," she found a way to play out the scene as one in which he helped her. She asked, "Which way is west?" and, on being told, replied, "Thank you. I'll just walk west."

From the point of view of getting directions, this encounter was absurd from start to finish. The woman didn't really need help, and the man wasn't in a position to give it. But getting directions really wasn't the main point. She had used the commonplace ritual of asking directions of a stranger not only—and not mostly—to find her way on emerging from the subway, but to reinforce her connection to the mass of people in the big city by making fleeting contact with one of them. Asking for help was simply an automatic way for her to do this.

"I'LL HELP YOU IF IT KILLS YOU"

Martha bought a computer and needed to learn to use it. After studying the manual and making some progress, she still had many questions, so she went to the store where she had bought it and asked for help. The man assigned to help her made her feel like the stupidest person in the world. He used technical language in explaining things, and each time she had to ask what a word meant she felt more incompetent, an impression reinforced by the tone of voice he used in his answer, a tone that sent the metamessage "This is obvious; everyone knows this." He explained things so quickly, she couldn't possibly remember them. When she went home, she discovered she couldn't recall what he had demonstrated, even in cases where she had followed his explanation at the time.

Still confused, and dreading the interaction, Martha returned to the store a week later, determined to stay until she got the information she needed. But this time a woman was assigned to help her. And the experience of getting help was utterly transformed. The woman avoided using technical terms for the most part, and if she did use one, she asked whether Martha knew what it meant and explained simply and clearly if she didn't. When the woman answered questions, her tone never implied that everyone should know this. And when showing how to do something, she had Martha do it, rather than demonstrating while Martha watched. The different style of this "teacher" made Martha feel like a different "student": a competent rather than stupid one, not humiliated by her ignorance.

Surely not all men give information in a way that confuses and humiliates their students. There are many gifted teachers who also happen to be men. And not all women give information in a way that makes it easy for students to understand. But many women report experiences similar to Martha's, especially in dealing with computers, automobiles, and other mechanical equipment; they claim that they feel more comfortable having women explain things to them. The different meanings that giving help entails may explain why. If women are focusing on connections, they will be motivated to minimize the difference in expertise and to be as comprehensible as possible. Since their goal is to maintain the appearance of similarity and equal status, sharing knowledge helps even the score. Their tone of voice sends metamessages of support rather than disdain, although "support" itself can be experienced as condescension.

If a man focuses on the negotiation of status and feels someone must have the upper hand, he may feel more comfortable when he has it. His attunement to the fact that having more information, knowledge, or skill puts him in a one-up position comes through in his way of talking. And if sometimes men seem intentionally to explain in a way that makes what they are explaining difficult to understand, it may be because their pleasant feeling of knowing more is reinforced when the student *does not* understand. The comfortable margin of superiority diminishes with every bit of knowledge the student gains. Or it may simply be that they are more concerned with displaying their superior knowledge and skill than with making sure that the knowledge is shared.

A colleague familiar with my ideas remarked that he'd seen evidence of this difference at an academic conference. A woman delivering a paper kept stopping and asking the audience, "Are you with me so far?" My colleague surmised that her main concern seemed to be that the audience understand what she was saying. When he gave his paper, his main concern was that he not be put down by members of the audience—and as far as he could tell, a similar preoccupation was motivating the other men presenting papers as well. From this point of view, if covering one's tracks to avoid attack entails obscuring one's point, it is a price worth paying.

This is not to say that women have no desire to feel knowledgeable or powerful. Indeed, the act of asking others whether they are able to follow your argument can be seen to frame you as superior. But it seems that having information, expertise, or skill at manipulating objects is not the primary measure of power for most women. Rather, they feel their power enhanced if they can be of help. Even more, if they are focusing on connection rather than independence and self-reliance, they feel stronger when the community is strong.

"TRUST ME"

A woman told me that she was incredulous when her husband dredged up an offense from years before. She had been unable to get their VCR to record movies aired on HBO. Her husband had looked at the VCR and declared it incapable of performing this function. Rather than accepting his judgment, she asked their neighbor, Harry, to take a look at it, since he had once fixed her VCR in the past. Harry's conclusion was the same as that of her husband, who was, however, incensed that his wife had not trusted his expertise. When he brought it up years later, the wife exclaimed in disbelief, "You still remember that? Harry is dead!" The incident, though insignificant to the wife, cut to the core of the husband's self-respect, because it called into question his knowledge and skill at managing the mechanical world.

Trust in a man's skill is also at issue between Felicia and Stan, another couple. Stan is angered when Felicia gasps in fear while he is driving. "I've never had an acident!" he protests. "Why can't you trust my driving?" Felicia cannot get him to see her point of view—that she does not distrust *his* driving in particular but is frightened of driving in general. Most of all, she cannot understand why the small matter of involuntarily sucking in her breath should spark such a strong reaction.

"BE NICE"

Having expertise and skill can reinforce both women's and men's sense of themselves. But the stance of expert is more fundamental to our notion of masculinity than to our concept of femininity. Women, according to convention, are more inclined to be givers of praise than givers of information. That women are expected to praise is reflected in a poster that was displayed in every United States post office branch inviting customers to send criticism, suggestions, questions, and compliments. Three of these four linguistic acts were represented by sketches of men; only compliments were represented by a sketch of a woman with a big smile on her face, a gesture of approval on her fingers, and a halo around her head. The halo is especially interesting. It shows that the act of complimenting frames the speaker as "nice."

Giving praise, like giving information, is also inherently asymmetrical. It too frames the speaker as one-up, in a position to judge someone else's performance. Women can also be framed as one-up by their classic helping activities as mothers, social workers, nurses, counselors, and psychologists. But in many of these roles—especially mothers and nurses—they may also be seen as doing others' bidding.

OVERLAPPING MOTIVATIONS

When acting as helpers, women and men typically perform different kinds of tasks. But even the same task can be approached with eyes on different goals, and this difference is likely to result in misjudgments of others' intentions. The end of my camera story underlines this. At a family gathering, I brought the camera to my brother-in-law, who has a reputation in the family for mechanical ability. He took it to his workshop and returned an hour and a half later, having fixed it. Delighted and grateful, I commented to his daughter, "I knew he would enjoy the challenge." "Especially," she pointed out, "when it involves helping someone." I felt then that I had mistaken his displayed concern with the mechanics of the recalcitrant battery cover as reflecting his ultimate concern. But fixing the camera was a way of showing concern for me, of helping me with his effort. If women directly offer help, my brother-in-law was indirectly offering help, through the mediation of my camera.

A colleague who heard my analysis of this experience thought I had missed an aspect of my broken-camera episode. He pointed out that many men get a sense of pleasure from fixing things because it reinforces their feeling of being in control, self-sufficient, and able to dominate the world of objects. (This is the essence of Evelyn Fox Keller's thesis that the conception of science as dominating and controlling nature is essentially masculine in spirit.) He told me of an incident in which a toy plastic merry-go-round, ordered for his little boy, arrived in pieces, having come apart during shipping. His wife gave the toy to her uncle, renowned in the family as a fixer and helper. Her uncle worked for several hours and repaired the toy—even though it was probably not worth more than a few dollars. The uncle brought this up again the next time he saw them, and said he would have stayed up all night rather than admit he couldn't put it together. My colleague was convinced that the motivation to gain dominion over the plastic object had been stronger than the motivation to help his sister and nephew, though both had been present.

Furthermore, this man pointed out that he, and many other men, take special pleasure in showing their strength over the world of objects for the benefit of attractive women, because the thanks and admiration they receive is an added source of pleasure and satisfaction. His interpretation of my revised analysis was that my niece and I, both women, would be inclined to see the helping aspect of an act as the "real" or main motive, whereas he still was inclined to see the pleasure of demonstrating skill, succeeding where the camera expert had failed, and whacking the recalcitrant battery lid into line as the main ones.

The element of negotiating status that characterizes many men's desire to show they are knowledgeable and skillful does not negate the connection implied in helping. These elements coexist and feed each other. But women's and men's tendencies to place different relative weights on status versus connection result in asymmetrical roles. Attuned to the metamessage of connection, many women are comfortable both receiving help and giving it, though surely there are many women who are comfortable only in the role of giver of help and support. Many men, sensitive to the dynamic of status, the need to help women, and the need to be self-reliant, are comfortable in the role of giving information and help but not in receiving it.

THE VIEW FROM A DIFFERENT MOUNTAIN

In a story by Alice Mattison, "The Colorful Alphabet," a man named Joseph invites another man, Gordon, to visit his family in the country, because Gordon's wife has just left him. During the visit, they all climb a mountain. On the way down, they stop to rest, and Gordon realizes that he left his beloved old knapsack on the mountaintop. Joseph volunteers to climb back up to get it, because Gordon is not used to climbing and his feet are sore. Joseph's wife goes with him, but she is too tired to climb all the way to the top, and he leaves her on the path to complete the mission himself. When he finds her again, he is empty-handed: The bag wasn't there. He says then that he knew it wouldn't be, because he had seen a man carrying the bag pass them when they all stopped to rest. He explains why he didn't just say that he had seen someone go by with the bag: "I couldn't tell him I'd seen it and hadn't been smart enough to get it back for him." Instead, he says, "I had to *do* something."

Exhausted and frustrated, the wife is not so much angry as incredulous. She can't understand how he could have preferred reclimbing the mountain (and making her reclimb it too) to admitting that he had seen someone carrying Gordon's bag. "I would never have done that," she says, but she speaks "more in wonder than anger." She explains, "I'd have just blurted it out. I'd have been upset about making the mistake—but not about people *knowing*. That part's not a big deal to me." Her husband says, "Oh, is it ever a big deal to me."

This story supports the view of men's style that I have been proposing. Joseph wanted to help Gordon, and he did not want to let it be known that he had done something he thought stupid. His impulse to do something to solve the problem was stronger than his impulse not to climb a mountain twice. But what struck me most strongly about the story was the wife's reflections on the experience. She thinks:

> It was one of the occasional moments when I'm certain I haven't imagined him: I would never have done what he'd done, wouldn't have dreamt it or invented it—Joseph was, simply, *not me*.

This excerpt reflects what may be the subtlest yet deepest source of frustration and puzzlement arising from the different ways that women and men approach the world. We feel we know how the world is, and we look to others to reinforce that conviction. When we see others acting as if the world were an entirely different place from the one we inhabit, we are shaken.

We look to our closest relationships as a source of confirmation and reassurance. When those closest to us respond to events differently than we do, when they seem to see the same scene as part of a different play, when they say things that we could not imagine saying in the same circumstances, the ground on which we stand seems to tremble and our footing is suddenly unsure. Being able to understand why this happens—*why* and *how* our partners and friends, though like us in many ways, are *not* us, and different in other ways—is a crucial step toward feeling that our feet are planted on firm ground.

THREE

"Put Down That Paper and Talk to Me!": Rapport-talk and Report-talk

I was sitting in a suburban living room, speaking to a women's group that had invited men to join them for the occasion of my talk about communication between women and men. During the discussion, one man was particularly talkative, full of lengthy comments and explanations. When I made the observation that women often complain that their husbands don't talk to them enough, this man volunteered that he heartily agreed. He gestured toward his wife, who had sat silently beside him on the couch throughout the evening, and said, "She's the talker in our family."

Everyone in the room burst into laughter. The man looked puzzled and hurt. "It's true," he explained. "When I come home from work, I usually have nothing to say, but she never runs out.

If it weren't for her, we'd spend the whole evening in silence." Another woman expressed a similar paradox about her husband: "When we go out, he's the life of the party. If I happen to be in another room, I can always hear his voice above the others. But when we're home, he doesn't have that much to say. I do most of the talking."

Who talks more, women or men? According to the stereotype, women talk too much. Linguist Jennifer Coates notes some proverbs:

> A woman's tongue wags like a lamb's tail.
>
> Foxes are all tail and women are all tongue.
>
> The North Sea will sooner be found wanting in water than a woman be at a loss for a word.

Throughout history, women have been punished for talking too much or in the wrong way. Linguist Connie Eble lists a variety of physical punishments used in Colonial America: Women were strapped to ducking stools and held underwater until they nearly drowned, put into the stocks with signs pinned to them, gagged, and silenced by a cleft stick applied to their tongues.

Though such institutionalized corporal punishments have given way to informal, often psychological ones, modern stereotypes are not much different from those expressed in the old proverbs. Women are believed to talk too much. Yet study after study finds that it is men who talk more—at meetings, in mixed-group discussions, and in classrooms where girls or young women sit next to boys or young men. For example, communications researchers Barbara and Gene Eakins tape-recorded and studied seven university faculty meetings. They found that, with one exception, men spoke more often and, without exception, spoke for a longer time. The men's turns ranged from 10.66 to 17.07 seconds, while the women's turns ranged from 3 to 10 seconds. In other words, the women's longest turns were still shorter than the men's shortest turns.

When a public lecture is followed by questions from the floor, or a talk show host opens the phones, the first voice to be heard asking a question is almost always a man's. And when they ask questions or offer comments from the audience, men tend to talk longer. Linguist Marjorie Swacker recorded question-and-answer sessions at academic conferences. Women were highly visible as speakers at the conferences studied; they presented 40.7 percent of the papers at the conferences studied and made up 42 percent of the audiences. But when it came to volunteering and being called on to ask questions, women contributed only 27.4 percent. Furthermore, the women's questions, on the average, took less than half as much time as the men's. (The mean was 23.1 seconds for women, 52.7 for men.) This happened, Swacker shows, because men (but not women) tended to preface their questions with statements, ask more than one question, and follow up the speaker's answer with another question or comment.

I have observed this pattern at my own lectures, which concern issues of direct relevance to women. Regardless of the proportion of women and men in the audience, men almost invariably ask the first question, more questions, and longer questions. In these situations, women often feel that men are talking too much. I recall one discussion period following a lecture I gave to a group assembled in a bookstore. The group was composed mostly of women, but most of the discussion was being conducted by men in the audience. At one point, a man sitting in the middle was talking at such great length that several women in the front rows began shifting in their seats and rolling their eyes at me. Ironically, what he was going on about was how frustrated he feels when he has to listen to women going on and on about topics he finds boring and unimportant.

RAPPORT-TALK AND REPORT-TALK

Who talks more, then, women or men? The seemingly contradictory evidence is reconciled by the difference between what I call *public* and *private speaking*. More men feel comfortable doing "public speaking," while more women feel comfortable doing "private" speaking. Another way of capturing these differences is by using the terms *report-talk* and *rapport-talk*.

For most women, the language of conversation is primarily a language of rapport: a way of establishing connections and negotiating relationships. Emphasis is placed on displaying similarities and matching experiences. From childhood, girls criticize peers who try to stand out or appear better than others. People feel their closest connections at home, or in settings where they *feel* at home—with one or a few people they feel close to and comfortable with—in other words, during private speaking. But even the most public situations can be approached like private speaking.

For most men, talk is primarily a means to preserve independence and negotiate and maintain status in a hierarchical social order. This is done by exhibiting knowledge and skill, and by holding center stage through verbal performance such as storytelling, joking, or imparting information. From childhood, men learn to use talking as a way to get and keep attention. So they are more comfortable speaking in larger groups made up of people they know less well—in the broadest sense, "public speaking." But even the most private situations can be approached like public speaking, more like giving a report than establishing rapport.

PRIVATE SPEAKING: THE WORDY WOMAN AND THE MUTE MAN

What is the source of the stereotype that women talk a lot? Dale Spender suggests that most people feel instinctively (if not consciously) that women, like children, should be seen and not heard, so any amount of talk from them seems like too much. Studies have shown that if women and men talk equally in a group, people think the women talked more. So there is truth to Spender's view. But another explanation is that men think women talk a lot because they hear women talking in situations where men would not: on the telephone; or in social situations with friends, when they are not discussing topics that men find inherently interesting; or, like the couple at the women's group, at home alone—in other words, in private speaking.

Home is the setting for an American icon that features the silent man and the talkative woman. And this icon, which grows out of the different goals and habits I have been describing, explains why the complaint most often voiced by women about the men with whom they are intimate is "He doesn't talk to me"—and the second most frequent is "He doesn't listen to me."

A woman who wrote to Ann Landers is typical:

> My husband never speaks to me when he comes home from work. When I ask, "How did everything go today?" he says, "Rough . . ." or "It's a jungle out there." (We live in Jersey and he works in New York City.)
>
> It's a different story when we have guests or go visiting. Paul is the gabbiest guy in the crowd—a real spellbinder. He comes up with the most interesting stories. People hang on every word. I think to myself, "Why doesn't he ever tell *me* these things?"
>
> This has been going on for 38 years. Paul started to go quiet on me after 10 years of marriage. I could never figure out why. Can you solve the mystery?
>
> —The Invisible Woman

Ann Landers suggests that the husband may not want to talk because he is tired when he comes home from work. Yet women who work come home tired too, and they are nonetheless eager to tell their partners or friends everything that happened to them during the day and what these fleeting, daily dramas made them think and feel.

Sources as lofty as studies conducted by psychologists, as down to earth as letters written to advice columnists, and as sophisticated as movies and plays come up with the same insight: Men's silence at home is a disappointment to women. Again and again, women complain, "He seems to have everything to say to everyone else, and nothing to say to me."

The film *Divorce American Style* opens with a conversation in which Debbie Reynolds is claiming that she and Dick Van Dyke don't communicate, and he is protesting that he tells her everything that's on his mind. The doorbell interrupts their quarrel, and husband and wife compose themselves before opening the door to greet their guests with cheerful smiles.

Behind closed doors, many couples are having conversations like this. Like the character played by Debbie Reynolds, women feel men don't communicate. Like the husband played by Dick Van Dyke, men feel wrongly accused. How can she be convinced that he doesn't tell her anything, while he is equally convinced he tells her everything that's on his mind? How can women and men have such different ideas about the same conversations?

When something goes wrong, people look around for a source to blame: either the person they are trying to communicate with ("You're demanding, stubborn, self-centered") or the group that the other person belongs to ("All women are demanding"; "All men are self-centered"). Some generous-minded people blame the relationship ("We just can't communicate"). But underneath, or overlaid on these types of blame cast outward, most people believe that something is wrong with them.

If individual people or particular relationships were to blame, there wouldn't be so many different people having the same problems. The real problem is conversational style. Women and men have different ways of talking. Even with the best intentions, trying to settle the problem through talk can only make things worse if it is ways of talking that are causing trouble in the first place.

BEST FRIENDS

Once again, the seeds of women's and men's styles are sown in the ways they learn to use language while growing up. In our culture, most people, but especially women, look to their closest relationships as havens in a hostile world. The center of a little girl's social life is her best friend. Girls' friendships are made and maintained by telling secrets. For grown women too, the essence of friendship is talk, telling each other what they're thinking and feeling, and what happened that day: who was at the bus stop, who called, what they said, how that made them feel. When asked who their best friends are, most women name other women they talk to regularly. When asked the same question, most men will say it's their wives. After that, many men name other men with whom they do things such as play tennis or baseball (but never just sit and talk) or a chum from high school whom they haven't spoken to in a year.

When Debbie Reynolds complained that Dick Van Dyke didn't tell her anything, and he protested that he did, both were right. She felt he didn't tell her anything because he didn't tell her the fleeting thoughts and feelings he experienced throughout the day— the kind of talk she would have with her best friend. He didn't tell her these things because to him they didn't seem like anything to tell. He told her anything that seemed important—anything he would tell his friends.

Men and women often have very different ideas of what's important—and at what point "important" topics should be raised. A woman told me, with lingering incredulity, of a conversation with her boyfriend. Knowing he had seen his friend Oliver, she asked, "What's new with Oliver?" He replied, "Nothing." But later in the conversation it came out that Oliver and his girlfriend had decided to get married. "That's nothing?" the woman gasped in frustration and disbelief.

For men, "Nothing" may be a ritual response at the start of a conversation. A college woman missed her brother but rarely called him because she found it difficult to get talk going. A typical conversation began with her asking, "What's up with you?" and his replying, "Nothing." Hearing his "Nothing" as meaning "There is nothing personal I want to talk about," she supplied talk by filling him in on her news and eventually hung up in frustration. But when she thought back, she remembered that later in the conversation he had mumbled, "Christie and I got into another fight." This came so late and so low that she didn't pick up on it. And he was probably equally frustrated that she didn't.

Many men honestly do not know what women want, and women honestly do not know why men find what they want so hard to comprehend and deliver.

"TALK TO ME!"

Women's dissatisfaction with men's silence at home is captured in the stock cartoon setting of a breakfast table at which a husband and wife are sitting: He's reading a newspaper; she's glaring at the back of the newspaper. In a Dagwood strip, Blondie complains, "Every morning all he sees is the newspaper! I'll bet you don't even know I'm here!" Dagwood reassures her, "Of course I know you're here. You're my wonderful wife and I love you very much." With this, he unseeingly pats the paw of the family dog, which the wife has put in her place before leaving the room. The cartoon strip shows that Blondie is justified in feeling like the woman who wrote to Ann Landers: invisible.

Another cartoon shows a husband opening a newspaper and asking his wife, "Is there anything you would like to say to me before I begin reading the newspaper?" The reader knows that there isn't—but that as soon as he begins reading the paper, she will think of something. The cartoon highlights the difference in what women and men think talk is for: To him, talk is for information. So when his wife interrupts his reading, it must be to inform him of something that he needs to know. This being the case, she might as well tell him what she thinks he needs to know before he starts reading. But to her, talk is for interaction. Telling things is a way to show involvement, and listening is a way to show interest and caring. It is not an odd coincidence that she always thinks of things to tell him when he is reading. She feels the need for verbal interaction most keenly when he is (unaccountably, from her point of view) buried in the newspaper instead of talking to her.

Yet another cartoon shows a wedding cake that has, on top, in place of the plastic statues of bride and groom in tuxedo and gown, a breakfast scene in which an unshaven husband reads a newspaper across the table from his disgruntled wife. The cartoon reflects the enormous gulf between the romantic expectations of marriage represented by the plastic couple in traditional wedding costume, and the often disappointing reality represented by the two sides of the newspaper at the breakfast table—the front, which he is reading, and the back, at which she is glaring.

These cartoons, and many others on the same theme, are funny because people recognize their own experience in them. What's not funny is that many women are deeply hurt when men don't talk to them at home, and many men are deeply frustrated by feeling they have disappointed their partners, without understanding how they failed or how else they could have behaved.

Some men are further frustrated because, as one put it, "When in the world am I supposed to read the morning paper?" If many women are incredulous that many men do not exchange personal information with their friends, this man is incredulous that many women do not bother to read the morning paper. To him, reading the paper is an essential part of his morning ritual, and his whole day is awry if he doesn't get to read it. In his words, reading the newspaper in the morning is as important to him as putting on makeup in the morning is to many women he knows. Yet many women, he observed, either don't subscribe to a paper or don't read it until they get home in the evening. "I find this very puzzling," he said. "I can't tell you how often I have picked up a woman's morning newspaper from her front door in the evening and handed it to her when she opened the door for me."

To this man (and I am sure many others), a woman who objects to his reading the morning paper is trying to keep him from doing something essential and harmless. It's a violation of his independence—his freedom of action. But when a woman who expects her partner to talk to her is disappointed that he doesn't, she perceives his behavior as a failure of intimacy: He's keeping things from her; he's lost interest in her; he's pulling away. A woman I will call Rebecca, who is generally quite happily married, told me that this is the one source of serious dissatisfaction with her husband, Stuart. Her term for his taciturnity is *stinginess of spirit*. She tells him what she is thinking, and he listens silently. She asks him what he is thinking, and he takes a long time to answer, "I don't know." In frustration she challenges, "Is there nothing on your mind?"

For Rebecca, who is accustomed to expressing her fleeting thoughts and opinions as they come to her, *saying* nothing means *thinking* nothing. But Stuart does not assume that his passing thoughts are worthy of utterance. He is not in the habit of uttering his fleeting ruminations, so just as Rebecca "naturally" speaks her thoughts, he "naturally" dismisses his as soon as they occur to him. Speaking them would give them more weight and significance than he feels they merit. All her life she has had practice in verbalizing her thoughts and feelings in private conversations with people she is close to; all his life he has had practice in dismissing his and keeping them to himself.

WHAT TO DO WITH DOUBTS

In the above example, Rebecca was not talking about any particular kind of thoughts or feelings, just whatever Stuart might have had in mind. But the matter of giving voice to thoughts and feelings becomes particularly significant in the case of negative feelings or doubts about a relationship. This difference was highlighted for me when a fifty-year-old divorced man told me about his experiences in forming new relationships with women. On this matter, he was clear: "I do not value my fleeting thoughts, and I do not value the fleeting thoughts of others." He felt that the relationship he was currently in had been endangered, even permanently weakened, by the woman's practice of tossing out her passing thoughts, because, early in their courtship, many of her thoughts were fears about their relationship. Not surprisingly, since they did not yet know each other well, she worried about whether she could trust him, whether their relationship would destroy her independence, whether this relationship was really right for her. He felt she should have kept these fears and doubts to herself and waited to see how things turned out.

As it happens, things turned out well. The woman decided that the relationship was right for her, she could trust him, and she did not have to give up her independence. But he felt, at the time that he told me of this, that he had still not recovered from the wear and tear of coping with her earlier doubts. As he put it, he was still dizzy from having been bounced around like a yo-yo tied to the string of her stream of consciousness.

In contrast, this man admitted, he himself goes to the other extreme: He never expresses his fears and misgivings about their relationship at all. If he's unhappy but doesn't say anything about it, his unhappiness expresses itself in a kind of distancing coldness. This response is just what women fear most, and just the reason they prefer to express dissatisfactions and doubts—as an antidote to the isolation and distance that would result from keeping them to themselves.

The different perspectives on expressing or concealing dissatisfactions and doubts may reflect a difference in men's and women's awareness of the power of their words to affect others. In repeatedly telling him what she feared about their relationship, this woman spoke as though she assumed he was invulnerable and could not be hurt by what she said; perhaps she was underestimating the power of her words to affect him. For his part, when he refrains from expressing negative thoughts or feelings, he seems to be overestimating the power of his words to hurt her, when, ironically, she is more likely to be hurt by his silence than his words.

These women and men are talking in ways they learned as

children and reinforced as young adults and then adults, in their same-gender friendships. For girls, talk is the glue that holds relationships together. Boys' relationships are held together primarily by activities: doing things together, or talking about activities such as sports or, later, politics. The forums in which men are most inclined to talk are those in which they feel the need to impress, in situations where their status is in question.

MAKING ADJUSTMENTS

Such impasses will perhaps never be settled to the complete satisfaction of both parties, but understanding the differing views can help detoxify the situation, and both can make adjustments. Realizing that men and women have different assumptions about the place of talk in relationships, a woman can observe a man's desire to read the morning paper at the breakfast table without interpreting it as a rejection of her or a failure of their relationship. And a man can understand a woman's desire for talk without interpreting it as an unreasonable demand or a manipulative attempt to prevent him from doing what he wants to do.

A woman who had heard my interpretations of these differences between women and men told me how these insights helped her. Early in a promising relationship, a man spent the night at her apartment. It was a weeknight, and they both had to go to work the next day, so she was delighted when he made the rash and romantic suggestion that they have breakfast together and report late for work. She happily prepared breakfast, looking forward to the scene shaped in her mind: They would sit facing each other across her small table, look into each other's eyes, and say how much they liked each other and how happy they were about their growing friendship. It was against the backdrop of this heady expectation that she confronted an entirely different scene: As she placed on the table an array of lovingly prepared eggs, toast, and coffee, the man sat across her small table—and opened the newspaper in front of his face. If suggesting they have breakfast together had seemed like an invitation to get closer, in her view (or obstructing her view) the newspaper was now erected as a paper-thin but nonetheless impenetrable barrier between them.

Had she known nothing of the gender differences I discuss, she would simply have felt hurt and dismissed this man as yet another clunker. She would have concluded that, having enjoyed the night with her, he was now availing himself of her further services as a short-order cook. Instead, she realized that, unlike her, he did not feel the need for talk to reinforce their intimacy. The companionability of her presence was all he needed, and that did not mean that he didn't cherish her presence. By the same token, had he understood the essential role played by talk in women's definition of intimacy, he could have put off reading the paper—and avoided putting her off.

THE COMFORT OF HOME

For everyone, home is a place to be offstage. But the comfort of home can have opposite and incompatible meanings for women and men. For many men, the comfort of home means freedom from having to prove themselves and impress through verbal display. At last, they are in a situation where talk is not required. They are free to remain silent. But for women, home is a place where they are free to talk, and where they feel the greatest need for talk, with those they are closest to. For them, the comfort of home means the freedom to talk without worrying about how their talk will be judged.

This view emerged in a study by linguist Alice Greenwood of the conversations that took place among her three preadolescent children and their friends. Her daughters and son gave different reasons for their preferences in dinner guests. Her daughter Stacy said she would not want to invite people she didn't know well because then she would have to be "polite and quiet" and put on good manners. Greenwood's other daughter, Denise, said she liked to have her friend Meryl over because she could act crazy with Meryl and didn't have to worry about her manners, as she would with certain other friends who "would go around talking to people probably." But Denise's twin brother, Dennis, said nothing about having to watch his manners or worry about how others would judge his behavior. He simply said that he liked to have over friends with whom he could joke and laugh a lot. The girls' comments show that for them being close means being able to talk freely. And being with relative strangers means having to watch what they say and do. This insight holds a clue to the riddle of who talks more, women or men.

PUBLIC SPEAKING: THE TALKATIVE MAN AND THE SILENT WOMAN

So far I have been discussing the private scenes in which many men are silent and many women are talkative. But there are other scenes in which the roles are reversed. Returning to Rebecca and Stuart, we saw that when they are home alone, Rebecca's thoughts find their way into words effortlessly, whereas Stuart finds he can't come up with anything to say. The reverse happens when they are in other situations. For example, at a meeting of the neighborhood council or the parents' association at their children's school, it is Stuart who stands up and speaks. In that situation, it is Rebecca who is silent, her tongue tied by an acute awareness of all the negative reactions people could have to what she might say, all the mistakes she might make in trying to express her ideas. If she musters her courage and prepares to say something, she needs time to formulate it and then waits to be recognized by the chair. She cannot just jump up and start talking the way Stuart and some other men can.

Eleanor Smeal, president of the Fund for the Feminist Majority, was a guest on a call-in radio talk show, discussing abortion. No subject could be of more direct concern to women, yet during the hour-long show, all the callers except two were men. Diane Rehm, host of a radio talk show, expresses puzzlement that although the audience for her show is evenly split between women and men, 90 percent of the callers to the show are men. I am convinced that the reason is not that women are uninterested in the subjects discussed on the show. I would wager that women listeners are bringing up the subjects they heard on *The Diane Rehm Show* to their friends and family over lunch, tea, and dinner. But fewer of them call in because to do so would be putting themselves on display, claiming public attention for what they have to say, catapulting themselves onto center stage.

I myself have been the guest on innumerable radio and television talk shows. Perhaps I am unusual in being completely at ease in this mode of display. But perhaps I am not unusual at all, because, although I am comfortable in the role of invited expert, I have never called in to a talk show I was listening to, although I have often had ideas to contribute. When I am the guest, my position of authority is granted before I begin to speak. Were I to call in, I would be claiming that right on my own. I would have to establish my credibility by explaining who I am, which might seem self-aggrandizing, or not explain who I am and risk having my comments ignored or not valued. For similar reasons, though I am comfortable lecturing to groups numbering in the thousands, I rarely ask questions following another lecturer's talk, unless I know both the subject and the group very well.

My own experience and that of talk show hosts seems to hold a clue to the difference in women's and men's attitudes toward talk: Many men are more comfortable than most women in using talk to claim attention. And this difference lies at the heart of the distinction between report-talk and rapport-talk.

REPORT-TALK IN PRIVATE

Report-talk, or what I am calling public speaking, does not arise only in the literally public situation of formal speeches delivered to a listening audience. The more people there are in a conversation, the less well you know them, and the more status differences among them, the more a conversation is *like* public speaking or report-talk. The fewer the people, the more intimately you know them, and the more equal their status, the more it is like private speaking or rapport-talk. Furthermore, women feel a situation is more "public"—in the sense that they have to be on good behavior—if there are men present, except perhaps for family members. Yet even in families, the mother and children may feel their home to be "backstage" when Father is not home, "onstage" when he is: Many children are instructed to be on good behavior when Daddy is home. This may be because he is not home often, or because Mother—or Father—doesn't want the children to disturb him when he is.

The difference between public and private speaking also explains the stereotype that women don't tell jokes. Although some women are great raconteurs who can keep a group spellbound by recounting jokes and funny stories, there are fewer such personalities among women than among men. Many women who do tell jokes to large groups of people come from ethnic backgrounds in which verbal performance is highly valued. For example, many of the great women stand-up comics, such as Fanny Brice and Joan Rivers, came from Jewish backgrounds.

Although it's not true that women don't tell jokes, it is true that many women are less likely than men to tell jokes in large groups, especially groups including men. So it's not surprising that men get the impression that women never tell jokes at all. Folklorist Carol Mitchell studied joke telling on a college campus. She found that men told most of their jokes to other men, but they also told many jokes to mixed groups and to women. Women, however, told most of their jokes to other women, fewer to men, and very few to groups that included men as well as women. Men preferred and were more likely to tell jokes when they had an audience: at least two, often four or more. Women preferred a small audience of one or two, rarely more than three. Unlike men, they were reluctant to tell jokes in front of people they didn't know well. Many women flatly refused to tell jokes they knew if there were four or more in the group, promising to tell them later in private. Men never refused the invitation to tell jokes.

All of Mitchell's results fit in with the picture I have been drawing of public and private speaking. In a situation in which there are more people in the audience, more men, or more strangers, joke telling, like any other form of verbal performance, requires speakers to claim center stage and prove their abilities. These are the situations in which many women are reluctant to talk. In a situation that is more private, because the audience is small, familiar, and perceived to be members of a community (for example, other women), they are more likely to talk.

The idea that telling jokes is a kind of self-display does not imply that it is selfish or self-centered. The situation of joke telling illustrates that status and connection entail each other. Entertaining others is a way of establishing connections with them, and telling jokes can be a kind of gift giving, where the joke is a gift that brings pleasure to receivers. The key issue is asymmetry: One person is the teller and the others are the audience. If these roles are later exchanged—for example, if the joke telling becomes a round in which one person after another takes the role of teller—then there is symmetry on the broad scale, if not in the individual act. However, if women habitually take the role of appreciative audience and never take the role of joke teller, the asymmetry of the individual joke telling is diffused through the larger interaction as well. This is a hazard for women. A hazard for men is that continually telling jokes can be distancing. This is the effect felt by a man who complained that when he talks to his father on the phone, all his father does is tell him jokes. An extreme instance of a similar phenomenon is the class clown, who, according to teachers, is nearly always a boy.

RAPPORT-TALK IN PUBLIC

Just as conversations that take place at home among friends can be like public speaking, even a public address can be like private speaking: for example, by giving a lecture full of personal examples and stories.

At the executive committee of a fledgling professional organization, the outgoing president, Fran, suggested that the organization adopt the policy of having presidents deliver a presidential address. To explain and support her proposal, she told a personal anecdote: Her cousin was the president of a more established professional organization at the time that Fran held the same position in this one. Fran's mother had been talking to her cousin's mother on the telephone. Her cousin's mother told Fran's mother that her daughter was preparing her presidential address, and she asked when Fran's presidential address was scheduled to be. Fran was embarrassed to admit to her mother that she was not giving one. This made her wonder whether the organization's professional identity might not be enhanced if it emulated the more established organizations.

Several men on the committee were embarrassed by Fran's reference to her personal situation and were not convinced by her argument. It seemed to them not only irrelevant but unseemly to talk about her mother's telephone conversations at an executive committee meeting. Fran had approached the meeting—a relatively public context—as an extension of the private kind. Many women's tendency to use personal experience and examples, rather than abstract argumentation, can be understood from the perspective of their orientation to language as it is used in private speaking.

A study by Celia Roberts and Tom Jupp of a faculty meeting

at a secondary school in England found that the women's arguments did not carry weight with their male colleagues because they tended to use their own experience as evidence, or argue about the effect of policy on individual students. The men at the meeting argued from a completely different perspective, making categorical statements about right and wrong.

The same distinction is found in discussions at home. A man told me that he felt critical of what he perceived as his wife's lack of logic. For example, he recalled a conversation in which he had mentioned an article he had read in *The New York Times* claiming that today's college students are not as idealistic as students were in the 1960s. He was inclined to accept this claim. His wife questioned it, supporting her argument with the observation that her niece and her niece's friends were very idealistic indeed. He was incredulous and scornful of her faulty reasoning; it was obvious to him that a single personal example is neither evidence nor argumentation—it's just anecdote. It did not occur to him that he was dealing with a different logical system, rather than a lack of logic.

The logic this woman was employing was making sense of the world as a more private endeavor—observing and integrating her personal experience and drawing connections to the experiences of others. The logic the husband took for granted was a more public endeavor—more like gathering information, conducting a survey, or devising arguments by rules of formal logic as one might in doing research.

Another man complained about what he and his friends call women's "shifting sands" approach to discussion. These men feel that whereas they try to pursue an argument logically, step by step, until it is settled, women continually change course in midstream. He pointed to the short excerpt from *Divorce American Style* quoted above as a case in point. It seemed to him that when Debbie Reynolds said, "I can't argue now. I have to take the French bread out of the oven," she was evading the argument because she had made an accusation—"All you do is criticize"— that she could not support.

This man also offered an example from his own experience. His girlfriend had told him of a problem she had because her boss wanted her to do one thing and she wanted to do another. Taking the boss's view for the sake of argumentation, he pointed out a negative consequence that would result if she did what she wanted. She countered that the same negative consequence would result if she did what the boss wanted. He complained that she was shifting over to the other field of battle—what would happen if she followed her boss's will—before they had made headway with the first—what would happen if she followed her own.

SPEAKING FOR THE TEAM

A final puzzle on the matter of public and private speaking is suggested by the experience I related at the opening of this chapter, in which a woman's group I addressed had invited men to participate, and a talkative man had referred to his silent wife as "the talker in our family." Following their laughter, other women in the group commented that this woman was not usually silent. When their meetings consisted of women only, she did her share of talking. Why, then, was she silent on this occasion?

One possibility is that my presence transformed the private-speaking group into a public-speaking event. Another transformation was that there were men in the group. In a sense, most women feel they are "backstage" when there are no men around. When men are present women are "onstage," insofar as they feel they must watch their behavior more. Another possibility is that it was not the presence of men in general that affected this woman's behavior, but the presence of *her husband*. One interpretation is that she was somehow cowed, or silenced, by her husband's presence. But another is that she felt they were a team. Since he was talking a lot, the team would be taking up too much time if she spoke too. She also may have felt that because he was representing their team, she didn't have to, much as many women let their husbands drive if they are in the car, but do the driving themselves if their husbands are not there.

Obviously, not every woman becomes silent when her husband joins a group; after all, there were many women in the group who talked a lot, and many had brought spouses. But several other couples told me of similar experiences. For example, when one couple took evening classes together, he was always an active participant in class discussion, while she said very little. But one semester they had decided to take different classes, and then she found that she was a talkative member of the class she attended alone.

Such a development can be viewed in two different ways. If talking in a group is a good thing—a privilege and a pleasure—then the silent woman will be seen as deprived of her right to speak, deprived of her voice. But the pleasures of report-talk are not universally admired. There are many who do not wish to speak in a group. In this view, a woman who feels she has no need to speak because her husband is doing it for her might feel privileged, just as a woman who does not like to drive might feel lucky that she doesn't have to when her husband is there—and a man who does not like to drive might feel unlucky that he has to, like it or not.

AVOIDING MUTUAL BLAME

The difference between public and private speaking, or report-talk and rapport-talk, can be understood in terms of status and connection. It is not surprising that women are most comfortable talking when they feel safe and close, among friends and equals, whereas men feel comfortable talking when there is a need to establish and maintain their status in a group. But the situation is complex, because status and connection are bought with the same currency. What seems like a bid for status could be intended as a display of closeness, and what seems like distancing may have been intended to avoid the appearance of pulling rank. Hurtful and unjustified misinterpretations can be avoided by understanding the conversational styles of the other gender.

When men do all the talking at meetings, many women—including researchers—see them as "dominating" the meeting, intentionally preventing women from participating, publicly flexing their higher-status muscles. But the *result* that men do most of the talking does not necessarily mean that men *intend* to prevent women from speaking. Those who readily speak up assume that others are as free as they are to take the floor. In this sense, men's speaking out freely can be seen as evidence that they assume women are at the same level of status: "We are all equals," the metamessage of their behavior could be, "competing for the floor." If this is indeed the intention (and I believe it often, though not always, is), a woman can recognize women's lack of participation at meetings and take measures to redress the imbalance, without blaming men for intentionally locking them out.

The culprit, then, is not an individual man or even men's styles alone, but the difference between women's and men's styles. If that is the case, then both can make adjustments. A woman can push herself to speak up without being invited, or begin to speak without waiting for what seems a polite pause. But the adjustment should not be one-sided. A man can learn that a woman who is not accustomed to speaking up in groups is *not* as free as he is to do so. Someone who is waiting for a nice long pause before asking her question does not find the stage set for her appearance, as do those who are not awaiting a pause, the moment after (or before) another speaker stops talking. Someone who expects to be invited to speak ("You haven't said much, Millie. What do you think?") is not accustomed to leaping in and claiming the floor for herself. As in so many areas, being admitted as an equal is not in itself assurance of equal opportunity, if one is not accustomed to playing the game in the way it is being played. Being admitted to a dance does not ensure the participation of someone who has learned to dance to a different rhythm.

FOUR

Gossip

The impression that women talk too freely and too much in private situations is summed up in a word: *gossip*. Although gossip can be destructive, it isn't always; it can serve a crucial function in establishing intimacy—especially if it is not "talking against" but simply "talking about."

The label "gossip" casts a critical light on women's interest in talking about the details of people's lives. Evidence that the negativity of the term reflects men's interpretation of women's ways of talking can be seen in the following excerpt from Marge Piercy's novel *Fly Away Home*. Daria falls in love with Tom partly because he differs from her former husband, Ross, in this respect:

> It surprised her what he knew about the people around him. Ross would never have known that Gretta disliked her

son's teacher, or that Fay had just given walking papers to her boyfriend because he drank too much in front of her boys. For a man, Tom had an uncommon interest in the details of people's lives. Gossip, Ross would call it, but she thought it was just being interested in people.

Not only men disparage an interest in the details of people's lives as "gossip." The great southern writer Eudora Welty, remembering her Mississippi childhood, writes that her mother tried to keep a talkative seamstress from telling stories about local people in front of her little girl: " 'I don't want her exposed to gossip,' " Welty recalls her mother saying, "as if gossip were the measles and I could catch it." But far from having a bad influence on the child, the gossipy stories about people that Welty loved to hear inspired her to become a writer. When people talk about the details of daily lives, it is gossip; when they write about them, it is literature: short stories and novels.

Mary Catherine Bateson draws another parallel—between gossip and anthropology, the academic discipline that makes a career of documenting the details of people's lives. She recalls that her mother, Margaret Mead, told her she would never make an anthropologist because she wasn't interested enough in gossip.

IN GOSSIP BEGINS FRIENDSHIP

Telling details of others' lives is partly the result of women's telling their friends details of their own lives. These details become gossip when the friend to whom they are told repeats them to someone else—presumably another friend. Telling what's happening in your life and the lives of those you talk to is a grown-up version of telling secrets, the essence of girls' and women's friendships.

In Alice Mattison's story "New Haven," which I quoted in Chapter Two, Eleanor tells Patsy that she is falling in love with a married man. As soon as these words are out, Eleanor feels "a little ashamed to lack her secret suddenly," but "she also feels pleased; she doesn't have to guard it, for once. And it's exhilarating to talk about Peter." I was struck by Mattison's phrasing—"to lack her secret"—which captures the way that *having* a secret makes a person feel enhanced, and telling it is giving something away—in the sense of possession as well as the idiomatic sense of revelation. Mattison also captures the pleasure in not having to hide something, and being able to talk about what's really on your mind.

Not only is telling secrets evidence of friendship; it *creates* a friendship, when the listener responds in the expected way. Eleanor does not know Patsy well, but she would like to. There is an affinity and a budding friendship between them; they have taken to going together for coffee and ice cream following the rehearsals of the musical group in which they both play. By telling Patsy what was going on in her life, telling her secret, Eleanor promoted Patsy from acquaintance to friend.

Keeping friends up to date about the events in one's life is not only a privilege; for many women it is an obligation. One woman explained that she didn't enjoy telling the story of her breakup with her boyfriend over and over, but she had to, because if she had failed to inform any of her close friends about such an important development, they would have been deeply hurt when they found out. They would have taken her secrecy as a sign that she was curtailing their friendship, clipping its wings. The woman, furthermore, was incredulous when she learned that her boyfriend had not told anyone at all about their breakup. He had gone to work, gone to his gym, and played squash with his friends, all as if nothing had happened to change his life.

Because telling secrets is an essential part of friendship for most women, they may find themselves in trouble when they have no secrets to tell. For example, a woman I'll call Carol had several women friends she talked to every few days, exchanging stories about dates with men. They would share their excitement before a new date, and after the date took place, they would report in detail what had been said and done. So when Carol fell in love and formed a lasting relationship with a man, she ran out of material for talks with her friends. She also had less time to talk on the phone, since she now spent most of her free time with the man. This put a strain on her friendships; it was as if she had gathered up her marbles, reneging on her part in the partnership of talk that constituted the friendship.

Situations in which one person feels abandoned because the other forms a permanent relationship are not limited to women friends. In the story "Mendocino" by Ann Packer, the narrator, Bliss, finds it sad to visit her brother, who now lives with a woman, because his intimacy with the woman has diminished his intimacy with her. Bliss recalls their former closeness, when

> they would exchange work stories, and, into a second bottle of wine, confide in each other the news of their most recent failures at love. It amazes Bliss that until this moment she never once realized it was because they were failures that they talked about them. Now Gerald has his success, and it is as if the two of them had never been anything but what they are now: wary, cordial.

Because they are not exchanging secrets about relationships in one-on-one conversation, Bliss perceives her conversations with Gerald, now taking place in a group of three, to be wary and cordial—in a way, more like public speaking.

Many things conspire to separate people from their single friends if they find a stable relationship. I had a friend, a man, who had been single for many years and had developed a wide and strong network of women friends to whom he talked frequently. When he developed a stable relationship with a woman and they moved in together, his friends complained that he did not tell them anything anymore. "It's not that I'm keeping things from them," he told me. "It's just that Naomi and I get along fine and there's nothing to tell." By saying this, he did, however, tell me about a problem in his relationships—although it involved not his partner but his friends.

RAPPORT-TALK AS LAMENT

A folklorist, Anna Caraveli, studied women's laments in the villages of Greece. Laments are spontaneous, ritualized, oral poems that some Greek women chant to express grief over the loss of loved ones to expatriation or death. According to Caraveli, women typically recite laments in the company of other women. Even more significant, women feel they *need* other women to participate for the lament to be successful. One woman who performed a lament for Caraveli to tape remarked that she could have done it better if she'd had other women there to help her.

When the Greek women gather to share laments, each one's expression of grief reminds the others of their own suffering, and they intensify each other's feelings. Indeed, both Caraveli and anthropologist Joel Kuipers, who has studied a similar lament tradition in Bali, note that women judge each other's skill in this folk art by their ability to move others, to involve them in the experience of grieving. Expressing the pain they feel in losing loved ones bonds the women to each other, and their bonding is a salve against the wound of loss. According to anthropologist Joel Sherzer, the performance of "tuneful weeping" over dead loved ones is the exclusive domain of women in vastly differing societies all over the world.

Folk rituals of lament are parallel to the less formal but equally widespread ritual by which modern American and European women get together for troubles talk. They too bond in pain. This may explain why troubles make such good talk. Bonding through troubles is widespread among women and common between women and men. It seems to be far less common between men.

Some of the men I interviewed said they did not discuss their problems with anyone. Most of those who said they did told me they tended to discuss them with women friends. Some men said that they had a man friend with whom they discussed problems. But there were differences that indicated they were somewhere farther on the continuum from the pole of intimacy than most women. First of all, they had one friend, at most two, with whom they discussed problems, not several, or even many, as was the case with many women I talked to. Second, they often said they had not spoken to that friend in a while—days, weeks, months, or even longer—but they knew that if they needed him, he would be there. Most women were in constant touch with their closest friends, and frequently discussed even minor decisions and developments in their lives. One man told me he does have a friend that he tells his troubles to, but if he does not have a serious problem, he does not call his friend; that's why so much time can pass without their talking.

One woman, whom I will call Shirley, told me of her surprise at receiving a call from a man who had broken her heart; he said he wanted to come over and talk. It turned out that what he wanted to talk about was that he had just had his heart broken—by another woman. Shirley asked why he had come to her. He said there was no one else he could talk to about how he felt. What about his friends? He just didn't feel comfortable talking to them about something like this.

When most men talk to their friends on the phone, they may discuss what's happening in business, the stock market, the soccer match, or politics. They do gossip (although they may not call it that) in the sense of talking about themselves and other people. But they tend to talk about political rather than personal relationships: institutional power, advancement and decline, a proposal that may or may not get through the committee, a plan for making money. If men do mention their wives and families, the mention is likely to be brief, not belabored and elaborated in depth or detail. If they make reference to a difficult personal situation, it will likely be minimal and vague ("It's been rough").

A man described his Thanksgiving to me. Three generations of his wife's family had gathered: brothers and sisters, their children, and their parents. The men went outside to play football, while the women stayed inside and talked. The older women ended up telling the youngest granddaughter she was too young to get married.

Earlier we saw that women's inclination to engage in troubles talk is confusing to men, who mistake the ritual lament for a request for advice. Now we can see that troubles talk is just one aspect of the ongoing intimate conversation that can be called gossip. Not only is providing solutions to minor problems beside the point, but it cuts short the conversation, which *is* the point. If one problem is solved, then another must be found, to keep the intimate conversation going.

SMALL TALK SERVES A BIG PURPOSE

Small talk is crucial to maintain a sense of camaraderie when there is nothing special to say. Women friends and relatives keep the conversational mechanisms in working order by talking about small things as well as large. Knowing they will have such conversations later makes women feel they are not alone in life. If they do not have someone to tell their thoughts and impressions to, they *do* feel alone. This is dramatized in a short story by Ursula Le Guin titled "In and Out." A woman who is becoming interested in doing ceramics gets some help and advice from a local potter. He gives her more attention than she sought, and she finds it difficult to get away. When she finally drives off, he calls after her, saying that

> if she wanted to try bringing pots up on his wheel she could come over any evening, which left her really wishing she was at the office, where she could tell somebody. "He said, 'Come over and bring pots up on my wheel'!"

Like a writer who sees small events in her life as material for a story, Le Guin's character sees her life as material for conversations.

Students in my class on gender differences recorded casual conversations between women friends and men friends. It was easy to get recordings of women friends talking, partly because most of the students were women, but also because the request to "record a conversation with your friend" met with easy compliance from the students' female friends and family members. But asking men to record conversations with their friends had mixed results. One woman's mother agreed readily, but her father insisted that he didn't have conversations with his friends. "Don't you ever call Fred on the phone?" she asked, naming a man she knew to be his good friend. "Not often," he said. "But if I do, it's because I have something to ask, and when I get the answer, I hang up."

Another woman's husband delivered a tape to her with great satisfaction and pride. "This is a good conversation," he announced, "because it's not just him and me shooting the breeze, like 'Hi, how are you? I saw a good movie the other day,' and stuff. It's a problem-solving task. Each line is meaningful." When the woman listened to the tape, she heard her husband and his friend trying to solve a computer problem. Everything they said was technical and impersonal. Not only did she not consider it "a good conversation," she didn't really regard it as a conversation at all. His idea of a good conversation was one with impersonal, factual, task-focused content. Hers was one with personal content.

These differences also show up in relations between parents and children. My students tell me that when they talk to "their parents" on the phone, they spend most of the time talking to their mothers. Their fathers typically join the conversation only when they have a business matter to discuss or report. This happens in writing as well as in speaking, and apparently it is not limited to American families. A German student showed me a card she had received that her mother had covered with handwritten "conversation" inquiring about her daughter's life and health and filling her in on family news. Folded into the card was a brief typewritten note from her father, telling her to go to the university registrar and obtain a form that he needed for tax purposes.

In response to an article I had written, a journalist remarked that my claim that many men have little use for small talk, since they believe talk is designed to convey information, rang a bell with him. He deplores chit-chat and believes that talk should have significant content, be interesting and meaningful. This is fine so long as there is a business meeting with lots of substance to discuss. But he finds himself verbally hamstrung when the meeting breaks up, and he has to embark on the long walk down the hall with a stranger. Opposed in principle to, and simply unpracticed in, making small talk, he is at a loss when there is no "big talk" available.

For most women, getting together and telling about their feelings and what is happening in their lives is at the heart of friendship. Having someone to tell your secrets to means you are not alone in the world. But telling secrets is not an endeavor without risks. Someone who knows your secrets has power over you: She can tell your secrets to others and create trouble for you. This is the source of the negative image of gossip.

WHEN GOSSIP IS RUMOR

The most negative image of gossip reflects a situation in which destructive rumors that have no basis in fact are spread. An extreme illustration of such a situation is described in Edna O'Brien's story "The Widow." In this story, a woman named Biddy, whose beloved husband has drowned, finally finds happiness in a new relationship. The people of the town watch her every move and criticize her new love interest, predicting disaster, but she has what she thinks is the last laugh when she becomes engaged. A week before the wedding, the happy couple visit the local pub and stand everyone to drinks.

> Then Biddy, being a little tipsy, tapped her glass with her engagement ring and said she was going to give a little reci-

tation. Without further ado, she stood up, smiled that sort of urchin smile of hers, ran her tongue over her lips, another habit, and recited a poem entitled "People Will Talk." It was a lunge at all those mischievous, prurient people who begrudged her her little flourish. It may have been—indeed, many people said that it was—this audacious provocation that wreaked the havoc of the next weeks. Had she confided in a few local women, she might have been saved, but she did not confide; she stood aloof with her man, her eyes gleaming, her happiness assured.

Far from assured, Biddy's happiness is doomed. She is undone by malicious and unfounded gossip. The rumor is spread that her first husband committed suicide because she made his life intolerable. Biddy tries desperately to prevent her fiancé from hearing the false rumors, and one of her efforts in this regard leads to her death. O'Brien implies that spreading the malicious rumor was the townspeople's way of punishing Biddy for thumbing her nose at the power of their tongues, and for holding herself aloof from them by not confiding in other women—in other words, they undid her with gossip because she had not shown the proper respect for it.

In many ways, our society is becoming more private than public in orientation, more gossiplike in public domains. Most forms of public communication, such as television news and public officials' press conferences, are becoming more informal in style, with remarks being made (or made to seem) off the cuff rather than prepared. One result of this is the need for frequent public apologies, and even resignations, by people who have spoken off the cuff, making the kinds of comments that are common in private conversations but unacceptable in public. Another aspect of this development is increased interest in the private lives of public people. It is perhaps not surprising that an aspect of this interest—perhaps a byproduct of it—is the role of rumor in public life.

A *Washington Post* article headlined THE PUBLIC POLITICS OF RUMOR notes that whereas rumors have long been "a staple of politics," only recently have they been readily reported by the media, whether or not the reporter has been able to confirm their truth. The incident that sparked this article was one in which the Republican National Committee's communication director resigned after having written and distributed a memo implying—not stating—that the newly installed Democratic Speaker of the House was homosexual. The *Post* writer comments that rumors are effective even if they are later disproved and retracted; the damage is done by their mere existence, because most people assume "where there's smoke, there's fire." The American public arena has become a little more like the Irish community of Edna O'Brien's story.

THE USES OF GOSSIP

These are dramatic examples of the destructive potential of gossip. Nora Ephron describes the more circumscribed danger of telling one's secrets to friends in her novel *Heartburn*. The heroine, Rachel, runs into her friend Meg Roberts on a plane to Washington from New York. Meg mentions their friend Betty's birthday party, and Rachel is aghast to realize she forgot all about the party. She has an unassailable excuse: She left her husband and flew to New York because she had learned that he was passionately in love and having an affair with another woman. Now, however, she is on her way back home with her husband, intending to resume her marriage. She doesn't want to make use of her excellent excuse because it would be too good as gossip:

> The only way Betty would ever forgive me would be for me to tell her why, and if I told her why she'd tell everyone in Washington, and then everyone in town would know something about our marriage that I didn't want them to know. I know all about Meg Roberts' marriage, for example, because Meg confides in her friend Ann, who confides in Betty, who confides in me.

True friends, everyone feels, do not repeat their friends' secrets to others. Revealing a secret can be the basis for the end of a friendship. And yet people do often repeat what is told to them in confidence by their friends. Why is this so?

Penelope Eckert, an anthropologist, spent time with high school girls and got to know their social worlds. Donna Eder, a sociologist, did the same in junior high. Both noticed that girls get status by being friends with high-status girls: the cheerleaders, the pretty ones, the ones who are popular with boys. If being friends with those of high status is a way to get status for yourself, how are you to prove to others that a popular girl is your friend? One way is to show that you know her secrets, because it is in the context of friendship that secrets are revealed.

A few high school girls told Eckert that they prefer to have boys as friends because boys don't try to get juicy details and are less likely to spread them around. The girls may think that this demonstrates the moral superiority of boys. But Eckert points out that the reason a boy is less likely to scavenge for gossip and distribute his findings is that he has much less to gain by it. Boys' main access to status is less a matter of whom they are close to than of their achievements and skill, primarily at sports, and their ability to prevail in a fight (though the older a boy gets, the more his fights tend to be verbal rather than physical).

There is yet another way that the desire to forge connections may be at work in creating gossip. Talking about someone who is not there is a way of establishing rapport with someone who *is* there. By agreeing about their evaluation of someone else, people reinforce their shared values and world views.

GOSSIP AS SOCIAL CONTROL

The reinforcement of values by talking about other people also works in another way. We measure our behavior against the potential for gossip, hearing in our minds how others are likely to talk about us. In trying to decide what to do, we automatically project contemplated actions onto the backdrop of this imagined dialogue, and our decisions about how to act are influenced by what we think others would say about them. Having decided, we hide, adjust or display our behavior to prevent criticism and ensure being praised. Those who are of a rebellious nature and age may defy expectations evidenced in gossip. Regardless of the stance taken toward them, the assumptions underlying "what people will say" plant in us an image of what a good person is and does. Hearing people praised for being generous and self-effacing, we get the idea that these are good things to be. Hearing people criticized for being stingy, disloyal, or ugly, we get the idea that these are not good things to be.

Girls and women feel it is crucial that they be liked by their peers, a form of involvement that focuses on symmetrical connections. Boys and men feel it is crucial that they be respected by their peers, a form of involvement that focuses on asymmetrical status. Being disliked is a more devastating punishment for girls and women, because of their need for affiliation. Marjorie Harness Goodwin, in her study of teen and preteen boys and girls at play, found that when a girl's behavior was strongly disapproved, the other girls ostracized her for a month and a half—the ultimate means of social control. In contrast, although boys sometimes left the group when they felt they were insulted too much, Goodwin did not find boys excluded for an extended period of time.

LETTING IT SHOW

The need to be liked and approved of can be at odds with the need to reveal secrets, since secrets expose one's weaknesses. In an example I gave earlier, a woman's former boyfriend had his heart broken and he wanted to talk about it—so much that he went to her, even though he had left her long before. Why didn't he feel comfortable talking to his friends about problems? Maybe for the same reason that many men interviewed by Catherine Kohler Riessman did not talk to anyone about their divorce. One of the men told her, "I think everybody hates to have anybody know that they have problems. . . . You always try and keep your problems to yourself." These men, like many others, are keenly aware of the imbalance in power that can result from telling secrets. For one thing, those who show weakness can feel they have put themselves in a one-down position. For another, they are giving away information that could be used against them.

Women are aware of this danger too. Robinette Kennedy, a psychologist who studied women's friendships in a village in Crete, found that women are keenly aware of the danger of malicious gossip resulting from exchanging secrets. She asked twelve schoolgirls to write what qualities they valued in a friend, and every single one wrote: not betraying secrets. Kennedy found that some women actually avoided having friendships for this reason, but they missed having friends. In a society where women and men lived in separate spheres and had to take clearly defined roles in relation to each other, having a woman friend meant that there was at least one relationship in which a woman could be completely herself, and be understood and accepted. If she had no one to whom she could tell her true feelings, she felt painfully isolated.

The women and girls in the Greek village and the American schoolgirls that Eder and Eckert studied had the same dilemma: They needed friends to talk to, but they knew that talking to friends is risky. Girls and women, more often than boys and men, are willing to take the risk, because their eyes are on the payoff in rapport. The possibilities of appearing vulnerable and of losing independence are in the corner of the eye. Men are less likely to take the risk because for them preventing vulnerability and protecting their independence are in the foreground, and issues of intimacy in the background.

Many men resent their wives' or girlfriends' talking about their relationships to friends. To these men, talking about a personal relationship to others is an act of disloyalty. One man I interviewed waxed eloquent on this point. He said he regarded telling intimate details about a relationship—especially those that showed a partner's weaknesses—as a breach of trust, pure and simple. He expressed disdain for anyone who would need to stoop to such a level in order to create rapport with friends. Such strong reactions support the claim by anthropologist Jill Dubisch (writing about Greek culture) that talking about family matters to nonfamily members is taboo because it destroys a sacred boundary between inside and outside, taking outside the home what properly belongs inside it.

Dubisch also points out the symbolic connection between verbal and sexual pollution: Allowing strangers into the house by telling them the family's secrets is like "illicit sexual penetration." This seems to capture the dilemma of widows in Greece as seen in a line from a lament that Caraveli recorded: "Widow in the house, gossips at the door." The widow is confined to the house, because if she steps outside, anything she does will expose her to the sexual accusations of gossip.

To say that many men do not exchange secrets about their own and others' lives for the purpose of establishing intimacy is certainly not to say that they do not have a need and a way to bond with others through talk. If women's source of involvement, talking about personal lives, is an irritant to men, then to find a source of men's involvement, we can inspect an aspect of their behavior that is an irritant to women: the daily newspaper.

NEWS AS GOSSIP

A retired professor met daily with several retired male friends at a local diner. He and his friends referred to their gatherings as "solving the world's problems"—and this gives a good indication of what they talked about.

Men's interest in the details of politics, news, and sports is parallel to women's interest in the details of personal lives. If

110

women are afraid of being left out by not knowing what is going on with this person or that, men are afraid of being left out by not knowing what is going on in the world. And exchanging details about public news rather than private news has the advantage that it does not make men personally vulnerable: The information they are bartering has nothing to do with them.

In a book about the history of news, Mitchell Stephens points out that men have long been obsessed with exchanging details about current events. He does not actually say he is talking about "men" but rather "the English"; however, it is clear from his description that it is English *men* to whom his comments apply.

> It might be surprising to learn that more than 275 years ago, the English—though they had no radio, television, satellites or computers, they obtained much of their news at the coffeehouse—thought *their* era was characterized by an obsession with news. The condition was described in a newspaper written in 1712 as "the furious itch of novelty," and it was said to have "proved fatal to many families; the meanest of shopkeepers and handicrafts spending whole days in coffee-houses, to hear news and talk politicks, whilst their wives and children wanted bread at home. . . ." Similar behavior had been noted in the mid-seventeenth century in Cambridge. "Scholars are so Greedy after news . . . that they neglect all for it," one concerned observer complained.

If "the English" are gathering in coffeehouses to "talk politicks" while their wives and children are at home, then "the English" are actually "English men." But how similar this picture of men gathering to exchange news is to the stereotype of women neglecting their household duties to gossip on the phone or meet over coffee in their kitchens.

THE POWER OF DETAILS

Discussing details about the news and exchanging details about private lives are coming together, as newspapers report more about the private lives of people in the news. The phenomenal success of *People* magazine is only the most extreme instance. Consider this article opening:

> Charles and Jeanne Atchison live near the Cowboy City dance bar on a gravel street in a peeling white and gold mobile home. Weeds sway in the breeze out front. It's a street with a melancholy down-on-one's-luck feel about it. The town is Azle, Tex., a tiny speck on the periphery of Fort Worth.
>
> A few years ago, the picture was a far prettier one. Charles (Chuck) Atchison was all set. He made good money— more than $1,000 a week—enough to pay for a cozy house, new cars, fanciful trips. But all that is gone. He's six months behind on rent for his land, and don't even ask about the legal bills.
>
> "It's sort of like I was barreling along and I suddenly shifted into reverse," Mr. Atchison said with a rueful smile. "Well, welcome to whistle blower country."
>
> Chuck Atchison is 44, with a stony face and a sparse mustache.

These lines are not from a short story or magazine article. The excerpt is from the front page of the "Business" section of *The New York Times*—that soberest section of the soberest of American newspapers. In reporting what happened to Atchison, a quality control inspector who exposed safety violations at a nuclear plant, the journalist gives a personal view of the whistle-blower: what he looked like, what his house looked like—details that involve the reader.

According to columnist Bob Greene, journalists began turning their attention to such mundane details in 1963, when Jimmy Breslin wrote a column entitled "A Death in Emergency Room One" describing the last moments of John Kennedy's life. Greene says Breslin's column "literally took his readers into the corridors and operating rooms of Parkland Hospital on that day." Greene observes, "Journalists today are trained to get those telling details quickly. . . ." The same brand of journalism is said to have established the career of columnist Russell Baker, whose coverage of Queen Elizabeth's coronation focused not on the public pageantry but on the backstage details—for example, as a reviewer noted, the "long lines of colonial potentates in animal skins and gold braid forming to use Westminster Abbey's toilets."

Why would readers want to feel that they were in the corridors and operating rooms of the hospital in which Kennedy lay? Why would they be interested in the lines outside the toilets at a coronation? Because such details give them a pleasurable sense of involvement, of being part of something, just as gossip does for women who talk about the details of their own and others' lives.

THE JOY OF INVOLVEMENT

Despite the growing appreciation of details in news stories, the usefulness of telling details in everyday conversation is not universally recognized. A woman told me that members of her family refer to her grandmother in a phrase that typifies the old woman's conversation: "I had a little ham, I had a little cheese." This affectionate yet disparaging mode of reference reveals that they find it boring when Grandmother tells them what she had for lunch. They wish she would give fewer details, or not report her lunch at all.

My great-aunt, for many years a widow, had a love affair when she was in her seventies. Obese, balding, her hands and legs misshapen by arthritis, she did not fit the stereotype of a woman romantically loved. But she was—by a man, also in his seventies, who lived in a nursing home but occasionally spent weekends with her in her apartment. In trying to tell me what this relationship meant to her, my great-aunt told of a conversation. One evening she had had dinner out, with friends. When she returned home, her male friend called and she told him about the dinner. He listened with interest and asked her, "What did you wear?" When she told me this, she began to cry: "Do you know how many years it's been since anyone asked me what I wore?"

When my great-aunt said this, she was saying that it had

been years since anyone had cared deeply—intimately—about her. The exchange of relatively insignificant details about daily life sends a metamessage of rapport and caring.

Attention to details associated with a person is often a sign of romantic interest. In a novel titled *The Jealous One,* by Celia Fremlin, a woman sends her husband, Geoffrey, next door to deliver a dinner invitation to their new neighbor, who has moved in that day. Geoffrey returns full of excitement, bubbling with admiration for and details about the new neighbor. He announces, starry-eyed, that the neighbor has invited *them* to dinner in her not-yet-furnished home, and he asks his wife if she has a red ribbon for Shang Low, the neighbor's Pekingese, explaining that *Shang Low* is the opposite of *Shang High*. The wife responds with irony, but Geoffrey is slow to join in her ironic denigration of the neighbor's airs in ribboning her dog:

> She giggled in terrible solitude for a fraction of a second; and then Geoffrey joined in, a tiny bit too late and a tiny bit too loud. And the joke did not lead to another joke. Murmuring something about "having promised . . .", Geoffrey hurried away out of the kitchen and out of the house, without any red ribbon. And this piece of red ribbon, which they didn't look for, didn't find, and probably hadn't got, became the very first of the objects which couldn't ever again be mentioned between them.

Geoffrey's romantic interest in the new neighbor leaks out in his enthusiastic, uncritical recounting of details about her, such as the breed and name of her dog.

If recalling a detail or name is a sign of caring, failure to recall a name can be seen as a sign of lack of caring. Complaints are frequent from people whose parents disapprove of their partners or friends and seem to display their disapproval subtly by habitually referring to them by the wrong names or failing to recall their names. The same phenomenon can be manipulated for positive ends. This was the case with a woman who remained friends with the wife of an acquaintance of her former husband's.

Her friend persisted in referring to the former husband's new wife as "what's her name." The divorced woman took the metamessage of this to be "Even though I see her occasionally, I don't really care about her. You are still the one who counts to me." Not remembering the new wife's name was offered as evidence of lack of caring about her—and, consequently, loyalty to the first wife.

Paying attention to details of a person's appearance can be a means of flirting. A woman had an appointment to meet a man she had met only once before, briefly. They were both married; the purpose of the meeting was business. But the man began their conversation by observing that she looked younger than he recalled, and her hair was different. "You were wearing a hat, then, weren't you?" he said. "And you were dressed in white then too." Simply saying that he had noticed her appearance the first time they had met was a kind of flirtation. It was not a displeasing one to her, though her husband found it displeasing when she recounted it to him.

The noticing of details shows caring and creates involvement. Men, however, often find women's involvement in details irritating. Because women are concerned first and foremost with establishing intimacy, they value the telling of details.

Conversely, many women complain that men don't tell enough details. A woman thus frustrated is Laura in Alice Mattison's story "Sleeping Giant." Laura and Dan are both troubled by their son-in-law's plan to buy an old, run-down house. In the past, when Laura tried to talk to her daughter about it, the daughter defended her husband. But Dan now assures Laura that their daughter sees her point of view, because she said as much to him. "Believe me," he says, "she's not happy about this." Laura wants more details about the conversation, but Dan won't supply them. Laura asks:

> "Well, why doesn't she tell him so?"
> He doesn't answer.
> "What did she say *exactly*?" Laura is searching in her

canvas bag for her car keys. She's chilly after all, and there's a flannel shirt in the trunk of the car. She waits, holding the keys and the bag, but Dan still doesn't answer, and she drops the bag on the bench. "What did she *say*?"

"Oh, I don't remember. General things."

"What did *you* say?"

"Oh, I don't know, Laura." Laura turns aside abruptly, opens the trunk, and stares into it for a moment, annoyed that Dan won't tell her more.

Laura sounds like innumerable flesh-and-blood women I've talked to. As one put it, "Men don't tell the whole story—who said what." Another complained of her husband: "It's like pulling teeth to get him to tell me, 'What did she *say*? What did he *say*?' "

Yet another woman recalled a time that her best friend's husband tried unsuccessfully to take part in one of their conversations. Breaking with tradition, he tried to tell about an experience that he thought was similar to the ones they were discussing. The two women plied him with questions he couldn't answer about exactly what had been said and how and why. He backed off from the story, and didn't try to tell any more. Perhaps he was wondering to himself why the women were interested in all these unimportant details.

"SKIP THE DETAILS"

Though many women value the recounting of subtle nuances in conversations with close friends, there are situations in which everyone feels oppressed by being told, or asked for, what seem like too many details. If interest in details is a sign of intimacy, a woman will resist such interest if it comes from someone she doesn't want to be intimate with. And everyone has had the experience of being told unwanted details—so many that they seem pointless, or demand longer or more intimate attention than one wants to give. Many of the examples I have collected of people piling on details in conversation involve old people. This may be because old people often want more involvement with young people than young people want with them, or because old people frequently cannot hear well, so they tell detailed stories to maintain interaction. Old people are also more inclined to reminisce about the past, consequently telling stories that are likely to include details.

It is a tenet of contemporary American psychology that mental health requires psychological separation from one's parents. One way of resisting overinvolvement, for some people at least, is resisting telling details. For example, one woman told me that her mother sought overinvolvement with her and had succeeded in achieving overinvolvement with her sister Jane. To support her claim, she said, "It's amazing, the details of Jane's life my mother knows." Later, she was explaining how she resists her mother's attempts to get overly involved in her life. As an example of her mother's prying, she said, "She's hungry for details. If I tell her I went somewhere, she asks, 'What did you wear?' "

The question that offended this woman was the same one that had brought my great-aunt such happiness. The difference is that my great-aunt was seeking involvement with the man who asked her what she wore. This woman was resisting what she perceived as the excessive involvement her mother sought with her. Presumably, however, when her sister Jane talks to their mother, she does not feel that the question "What did you wear?" is inappropriate. Perhaps, like my great-aunt, Jane values the show of caring and resulting involvement.

MIXING BUSINESS WITH GOSSIP

Many women mix talk about relatively important things, like business, with talk about relatively unimportant things, like clothes. On Monday morning, Marjorie walks into Beatrice's office to ask her opinion about a contract. After they have settled their business, or perhaps before, they bring each other up to date on their personal lives: Marjorie has her hands full with her ailing mother-in-law; Beatrice is feeling optimistic about a new relationship.

A woman who runs a counseling center noted that when she meets with women on her staff, it is not unusual for them to spend 75 percent of the time in personal talk and then efficiently take care of business in the remaining 25 percent. To men on the staff, this seems like wasting time. But the director places value on creating a warm, intimate working environment. She feels that such personal talk contributes to a sense of rapport that makes the women on her staff happy in their jobs and lays a foundation for the working relationship that enables them to conduct business so efficiently.

The mutual knowledge and trust that grows out of personal talk can precede a business relationship as well as grow out of it. A magazine article described a partnership between two women who own a construction company. The seed of their working relationship had been planted years before the business was founded, when the two women met regularly to exchange coffee and talk. When one of them decided to start a business, her working relationship with her partner was already in place.

For women who engage in frequent, regular social talk with friends, the machinery is up and running when a significant decision needs to be made. Elizabeth Loftus, a psychologist specializing in eyewitness testimony, was confronted with a moral dilemma when she was asked to testify on behalf of the man accused of being "Ivan the Terrible"—a notoriously sadistic Nazi war criminal. To be consistent, Loftus felt she should testify in this case as she had in many others. But her relatives and friends argued against it, and she recoiled at the prospect of undermining the testimony of the few witnesses who were alive to tell what Ivan had done—a mere fifty survivors of an estimated million of Ivan's victims. The dilemma was resolved when a friend dropped by for tea. Loftus recalls, "My friend, quoting Emerson, reminded me that 'A foolish consistency is the hobgoblin of little minds.' " With this comfort, Loftus decided not to testify. If women and men have different habits for social talk, they also make different use of it.

Differences in uses of social talk also begin early. One couple I talked to had different perspectives on their son's relationship with his best friend. The mother thought it odd that, despite the significant amount of time the boys spent together, for example playing football, their son found out what college his best friend was going to by reading it in their yearbook. One day a girl called him to ask whether his friend had a date for the prom. She was calling for *her* friend, who wanted to ask his friend, but not if he already had a date. Not only did their son not know whether his best friend had a date for the prom, but he was annoyed that the girl thought he should know. He gave her his friend's phone number and suggested she call to find out directly. He later commented that had he known his friend was going to the prom, he might have planned to go himself; not keeping up with such personal information deprived him of a chance to go.

All of this seemed very strange to the boy's mother, who could not imagine what it meant to be best friends if it didn't include knowing the basic developments in the other's life. To the boy's father, however, it seemed unremarkable.

TALKING-ABOUT VERSUS TALKING-AGAINST

The relatively positive or negative value that is placed on talking about personal details—of one's own life or others'— is reflected in the positive and negative views of gossip. One man commented that he and I seemed to have different definitions of gossip. He said, "To you it seems to be discussion of personal details about people known to the conversationalists. To me, it's a discussion of the weaknesses, character flaws, and failures of third persons, so that the participants in the conversation can feel superior to them. This seems unworthy, hence gossip is bad."

This man's view parallels that of a woman who told me she was troubled by one of the women in her child care co-op who gossiped too much. But it turned out that this woman's gossip was all negative: putting down other members of the co-op and criticizing them. It was not the talking-*about* that was disturbing, but the talking-*against*. This distances the speakers from those they are talking about, rather than bringing them closer. Furthermore, it is natural to assume that someone who has only negative things to say about others will also say negative things about you when you aren't there.

Gossip as talking-against is related to a verbal game that Christine Cheepen calls "scapegoat." In conversations she analyzed, Cheepen found that speakers talked against someone who wasn't there to redress imbalances of power that had erupted. "Scapegoat" was a way for speakers to achieve parity with each other by teaming up against someone else.

In Cheepen's examples, however, the third party whom the conversationalists teamed up against wasn't just anyone—it was their boss. And this brings us back to the view of the man who told me why he considers gossip to be bad. To the extent that talking about someone who is not there brings an absent party into the room, the effect is to establish connection. But if that party is brought into the room to be *put down,* then the effect is negotiation of status. As always, connection and status are operating at once, so both views are valid. They are different takes on the same scene.

WOMEN AND MEN ON THEIR OWN TERMS

What is the solution, then, if women and men are talking at cross-purposes, about gossip as about other matters? How are we to open lines of communication? The answer is for both men and women to try to take each other on their own terms rather than applying the standards of one group to the behavior of the other. This is not a "natural" thing to do, because we tend to look for a single "right" way of doing things. Understandably, experts are as liable to do this as anyone else.

A national audience-participation talk show featured a psychologist answering questions about couples' relationships. A woman in the audience voiced a complaint: "My husband talks to his mother, but he won't talk to me. If I want to know how his day was, I listen to his conversation with his mother." The psychologist told this woman, "He probably trusts his mother more than he trusts you."

This comment reinforced the woman's own suspicions and worst fears. And what the psychologist said was perfectly legitimate and reasonable—within the framework of talk in women's friendships: The friend to whom you talk daily, telling all the little experiences you had, is your best friend. But how reasonable an interpretation is it from the man's point of view? I would wager that her husband did not think he needed to do anything special to create intimacy with his wife, because he was with her every day. But because his mother was alone, he humored her by telling her unimportant little things that she seemed to want to hear. His mother's need to hear such details would make sense to her son because she was alone and needed them as a substitute for the real thing, like watching life from her window. He wouldn't understand why his wife would want and need to hear such talk. Although it is possible that this man trusts his mother more than his wife, the evidence given does not warrant such a conclusion.

This therapist was judging the man's way of talking by women's standards. In a sense, the values of therapy are those more typically associated with women's ways of talking than with men's. This may be why a study showed that among inexperienced therapists, women do better than men. But over time, with experience, this gender difference disappears. Eventually, perhaps, men therapists—and men in therapy—learn to talk like women. This is all to the good. Assertiveness training, on the other hand, teaches women to talk more like men, and this too is to the good. Women and men would both do well to learn strategies more typically used by members of the other group— not to switch over entirely, but to have more strategies at their disposal.

Habitual ways of talking are hard to change. Learning to respect others' ways of talking may be a bit easier. Men should accept that many women regard exchanging details about personal lives as a basic ingredient of intimacy, and women should accept that many men do not share this view. Mutual acceptance will at least prevent the pain of being told you are doing something wrong when you are only doing things your way.

FIVE

"I'll Explain It to You": Lecturing and Listening

At a reception following the publication of one of my books, I noticed a publicist listening attentively to the producer of a popular radio show. He was telling her how the studio had come to be built where it was, and why he would have preferred another site. What caught my attention was the length of time he was speaking while she was listening. He was delivering a monologue that could only be called a lecture, giving her detailed information about the radio reception at the two sites, the architecture of the station, and so on. I later asked the publicist if she had been interested in the information the producer had given her. "Oh, yes," she answered. But then she thought a moment and said, "Well, maybe he did go on a bit." The next day she told me, "I was thinking about what you asked. I couldn't have cared less about what he was saying. It's just that I'm so used to listening to men go on about things I don't care about, I didn't even realize how bored I was until you made me think about it."

I was chatting with a man I had just met at a party. In our conversation, it emerged that he had been posted in Greece with the RAF during 1944 and 1945. Since I had lived in Greece for several years, I asked him about his experiences: What had Greece been like then? How had the Greek villagers treated the British soldiers? What had it been *like* to be a British soldier in wartime Greece? I also offered information about how Greece had changed, what it is like now. He did not pick up on my remarks about contemporary Greece, and his replies to my questions quickly changed from accounts of his own experiences, which I found riveting, to facts about Greek history, which interested me in principle but in the actual telling left me profoundly bored. The more impersonal his talk became, the more I felt oppressed by it, pinned involuntarily in the listener position.

At a showing of Judy Chicago's jointly created art work *The Dinner Party,* I was struck by a couple standing in front of one of the displays: The man was earnestly explaining to the woman the meaning of symbols in the tapestry before them, pointing as he spoke. I might not have noticed this unremarkable scene, except that *The Dinner Party* was radically feminist in conception, intended to reflect women's experiences and sensibilities.

While taking a walk in my neighborhood on an early summer evening at twilight, I stopped to chat with a neighbor who was walking his dogs. As we stood, I noticed that the large expanse of yard in front of which we were standing was aglitter with the intermittent flickering of fireflies. I called attention to the sight, remarking on how magical it looked. "It's like the Fourth of July," I said. He agreed, and then told me he had read that the lights of fireflies are mating signals. He then explained to me details of how these signals work—for example, groups of fireflies fly at different elevations and could be seen to cluster in different parts of the yard.

In all these examples, the men had information to impart

and they were imparting it. On the surface, there is nothing surprising or strange about that. What is strange is that there are so many situations in which men have factual information requiring lengthy explanations to impart to women, and so few in which women have comparable information to impart to men.

The changing times have altered many aspects of relations between women and men. Now it is unlikely, at least in many circles, for a man to say, "I am better than you because I am a man and you are a woman." But women who do not find men making such statements are nonetheless often frustrated in their dealings with them. One situation that frustrates many women is a conversation that has mysteriously turned into a lecture, with the man delivering the lecture to the woman, who has become an appreciative audience.

Once again, the alignment in which women and men find themselves arrayed is asymmetrical. The lecturer is framed as superior in status and expertise, cast in the role of teacher, and the listener is cast in the role of student. If women and men took turns giving and receiving lectures, there would be nothing disturbing about it. What is disturbing is the imbalance. Women and men fall into this unequal pattern so often because of the differences in their interactional habits. Since women seek to build rapport, they are inclined to play down their expertise rather than display it. Since men value the position of center stage and the feeling of knowing more, they seek opportunities to gather and disseminate factual information.

If men often seem to hold forth because they have the expertise, women are often frustrated and surprised to find that when they have the expertise, they don't necessarily get the floor.

FIRST ME, THEN ME

I was at a dinner with faculty members from other departments in my university. To my right was a woman. As the dinner began, we introduced ourselves. After we told each other what departments we were in and what subjects we taught, she asked what my research was about. We talked about my research for a little while. Then I asked her about her research and she told me about it. Finally, we discussed the ways that our research overlapped. Later, as tends to happen at dinners, we branched out to others at the table. I asked a man across the table from me what department he was in and what he did. During the next half hour, I learned a lot about his job, his research, and his background. Shortly before the dinner ended there was a lull, and he asked me what I did. When I said I was a linguist, he became excited and told me about a research project he had conducted that was related to neurolinguistics. He was still telling me about his research when we all got up to leave the table.

This man and woman were my colleagues in academia. What happens when I talk to people at parties and social events, not fellow researchers? My experience is that if I mention the kind of work I do to women, they usually ask me about it. When I tell them about conversational style or gender differences, they offer their own experiences to support the patterns I describe. This is very pleasant for me. It puts me at center stage without my having to grab the spotlight myself, and I frequently gather anecdotes I can use in the future. But when I announce my line of work to men, many give me a lecture on language—for example, about how people, especially teenagers, misuse language nowadays. Others challenge me, for example questioning me about my research methods. Many others change the subject to something they know more about.

Of course not all men respond in this way, but over the years I have encountered many men, and very few women, who do. It is not that speaking in this way is *the* male way of doing things, but that it is *a* male way. There are women who adopt such styles, but they are perceived as speaking like men.

IF YOU'VE GOT IT, FLAUNT IT— OR HIDE IT

I have been observing this constellation in interaction for more than a dozen years. I did not, however, have any understanding of *why* this happens until fairly recently, when I developed the framework of status and connection. An experimental study that was pivotal in my thinking shows that expertise does not ensure women a place at center stage in conversation with men.

Psychologist H. M. Leet-Pellegrini set out to discover whether gender or expertise determined who would behave in what she terms a "dominant" way—for example, by talking more, interrupting, and controlling the topic. She set up pairs of women, pairs of men, and mixed pairs, and asked them to discuss the effects of television violence on children. In some cases, she made one of the partners an expert by providing relevant factual information and time to read and assimilate it before the videotaped discussion. One might expect that the conversationalist who was the expert would talk more, interrupt more, and spend less time supporting the conversational partner who knew less about the subject. But it wasn't so simple. On the average, those who had expertise did talk more, but men experts talked more than women experts.

Expertise also had a different effect on women and men with regard to supportive behavior. Leet-Pellegrini expected that the one who did not have expertise would spend more time offering agreement and support to the one who did. This turned out to be true—*except* in cases where a woman was the expert and her nonexpert partner was a man. In this situation, the women experts showed support—saying things like "Yeah" and "That's right"—far *more* than the nonexpert men they were talking to. Observers often rated the male nonexpert as more dominant than the female expert. In other words, the women in this experiment not only didn't wield their expertise as power, but tried to play it down and make up for it through extra assenting behavior. They acted as if their expertise were something to hide.

And perhaps it was. When the word *expert* was spoken in these experimental conversations, in all cases but one it was the man in the conversation who used it, saying something like "So, you're the expert." Evidence of the woman's superior knowledge sparked resentment, not respect.

Furthermore, when an expert man talked to an uninformed woman, he took a controlling role in structuring the conversation in the beginning *and* the end. But when an expert man talked to an uninformed man, he dominated in the beginning but not always in the end. In other words, having expertise was enough to keep a man in the controlling position if he was talking to a woman, but not if he was talking to a man. Apparently, when a woman surmised that the man she was talking to had more information on the subject than she did, she simply accepted the reactive role. But another man, despite a lack of information, might still give the expert a run for his money and possibly gain the upper hand by the end.

Reading these results, I suddenly understood what happens to me when I talk to women and men about language. I am assuming that my acknowledged expertise will mean I am automatically accorded authority in the conversation, and with women that is generally the case. But when I talk to men, revealing that I have acknowledged expertise in this area often invites challenges. I *might* maintain my position if I defend myself successfully against the challenges, but if I don't, I may lose ground.

One interpretation of the Leet-Pellegrini study is that women are getting a bum deal. They don't get credit when it's due. And in a way, this is true. But the reason is not—as it seems to many women—that men are bums who seek to deny women authority. The Leet-Pellegrini study shows that many men are inclined to jockey for status, and challenge the authority of others, when they are talking to men too. If this is so, then challenging a woman's authority as they would challenge a man's could be a sign of respect and equal treatment, rather than lack of respect and discrimination. In cases where this is so, the inequality of the treatment results not simply from the men's behavior alone but from the differences in men's and women's styles: Most women lack experience in defending themselves against challenges, which they misinterpret as personal attacks on their credibility.

Even when talking to men who are happy to see them in positions of status, women may have a hard time getting their due because of differences in men's and women's interactional goals. Just as boys in high school are not inclined to repeat information about popular girls because it doesn't get them what they want, women in conversation are not inclined to display their knowledge because it doesn't get them what they are after. Leet-Pellegrini suggests that the men in this study were playing a game of "Have I won?" while the women were playing a game of "Have I been sufficiently helpful?" I am inclined to put this another way: The game women play is "Do you like me?" whereas the men play "Do you respect me?" If men, in seeking respect, are less liked by women, this is an unsought side effect, as is the effect that women, in seeking to be liked, may lose respect. When a woman has a conversation with a man, her efforts to emphasize their similarities and avoid showing off can easily be interpreted, through the lens of status, as relegating her to a one-down position, making her appear either incompetent or insecure.

A SUBTLE DEFERENCE

Elizabeth Aries, a professor of psychology at Amherst College, set out to show that highly intelligent, highly educated young women are no longer submissive in conversations with male peers. And indeed she found that the college women did talk more than the college men in small groups she set up. But what they said was different. The men tended to set the agenda by offering opinions, suggestions, and information. The women tended to react, offering agreement or disagreement. Furthermore, she found that body language was as different as ever: The men sat with their legs stretched out, while the women gathered themselves in. Noting that research has found that speakers using the open-bodied position are more likely to persuade their listeners, Aries points out that talking more may not ensure that women will be heard.

In another study, Aries found that men in all-male discussion groups spent a lot of time at the beginning finding out "who was best informed about movies, books, current events, politics, and travel" as a means of "sizing up the competition" and negotiating "where they stood in relation to each other." This glimpse of how men talk when there are no women present gives an inkling of why displaying knowledge and expertise is something that men find more worth doing than women. What the women in Aries's study spent time doing was "gaining a closeness through more intimate self-revelation."

It is crucial to bear in mind that both the women and the men in these studies were establishing camaraderie, and both were concerned with their relationships to each other. But different aspects of their relationships were of primary concern: their place in a hierarchical order for the men, and their place in a network of intimate connections for the women. The consequence of these disparate concerns was very different ways of speaking.

Thomas Fox is an English professor who was intrigued by the differences between women and men in his freshman writing classes. What he observed corresponds almost precisely to the experimental findings of Aries and Leet-Pellegrini. Fox's method of teaching writing included having all the students read their essays to each other in class and talk to each other in small groups. He also had them write papers reflecting on the essays and the discussion groups. He alone, as the teacher, read these analytical papers.

To exemplify the two styles he found typical of women and men, Fox chose a woman, Ms. M, and a man, Mr. H. In her speaking as well as her writing, Ms. M. held back what she knew, appearing uninformed and uninterested, because she feared offending her classmates. Mr. H spoke and wrote with authority and apparent confidence because he was eager to persuade his peers. She did not worry about persuading; he did not worry about offending.

In his analytical paper, the young man described his own behavior in the mixed-gender group discussions as if he were describing the young men in Leet-Pellegrini's and Aries's studies:

> In my sub-group I am the leader. I begin every discussion by stating my opinions as facts. The other two members of the sub-group tend to sit back and agree with me. . . . I need people to agree with me.

Fox comments that Mr. H reveals "a sense of self, one that acts to change himself and other people, that seems entirely distinct from Ms. M's sense of self, dependent on and related to others."

Calling Ms. M's sense of self "dependent" suggests a negative view of her way of being in the world—and, I think, a view more typical of men. This view reflects the assumption that the alternative to independence is dependence. If this is indeed a male view, it may explain why so many men are cautious about becoming intimately involved with others: It makes sense to avoid humiliating dependence by insisting on independence. But there is another alternative: *inter*dependence.

The main difference between these alternatives is symmetry. Dependence is an asymmetrical involvement: One person needs the other, but not vice versa, so the needy person is one-down. Interdependence is symmetrical: Both parties rely on each other, so neither is one-up or one-down. Moreover, Mr. H's sense of self is also dependent on others. He requires others to listen, agree, and allow him to take the lead by stating his opinions first.

Looked at this way, the woman and man in this group are both dependent on each other. Their differing goals are complementary, although neither understands the reasons for the other's behavior. This would be a fine arrangement, except that their differing goals result in alignments that enhance his authority and undercut hers.

DIFFERENT INTERPRETATIONS— AND MISINTERPRETATIONS

Fox also describes differences in the way male and female students in his classes interpreted a story they read. These differences also reflect assumptions about the interdependence or independence of individuals. Fox's students wrote their responses to "The Birthmark" by Nathaniel Hawthorne. In the story, a woman's husband becomes obsessed with a birthmark on her face. Suffering from her husband's revulsion at the sight of her, the wife becomes obsessed with it too and, in a reversal of her initial impulse, agrees to undergo a treatment he has devised to remove the birthmark—a treatment that succeeds in removing the mark, but kills her in the process.

Ms. M interpreted the wife's complicity as a natural response to the demand of a loved one: The woman went along with her husband's lethal schemes to remove the birthmark because she wanted to please and be appealing to him. Mr. H blamed the woman's insecurity and vanity for her fate, and he blamed her for voluntarily submitting to her husband's authority. Fox points out that he saw her as individually responsible for her actions, just as he saw himself as individually responsible for his own actions. To him, the issue was independence: The weak wife voluntarily took a submissive role. To Ms. M, the issue was interdependence: The woman was inextricably bound up with her husband, so her behavior could not be separated from his.

Fox observes that Mr. H saw the writing of the women in the class as spontaneous—they wrote whatever popped into their heads. Nothing could be farther from Ms. M's experience as she described it: When she knew her peers would see her writing, she censored everything that popped into her head. In contrast, when she was writing something that only her professor would read, she expressed firm and articulate opinions.

There is a striking but paradoxical complementarity to Ms. M's and Mr. H's styles, when they are taken together. He needs someone to listen and agree. She listens and agrees. But in another sense, their dovetailing purposes are at cross-purposes. He misinterprets her agreement, intended in a spirit of connection, as a reflection of status and power: He thinks she is "indecisive" and "insecure." Her reasons for refraining from behaving as he does—firmly stating opinions as facts—have nothing to do with her attitudes toward her knowledge, as he thinks they do, but rather result from her attitudes toward her relationships with her peers.

These experimental studies by Leet-Pellegrini and Aries, and the observations by Fox, all indicate that, typically, men are more comfortable than women in giving information and opinions and speaking in an authoritative way to a group, whereas women are more comfortable than men in supporting others.

IS ANYBODY LISTENING?

In Jules Feiffer's play *Grown Ups,* a woman, Marilyn, tries to tell her parents, Jack and Helen, about something that happened to her, but she never succeeds in getting them to listen. Her explicit attempts to tell her story are highlighted by boldface type.

MARILYN: **This you gotta hear! I was coming home Wednesday on the bus from Philadelphia—**

JACK: Nobody said a word to me about Philadelphia.

HELEN: Marilyn, you want me to check the chicken for you?

MARILYN: Leave it, Mama.

HELEN: The old lady's trying to give a hand.

MARILYN: I'm like you; if somebody starts to help I forget what I'm doing. **Sit down, you'll love this: I was coming home from Philadelphia—**

JACK: [To Helen] Did you know she was out of town?

MARILYN: Two days!

JACK: Who took care of my grandchildren?

MARILYN: How should I know? Out of sight, out of mind. No, Rudy was here. He got them out of bed in the morning and back in bed at night. In between I don't even want to know what happened. **Am I ever going to be able to tell you this or not?**

HELEN: [Returning to table] You're going out of town, Marilyn?

Marilyn can't get her parents to pay attention to her story. They continually sidetrack the narration with comments about her cooking, her housekeeping, her family, her safety, and her brother, Jake:

HELEN: Where's Jake?

MARILYN: On the way. **So I caught the last bus back to the city—**

JACK: I don't like you taking a last bus, it's dangerous.

MARILYN: **It's not nearly as dangerous as trying to tell a story around here.**

Like the woman who wrote to Ann Landers that her husband doesn't talk to her, Marilyn feels invisible. She sees her parents' lack of interest in listening to her as symbolic of their inability to see and value her as a person, as she explains to Jake:

MARILYN: You at least, they know you're alive. No matter what I do you know how it feels? I'll put it this way: If *you* take them some place in your car, you're this wonderful success who can afford his own car; if I take them some place in my car, I'm the chauffeur. More than anything, you know what kills me? The thing I loved most was you and Mama in the kitchen with your stories. She'd tell one, you'd tell one, she'd tell one, you'd tell one. I thought someday I'll be old enough to have my

> own real experiences and then *I'll* have stories!
> To this day they will not allow me to tell a story.
> Isn't it crazy that I should still be bothered by
> that?
> JAKE: I told my stories to get away from her stories.

Jake's explanation of why he told stories as a child shows his
impulse to avoid being in the listening position. Whereas Marilyn
loved listening to their mother's stories, Jake says he learned to
hold the floor with his own stories in order to avoid listening to
hers.

Just as Marilyn believed that she would have stories to tell
when she grew up, I recall that when I was a child, there were
two skills I thought all adults had that I didn't have: whistling
and snapping their fingers. I assumed I would acquire these abilities with age and eagerly awaited the development. But I grew
up, and I still can't whistle or get my fingers to produce a snap
worth listening to. It never occurred to me when I was a child
that these skills did not magically appear, like the physical changes
of puberty. I realized too late that if I wanted to know how to
whistle and snap my fingers, I had to practice. The grown daughter in *Grown Ups* could not tell stories in a way to command
attention partly because she hadn't gotten any practice as a child.
What she'd done as a child was listen attentively and appreciatively as her mother and brother told stories. While Jake was
getting practice in commanding attention through verbal performance, Marilyn was getting practice in listening.

The skills Marilyn and Jake honed as children provided the
basis for their adult vocations. Jake became a journalist at *The
New York Times:* He made a career of writing news stories that
millions would read, another form of verbal display to an audience. Marilyn became a social worker: She made a career of sitting and listening to other people talk.

In Feiffer's play, Marilyn really is not as good a storyteller
as Jake—she gets bogged down in unimportant details and interrupts herself to fuss about accuracy when it doesn't make any

difference to the story. The scene ends with Jake triumphantly holding forth, retelling to a rapt audience a story that Marilyn has just botched. This implies that her own storytelling deficiencies are the cause of her failing to command attention. But it could well be that even if Marilyn had been able to tell a good story, her family wouldn't have listened, because they had long since come to assume that Jake tells stories and Marilyn doesn't. By the same process, since more men than women are comfortable holding forth to a crowd, it may well be that it is difficult for women to get center stage, regardless of how articulate they are, because a norm is established by which most people expect men, and not women, to command attention.

GROWING UP INVISIBLE

Anthropologists Frederick Erickson and Susan Florio recorded a real-life conversation that could have been a blueprint for the family created by Jules Feiffer in *Grown Ups*. Erickson studied the videotape they made of a dinner table conversation of an Italian family in Boston. The youngest boy in the family had fallen off his bicycle and he had a bruise to prove it. To comfort him, his father and brothers told him—and everyone present—about times they had fallen off their bikes. In their stories, they didn't just fall off, they "wiped out" their bikes, lending an air of glamour and daring to their accidents. The longest and most impressive story was told by the father, who had the biggest bike: a motorcycle. In this way, the older boys and men in the family gave the youngest brother a lesson in fearlessness as well as storytelling. Not only was doing dangerous things part of being a man, but so was crashing—and telling about it before an audience of other men and appreciative women.

Throughout this portion of the conversation, the boys and men told stories, while the women—the mother, the sister, and Susan Florio, the researcher-guest—took the role of audience. Florio was a particularly important member of the audience, because it was partly for her, an attractive young woman, that the young men were displaying their prowess at riding bikes, weathering crashes, and telling stories. When the daughter, the little boy's sister, tried to tell about falling off her bike, nobody paid any attention to her, and she never got past the first line, which is highlighted in the excerpt with boldface type.

FATHER: [About youngest brother Jimmy's bruise] That's really a good one, huh?

MOTHER: Yeah.

JIMMY: Yeah, and a scrape near the—

FATHER: You should keep a patch on that.

BROTHER 2: Go get the patch—

BROTHER 3: The patching kit. Scrape down— [Kidding Jimmy by analogy with a tire-patching kit]

SISTER: **I wiped out my bike on the hill.**

BROTHER 1: Last time I did it. That was a good wipeout.

BROTHER ?: /??/ was the last time I did this.

FATHER: I'll have to get you a helmet too.

BROTHER 1: [To brother 2] I think one of my best, my best wipeouts, was when I hit you when I was doing about twenty.

The little brother's wipeout—falling off his bike—is the object of a lot of attention. But the little girl's attempt to tell about her wipeout is completely ignored, just as Marilyn finds her attempts to tell about her experience ignored by her family in Feiffer's play.

There are many reasons this could happen. It could be that the way the little girl goes about getting a turn is different. After announcing that she wiped out her bike on the hill, she may have waited to be encouraged to continue, whereas the boys just pressed on until they got to tell their stories. She may have spoken too quietly and tentatively. Or it may simply be that the family is not interested in girls' stories in general, or girls' wipeouts in particular.

In his paper, Erickson shows that the wipeout stories are lessons in male behavior. Through attention to their stories, the boys are learning, and demonstrating for the youngest boy, that risking danger in riding a bike is good, getting hurt is unavoidable, sustaining injury bravely is commendable, technical knowledge and skill can be useful (there is a lot of talk about the mechanics of brakes and the engineering of roads), and telling about risking danger, sustaining injury, and applying and displaying technical expertise is a good way to get attention and impress people. Perhaps none of these lessons are deemed relevant for the sister. In any event, the net effect is that the boys in the family are learning to hold center stage by talking; the girl in the family is learning to listen.

LISTENER AS UNDERLING

Clearly men are not always talking and women are not always listening. I have asked men whether they ever find themselves in the position of listening to another man giving them a lecture, and how they feel about it. They tell me that this does happen. They may find themselves talking to someone who presses information on them so insistently that they give in and listen. They say they don't mind too much, however, if the information is interesting. They can store it away for future use, like remembering a joke to tell others later. Factual information is of less interest to women because it is of less use to them. They are unlikely to try to pass on the gift of information, more likely to give the gift of being a good audience.

Men as well as women sometimes find themselves on the receiving end of a lecture they would as soon not hear. But men tell me that it is most likely to happen if the other man is in a position of higher status. They know they have to listen to lectures from fathers and bosses.

That men can find themselves in the position of unwilling listener is attested to by a short opinion piece in which A. R.

Gurney bemoans being frequently "cornered by some self-styled expert who harangues me with his considered opinion on an interminable agenda of topics." He claims that this tendency bespeaks a peculiarly American inability to "converse"—that is, engage in a balanced give-and-take—and cites as support the French observer of American customs Alexis de Tocqueville, who wrote, "An American . . . speaks to you as if he was addressing a meeting." Gurney credits his own appreciation of conversing to his father, who "was a master at eliciting and responding enthusiastically to the views of others, though this resiliency didn't always extend to his children. Indeed, now I think about it, he spoke to us many times as if he were addressing a meeting."

It is not surprising that Gurney's father lectured his children. The act of giving information by definition frames one in a position of higher status, while the act of listening frames one as lower. Children instinctively sense this—as do most men. But when women listen to men, they are not thinking in terms of status. Unfortunately, their attempts to reinforce connections and establish rapport, when interpreted through the lens of status, can be misinterpreted as casting them in a subordinate position—and are likely to be taken that way by many men.

WHAT'S SO FUNNY?

The economy of exchanging jokes for laughter is a parallel one. In her study of college students' discussion groups, Aries found that the students in all-male groups spent a lot of time telling about times they had played jokes on others, and laughing about it. She refers to a study in which Barbara Miller Newman found that high school boys who were not "quick and clever" became the targets of jokes. Practical joking—playing a joke *on* someone—is clearly a matter of being one-up: in the know and in control. It is less obvious, but no less true, that *telling* jokes can also be a way of negotiating status.

Many women (certainly not all) laugh at jokes but do not

later remember them. Since they are not driven to seek and hold center stage in a group, they do not need a store of jokes to whip out for this purpose. A woman I will call Bernice prided herself on her sense of humor. At a cocktail party, she met a man to whom she was drawn because he seemed at first to share this trait. He made many funny remarks, which she spontaneously laughed at. But when she made funny remarks, he seemed not to hear. What had happened to his sense of humor? Though telling jokes and laughing at them are both reflections of a sense of humor, they are very different social activities. Making others laugh gives you a fleeting power over them: As linguist Wallace Chafe points out, at the moment of laughter, a person is temporarily disabled. The man Bernice met was comfortable only when he was making her laugh, not the other way around. When Bernice laughed at his jokes, she thought she was engaging in a symmetrical activity. But he was engaging in an asymmetrical one.

A man told me that sometime around tenth grade he realized that he preferred the company of women to the company of men. He found that his female friends were more supportive and less competitive, whereas his male friends seemed to spend all their time joking. Considering joking an asymmetrical activity makes it clearer why it would fit in with a style he perceived as competitive.

"WHO DO YOU THINK YOU'RE TALKING TO?"

Subtle asymmetries in listening and speaking may also shed light on the common complaint that men often don't talk to women at home. Gerry Philipsen is an anthropologist who spent two and a half years working among teenage boys in an urban Italian working-class neighborhood. These boys were loud and loquacious when hanging around with each other on the street corner or in the local bar. But they did not talk to superiors or inferiors.

If they wanted to get something from a person in a position of authority, they relied on intermediaries, just as they prayed to a saint for intercession rather than praying directly to God. To those in a subordinate position—children, women, or boys of lower status—they got their way by a show of physical power and, if necessary, violent action. To talk to someone of higher status would be cheeky, bold, out of order. To talk to someone of lower status would be weak, ineffectual, and inviting subordination.

There are two ways in which the culture of these "macho" teenage boys is similar to the culture of girls and women. Like girls, these boys gain status by affiliation: The more influential people they know, the more status they have. But the point of affiliation for them is power—they use their connections to get things done. For girls, affiliation is an end in itself: Their status goes up if they're friends with high-status girls. These boys are like girls in that they talk only when they feel comfortable, among peers. But why don't they want to talk to girls? It may be that they assume that the girls are lower in status, whereas the girls feel—or want to feel—that a partner, even a male one, is a peer.

Class differences may play a larger role in conversational styles than we think. Sociologist Mirra Komarovsky, in her classic study *Blue Collar Marriage,* found that the more middle class a couple was, the more the husband and wife considered each other friends. Among high school graduates, there was an expectation that a husband should talk to his wife. Among those who had not graduated from high school, wives who wanted their husbands to talk to them were thought to be inappropriately demanding. The expectation was that wives should talk to their female relatives and leave their husbands alone.

MUTUAL ACCUSATIONS

Considering these dynamics, it is not surprising that many women complain that their partners don't listen to them. But men make the same complaint about women, although less frequently. The accusation "You're not listening" often really means "You don't understand what I said in the way that I meant it," or "I'm not getting the response I wanted." Being listened to can become a metaphor for being understood and being valued.

In my earlier work I emphasized that women may get the impression men aren't listening to them even when the men really are. This happens because men have different habitual ways of showing they're listening. As anthropologists Maltz and Borker explain, women are more inclined to ask questions. They also give more listening responses—little words like *mhm, uh-uh*, and *yeah*—sprinkled throughout someone else's talk, providing a running feedback loop. And they respond more positively and enthusiastically, for example by agreeing and laughing.

All this behavior is doing the work of listening. It also creates rapport-talk by emphasizing connection and encouraging more talk. The corresponding strategies of men—giving fewer listener responses, making statements rather than asking questions, and challenging rather than agreeing—can be understood as moves in a contest by incipient speakers rather than audience members.

Not only do women give more listening signals, according to Maltz and Borker, but the signals they give have different meanings for men and women, consistent with the speaker/audience alignment. Women use "yeah" to mean "I'm with you, I follow," whereas men tend to say "yeah" only when they agree. The opportunity for misunderstanding is clear. When a man is confronted with a women who has been saying "yeah," "yeah," "yeah," and then turns out not to agree, he may conclude that she has been insincere, or that she was agreeing without really listening. When a woman is confronted with a man who does *not* say "yeah"—or much of anything else—she may conclude that *he* hasn't been listening. The men's style is more literally focused on the message level of talk, while the women's is focused on the relationship or metamessage level.

To a man who expects a listener to be quietly attentive, a woman giving a stream of feedback and support will seem to be talking too much for a listener. To a woman who expects a listener to be active and enthusiastic in showing interest, attention, and support, a man who listens silently will seem not to be listening at all, but rather to have checked out of the conversation, taken his listening marbles, and gone mentally home.

Because of these patterns, women may get the impression that men aren't listening when they really are. But I have come to understand, more recently, that it is also true that men listen to women less frequently than women listen to men, because the act of listening has different meanings for them. Some men really *don't* want to listen at length because they feel it frames them as subordinate. Many women do want to listen, but they expect it to be reciprocal—I listen to you now; you listen to me later. They become frustrated when they do the listening now and now and now, and later never comes.

MUTUAL DISSATISFACTION

If women are dissatisfied with always being in the listening position, the dissatisfaction may be mutual. That a woman feels she has been assigned the role of silently listening audience does not mean that a man feels he has consigned her to that role—or that he necessarily likes the rigid alignment either.

During the time I was working on this book, I found myself at a book party filled with people I hardly knew. I struck up a conversation with a charming young man who turned out to be a painter. I asked him about his work and, in response to his answer, asked whether there has been a return in contemporary art to figurative painting. In response to my question, he told me a lot about the history of art—so much that when he finished and said, "That was a long answer to your question," I had long since forgotten that I had asked a question, let alone what it was. I had not minded this monologue—I had been interested in it—but I realized, with something of a jolt, that I had just experienced the dynamic that I had been writing about.

I decided to risk offending my congenial new acquaintance

in order to learn something about his point of view. This was, after all, a book party, so I might rely on his indulgence if I broke the rules of decorum in the interest of writing a book. I asked whether he often found himself talking at length while someone else listened. He thought for a moment and said yes, he did, because he liked to explore ideas in detail. I asked if it happened equally with women and men. He thought again and said, "No, I have more trouble with men." I asked what he meant by trouble. He said, "Men interrupt. *They* want to explain to *me*."

Finally, having found this young man disarmingly willing to talk about the conversation we had just had and his own style, I asked which he preferred: that a woman listen silently and supportively, or that she offer opinions and ideas of her own. He said he thought he liked it better if she volunteered information, making the interchange more interesting.

When men begin to lecture other men, the listeners are experienced at trying to sidetrack the lecture, or match it, or derail it. In this system, making authoritative pronouncements may be a way to begin an *exchange* of information. But women are not used to responding in that way. They see little choice but to listen attentively and wait for their turn to be allotted to them rather than seizing it for themselves. If this is the case, the man may be as bored and frustrated as the woman when his attempt to begin an exchange of information ends in his giving a lecture. From his point of view, she is passively soaking up information, so she must not have any to speak of. One of the reasons men's talk to women frequently turns into lecturing is *because* women listen attentively and do not interrupt with challenges, sidetracks, or matching information.

In the conversations with male and female colleagues that I recounted at the outset of this chapter, this difference may have been crucial. When I talked to the woman, we each told about our own research in response to the other's encouragement. When I talked to the man, I encouraged him to talk about his work, and he obliged, but he did not encourage me to talk about mine. This may mean that he did not want to hear about it—but it also may not. In her study of college students' discussion groups, Aries found that women who did a lot of talking began to feel uncomfortable; they backed off and frequently drew out quieter members of the group. This is perfectly in keeping with women's desire to keep things balanced, so everyone is on an equal footing. Women expect their conversational partners to encourage them to hold forth. Men who do not typically encourage quieter members to speak up, assume that anyone who has something to say will volunteer it. The men may be equally disappointed in a conversational partner who turns out to have nothing to say.

Similarly, men can be as bored by women's topics as women can be by men's. While I was wishing the former RAFer would tell me about his personal experiences in Greece, he was probably wondering why I was boring him with mine and marveling at my ignorance of the history of a country I had lived in. Perhaps he would have considered our conversation a success if I had challenged or topped his interpretation of Greek history rather than listening dumbly to it. When men, upon hearing the kind of work I do, challenge me about my research methods, they are inviting me to give them information and show them my expertise—something I don't like to do outside of the classroom or lecture hall, but something they themselves would likely be pleased to be provoked to do.

The publicist who listened attentively to information about a radio station explained to me that she wanted to be nice to the manager, to smooth the way for placing her clients on his station. But men who want to ingratiate themselves with women are more likely to try to charm them by offering interesting information than by listening attentively to whatever information the women have to impart. I recall a luncheon preceding a talk I delivered to a college alumni association. My gracious host kept me entertained before my speech by regaling me with information about computers, which I politely showed interest in, while inwardly screaming from boredom and a sense of being weighed down by irrelevant information that I knew I would never remember. Yet I am sure he thought he was being interesting, and it is likely that at least some male guests would have thought that he was. I do not wish to imply that all women hosts have entertained me in the perfect way. I recall a speaking engagement before which I was taken to lunch by a group of women. They were so attentive to my expertise that they plied me with questions, prompting me to exhaust myself by giving my lecture over lunch before the formal lecture began. In comparison to this, perhaps the man who lectured to me about computers was trying to give me a rest.

The imbalance by which men often find themselves in the role of lecturer, and women often find themselves in the role of audience, is not the creation of only one member of an interaction. It is not something that men do to women. Neither is it something that women culpably "allow" or "ask for." The imbalance is created by the difference between women's and men's habitual styles.

HAMPERED BY STYLE

"War with Japan," a story by Frederick Barthelme, shows a man retreating into lecturing his son not because he wants to, but because it's familiar and safe. The story begins with the narrator announcing that he is going to move out of the house and into an apartment over the garage, because he and his wife have "been having a kind of trouble." He thinks about asking their twelve-year-old son to help him move his things:

> I think I'll take the opportunity to explain why I'm switching out to the garage, and then I think maybe I won't, because it won't come out clear. I don't know why I want to explain stuff to him—I guess I want to win him. . . .

When the narrator approaches his son and tells him he wants to have a talk with him, this is what he says:

> "What I want to tell you is that there are all these things wrong now, and they didn't use to be wrong. I'm figuring

you're going to notice that they're wrong and start wondering *why*, so I thought I'd get a step up, you know? Doing my duty."

He looks uncertain, so I say, "Let me give you an example. I was sitting inside here thinking about a war with the Japanese. Now, Charles, we're not about to have any war with the Japanese, you understand that, right?"

The father ends up lecturing his son about the Japanese, the Russians, the American government, and society. He makes jokes. He does not say anything about himself, his feelings, his move out of the house, or his relationship with the boy's mother and the boy. The story is ironic and sad because it is clear that this father will not "win" his son this way. The lecture he gives about war with Japan is of no interest to the boy, nor is it what the father really wanted to say. He slipped into explaining what was going on in the world because he found it more familiar, and hence easier to talk about, than explaining what was going on in the family.

This father seems to have succumbed to his fear that if he tried to explain why he was moving to the garage, it wouldn't "come out clear." He feels he should have precise answers and explanations, as he does about politics. Perhaps he would feel freer to say what is on his mind if he gave up the belief that he can't speak unless he has everything all worked out. His son would have benefited more from hearing his father's personal thoughts and feelings, even if they weren't perfectly clear. The man in this story was handicapped by his habitual style.

On the other hand, always taking the role of respondent rather than initiator is limiting to women. This tendency has significant consequences in sexual relations. Philip Blumstein and Pepper Schwartz, in their study *American Couples,* found that lesbians have sex less often than gay men and heterosexual couples. The sociologists believe that this happens because, as they found, in heterosexual couples the man almost always initiates sex, and the woman either complies or exercises veto power. Among gay men, at least one partner takes the role of initiator. But among lesbians, they found, often neither feels comfortable taking the role of initiator, because neither wants to be perceived as making demands.

HOPE FOR THE FUTURE

What is the hope for the future? Must we play out our assigned parts to the closing act? Although we tend to fall back on habitual ways of talking, repeating old refrains and familiar lines, habits can be broken. Women and men both can gain by understanding the other gender's style, and by learning to use it on occasion.

Women who find themselves unwillingly cast as the listener should practice propelling themselves out of that position rather than waiting patiently for the lecture to end. Perhaps they need to give up the belief that they must wait for the floor to be handed to them. If they have something to say on a subject, they might push themselves to volunteer it. If they are bored with a subject, they can exercise some influence on the conversation and change the topic to something they would rather discuss.

If women are relieved to learn that they don't always have to listen, there may be some relief for men in learning that they don't always have to have interesting information on the tips of their tongues if they want to impress a woman or entertain her. A journalist once interviewed me for an article about how to strike up conversations. She told me that another expert she had interviewed, a man, had suggested that one should come up with an interesting piece of information. I found this amusing, as it seemed to typify a man's idea of a good conversationalist, but not a woman's. How much easier men might find the task of conversation if they realized that all they have to do is listen. As a woman who wrote a letter to the editor of *Psychology Today* put it, "When I find a guy who asks, 'How was your day?' and really wants to know, I'm in heaven."

SIX

Community and Contest: Styles in Conflict

When two people's paths cross, there is bound to be a conflict of interest: We can't both stand on the same spot without one of us standing on the other's foot. If no one steps aside, someone will get stepped on. You and I are not the same person, so some of our wants will be different and conflict is inevitable. Because we can't both get our way, we may find ourselves in a power struggle.

It may seem at first that conflict is the opposite of rapport and affiliation. Much of what has been written about women's and men's styles claims that males are competitive and prone to conflict whereas females are cooperative and given to affiliation. But being in conflict also means being involved with each other. Although it is true that many women are more comfortable using language to express rapport whereas many men are more comfortable using it for self-display, the situation is really more complicated than that, because self-display, when part of a mutual struggle, is also a kind of bonding. And conflict may be valued as a way of creating involvement with others.

To most women, conflict is a threat to connection, to be avoided at all costs. Disputes are preferably settled without direct confrontation. But to many men, conflict is the necessary means by which status is negotiated, so it is to be accepted and may even be sought, embraced, and enjoyed.

Walter Ong, a scholar of cultural linguistics, shows in his book *Fighting for Life* that "adversativeness"—pitting one's needs, wants, or skills against those of others—is an essential part of being human, but "conspicuous or expressed adversativeness is a larger element in the lives of males than of females." He demonstrates that male behavior typically entails contest, which includes combat, struggle, conflict, competition, and contention. Pervasive in male behavior is ritual combat, typified by rough play and sports. Females, on the other hand, are more likely to use intermediaries or to fight for real rather than ritualized purposes. Friendship among men often has a large element of friendly aggression, which women are likely to mistake for the real thing.

Ong demonstrates the inextricable relationship between oral performance and "agonistic" relations. Oral disputation—from formal debate to the study of formal logic—is inherently adversative. With this in mind, we can see that the inclination of many men to expect discussions and arguments in daily conversation to adhere to rules of logic is a remnant of this tradition. Furthermore, oral performance in self-display—what I have been calling report-talk—is part of a larger framework in which many men approach life as a contest.

Because their imaginations are not captured by ritualized combat, women are inclined to misinterpret and be puzzled by the adversativeness of many men's ways of speaking and miss the *ritual* nature of friendly aggression. At the same time, the enactment of community can be ritualized just as easily as the enactment of combat. The appearance of community among women may mask power struggles, and the appearance of sameness may mask profound differences in points of view. Men can be as confused by women's verbal rituals as women are by men's. Such confusions abound in the verbal lives of couples.

"DON'T TELL ME WHAT TO DO"

A woman I'll call Diana often begins statements with "Let's." She might say, "Let's go out for brunch today," or "Let's clean up now, before we start lunch." This makes Nathan angry. He feels she is ordering him around, telling him what to do. Diana can't understand why he takes it that way. It is obvious to her that she is making suggestions, not demands. If he doesn't feel like doing what she proposes, all he has to do is say so. She would not press her preference if she knew it wasn't what he wanted.

Loraine frequently compliments Sidney and thanks him for doing things such as cleaning up the kitchen and doing the laundry. Instead of appreciating the praise, Sidney resents it. "It makes me feel like you're demanding that I do it all the time," he explains. Another man made a similar comment about his mother. She praised him for calling her, saying, "You're a very good person." He felt she was trying to ensure that he call her regularly by implying that if he neglected to call, he would be a bad person.

In their study of the private lives of American couples, Philip Blumstein and Pepper Schwartz quote a young man who, in discussing his sexual relationship with his girlfriend, told them, "We were in bed and she was saying, 'Do this lighter,' or 'Do this softer,' and I just told her that I was making love to her and she was going to have to let me do it my own way. . . . You don't want to feel bossed around. . . .'"

In all these examples, men complained that their independence and freedom were being encroached on. Their early warning system is geared to detect signs that they are being told what to do—even in so apparently affiliative an activity as making love. Such complaints surprise and puzzle women, whose early warning systems are geared to detect a different menace. Being on the lookout for threats to independence makes sense in the framework of an agonistic world, where life is a series of contests that test a man's skill and force him to struggle against others who are trying to bend his will to theirs. If a man experiences life as a fight for freedom, he is naturally inclined to resist attempts to control him and determine his behavior.

This world view has given rise to the concept of the henpecked husband: Many men resent any inkling that their wives want to get them to do things. Women's lives have historically been hemmed in at every turn by the demands of others—their families, their husbands—and yet, though individual women may complain of overbearing husbands, there is no parallel stereotype of a "roosterpecked wife." Why not? Seeing people as interdependent, women expect their actions to be influenced by others, and they expect people to act in concert. Their struggle is to keep the ties strong, keep everyone in the community, and accommodate to others' needs while making what efforts they can at damage control with respect to their own needs and preferences. If a man struggles to be strong, a woman struggles to keep the community strong.

LET'S GO BACK TO THE CHILDREN

The misunderstanding between Diana and Nathan can be traced to habitual conversational styles typical of women and men—styles that take shape with the first words children learn to use at play. Diana's tendency to make proposals beginning with "Let's" is not just idiosyncratic. Researchers who study children at play have found that girls of all ages tend to speak in this way.

Psychologist Jacqueline Sachs and her colleagues, studying

preschoolers between the ages of two and five, found that girls tended to make proposals for action by saying "Let's," whereas boys often gave each other commands. For example, in playing doctor, the little boys said things like:

"Lie down."

"Get the heart thing."

"Gimme your arm."

"Try to give me medicine."

When girls played doctor, they said things like "Let's sit down and use it."

Marjorie Harness Goodwin found exactly the same pattern in a completely different group—black children between the ages of six and fourteen, playing on the streets of a Philadelphia neighborhood. The boys, who were (agonistically) making sling-shots in preparation for a fight, gave each other orders:

"Gimme the pliers!"

"Man, don't come *in* here where I *am*."

"Give me that, man. After this, after you chop 'em, give 'em to me."

"Get off my steps."

The girls, who were making glass rings out of bottle necks, didn't issue commands. They made proposals beginning with "Let's":

"Let's go around Subs and Suds [a corner bar/restaurant]."

"Let's ask her, 'Do you have any bottles?' "

"Come on. Let's go find some."

"Come on. Let's turn back, y'all, so we can safe keep 'em."

"Let's move *these* out *first*."

Other ways the girls proposed activities were with "We gonna" ("We gonna make a *whole* display of rings"), "We could" ("We *could* use a sewer" [to sand down the glass surfaces of the rings]), "Maybe" ("Maybe we can slice them like that"), and "We gotta"

("We gotta find some more bottles"). All these are attempts to influence what the others do without telling them what to do. At the same time, they reinforce the identities of the girls as members of a community.

Children may be influenced by their parents' styles, just as adults are influenced by what they learned as children. Psycholinguist Jean Berko Gleason studied how parents talk to their young children, and found that fathers issue more commands to their children than mothers do, and they issue more commands to their sons than to their daughters. Sociolinguist Frances Smith observed a similar pattern in a public-speaking situation. Examining the practice sermons of male and female students at a Baptist seminary, she found that when referring to chapters and verses in their exegesis, the men frequently gave the audience orders, such as "Listen carefully as I read Luke, chapter seventeen." The women, on the other hand, rarely uttered imperatives but rather tended to invite the audience to participate, as in "Let's go back to verses fifteen and sixteen."

Given this pattern, Nathan is not far off the mark when he hears "Let's" as equivalent to a command. It *is* a way of getting others to do what someone wants. And yet Diana is also right when she says he should not feel coerced. The difference lies in the fundamentally different social structures of girls and boys, and women and men. In the hierarchical order that boys and men find or feel themselves in, status is indeed gained by telling others what to do and resisting being told what to do. So once Nathan has deciphered Diana's "Let's" as her way of saying what she wants him to do, his next step is to resist her. But girls and women find or feel themselves in a community that is threatened by conflict, so they formulate requests as proposals rather than orders to make it easy for others to express other preferences without provoking a confrontation. Not accustomed to having others try to bend their will simply to solidify a dominant position, girls do not learn to resist others' demands on principle and don't expect others to resist theirs on principle either.

It is not that women do not want to get their way, but that they do not want to purchase it at the cost of conflict. The irony of interactions like those between Diana and Nathan is that the differences between men's and women's styles doom their efforts. The very moves that women make to avoid confrontation have the effect of sparking it in conversation with some men. Insofar as men perceive that someone is trying to get them to do something without coming right out and saying so, they feel manipulated and threatened by an enemy who is all the more sinister for refusing to come out in the open.

"I'LL BE THE DOCTOR AND YOU BE THE BABY"

These differences in approaches to conflict have many other ramifications in ways of talking as well. In her study of preschoolers at play, Sachs found that when little boys played doctor, "I'll be the doctor" was the normal stance. Boys wanted to take the doctor role 79 percent of the time, and they often got into long arguments about which boy would get this high-status role. Others have found similar patterns. Linguist Elaine Anderson had preschoolers play out doctor-patient scenes with hand puppets. She too found that the boys wanted to take the high-status role of doctor and generally refused to be the patient or baby. The girls wanted to be the doctor only a third of the time; they often wanted to be the patient, the baby, or the mother.

In Sachs's study, in the vast majority of cases, boys told each other what role to take ("Come on, be a doctor"). Girls, on the other hand, usually asked each other what role they wanted ("Will you be the patient for a few minutes?") or made a joint proposal ("I'll be the nurse and you be the doctor"; "Now we can both be doctors"; "We both can be sick"; or "Okay, and I'll be the doctor for my baby and you be the doctor for your baby"). Many of these proposals, in addition to avoiding confrontation or telling others what to do, are creative ways of keeping the girls equal in status.

Do these experimental studies, in which children played in a laboratory setting, accurately reflect how children play in natural settings? Evidence that they do appears in an article written by a father, Rodger Kamenetz, that begins:

> My daughter Anya, six, and her friend Rosemary, seven, were playing together in Anya's room. The door was ajar, and when I heard some cooing noises, I peeked in and saw that each child was holding a Cabbage Patch doll, cradling it in her arms. "Now you change your baby," said Rosemary to Anya, "and I'll change mine."

In reading this I was struck by the symmetry of the girls' play. Rosemary was proposing that they both engage in the same activity at the same time. Instead of trying to cast Anya in the low-status role of baby, she reserved that role for the unprotesting Cabbage Patch dolls.

DIFFERENT SOCIAL STRUCTURES

Girls' and boys' different ways of trying to influence each other's behavior reflect—and create—different social structures. In getting ready for their slingshot fight, the boys in Goodwin's study evidenced a hierarchical organization: The leaders told the others what to do. Giving orders and getting others to follow them was the way that certain boys got to be and stay leaders. A command, by definition, distinguishes the speaker from the addressee and frames him as having more power. In contrast, the girls' groups were organized in an egalitarian way; according to Goodwin, "In accomplishing a task activity even among four- and five-year-olds, all participate jointly in decision making with minimal negotiation of status." By framing proposals with "Let's" and "We," the girls implied that their group was a community, and the results of compliance would increase the power of the community, not the individual power of the person making the suggestion.

Furthermore, the boys typically did not give reasons for their demands, other than their desires. For example, a boy who took a leadership role made demands like:

"PLIERS. I WANT THE PLIERS!"
"Look, man. I want the wire cutters right now."

But the girls gave reasons for their suggestions:

SHARON: We gotta *clean* 'em first. You know.
PAM: I know.
SHARON: 'Cause they got germs.
PAM: Wash 'em and stuff 'cause just in case they got germs on 'em.

Not giving reasons for their demands, the boys reinforced their orders as moves in a contest. Compliance indicated submission to the authority of the leader, although submission is an act of cooperation insofar as it reinforces the smooth working of the group. But the girls' methods of getting their way worked differently. Not only did they give reasons, but the reasons were for the general good: The bottles should be cleaned so no one would be harmed by germs. When Pam collaborated by echoing Sharon's suggestion and also her reason, she appeared to be participating in the decision making rather than following orders. This does not, however, mean that there may not be a pattern in whose suggestions tend to be taken up, or that someone whose suggestions are frequently taken up may not feel personal satisfaction and gain prestige in the group.

The different social structures that boys and girls maintained went along with the sorts of activities they preferred. Boys particularly liked to play openly competitive games, such as football and basketball. Even for activities that were not competitive by nature, the boys often broke into teams to facilitate competition. Girls were not much interested in organized sports or games. They preferred whole-group activities such as jump rope or hopscotch.

Goodwin found that the boys ranked themselves according to skill at different activities and often boasted and bragged about their abilities and possessions. Like the little boys in Sachs's study, arguing over who would get to be the doctor, the preteen and teenage boys in Goodwin's study argued about status—about relative skill and who had the power to tell whom what to do. The girls argued about their relative appearance, their relationships to others, and what others said about them. Whereas boys boasted that they were better, a girl who acted as if she was better than the others was criticized for "bragging" or "showing off."

Boys not only commanded but also insulted and threatened each other. If they had a complaint about another boy, they tended to voice it in his presence. Girls' complaints, however, were typically voiced in the absence of the accused.

The girls' preference to avoid direct confrontation resulted in behavior that is traditionally thought of in a negative way—talking behind someone's back. Expressing this negative view, one man remarked that girls sacrifice sincerity for harmony. The accusation of "insincerity" is commonplace in cross-cultural communication, because culturally different individuals don't talk in ways that seem obviously appropriate. Sparking direct confrontation by expressing criticism may seem "sincere" to those who believe that confrontation reinforces camaraderie. But in a system where confrontation causes rifts, it would not be "sincere" at all, since directly expressing criticism and sparking a fight would send a metamessage that one wants to weaken the bonds of friendship.

"YOU DIDN'T SAY WHY"

These differences in children's experience result in divergent expectations, assumptions, and attitudes that confuse adult conversations. For example, the following argument arose because the woman expected to hear reasons from a man who was not in the habit of giving them. Maureen and Philip were trying to set a date for a dinner party.

MAUREEN: The only weekend we seem to have free is October tenth.
PHILIP: That's the opening of hunting season.

158

MAUREEN: Well, let's do it Saturday or Sunday evening.

PHILIP: Okay, make it Saturday.

MAUREEN: Wouldn't you want to be able to hunt later on the first day of hunting?

PHILIP: [Annoyed] I *said* Saturday, so obviously that's the day I prefer.

MAUREEN: [Now also annoyed] I was just trying to be considerate of you. You didn't give a reason for choosing Saturday.

PHILIP: I'm taking off Thursday and Friday to hunt, so I figure I'll have had enough by Saturday night.

MAUREEN: Well, why didn't you say that?

PHILIP: I didn't see why I had to. And I found your question very intrusive.

MAUREEN: I found your response very offensive!

Since Philip didn't give a reason for choosing Saturday, Maureen assumed he might be accommodating to what he perceived to be her preference, as she might have done—indeed, as she was doing. She wanted to let him know that it wasn't necessary, and she was hurt by his objecting when she was being considerate. To Philip, being asked to explain his reasons feels like having to give an account of his time. He assumes that individuals watch out for their own interests, so her poking around in his interests is intrusive. Her attempts to ameliorate a potential conflict of interests actually sparked a conflict.

A GOOD KNOCK-DOWN DRAG-OUT FIGHT

Differences in attitudes toward conflict itself show up in daily conversations. Gail hates to argue. If Norman becomes angry and raises his voice, she is deeply upset. "I can't talk to you if you're yelling," she says. "Why can't we discuss this like mature people?" Norman can never figure this out. To him, being able to fight with someone is evidence of intimacy. In contrast, the endless monotonous discussions that she values as a sign of intimacy are anathema to him. They just wear him down, whereas he feels fine after a good knock-down, drag-out fight—which leaves her feeling weary and defeated. He regards such fighting as a form of ritual combat and values it as a sign of involvement, since only those who are intimately involved with each other argue.

Many cultures of the world see arguing as a pleasurable sign of intimacy, as well as a game. Americans in Greece often get the feeling that they are witnessing an argument when they are over-hearing a friendly conversation that is more heated than such a conversation would be if Americans were having it. Linguist Deborah Schiffrin showed that in the conversations of working-class Eastern European Jewish speakers—both male and female—in Philadelphia, friendly argument was a means of being sociable. Linguist Jane Frank analyzed the conversation of a Jewish couple who tended to polarize and take argumentative positions in social situations. But they were not fighting. They were staging a kind of public sparring, where both fighters were on the same side.

Greeks often show caring by telling people what to do. A Greek woman studying in the United States surprised and annoyed her dorm-mates by asking them questions like "Why are you keeping the refrigerator door open so long?" and "Why are you eating so little? You have to eat more than that." These questions would be common among friends in Greece and would be valued as a show of concern and involvement. To Americans, they are intrusive and critical. Her American dorm-mates responded by calling the Greek woman "Mom." What she intended as a sign of intimate caring was taken as a show of status characteristic of mothers talking to children.

Sociologists William Corsaro and Thomas Rizzo studied children in American and Italian nursery schools between the ages of two and four. They found that one of the Italian children's favorite activities was engaging in the kind of heated debate that Italians call *discussione* but Americans would regard as arguing. The researchers describe a typical instance of a routine that was played out several times a week, when the children were supposed to be quietly drawing with felt marking pens: A boy, Roberto, makes a display of searching for a red marker. Making sure everyone at his table is watching, he tries and discards all the red markers at his table, then gets up and takes one from another table. The children at the other table either don't notice or, more likely, pretend not to notice. But before long, a girl at that table, Antonia, asks loudly, "Where's red?" and *she* makes a show of searching for a red marker and displaying dissatisfaction with all those she and her tablemates can find.

Then the drama begins. This is how Corsaro and Rizzo describe it:

> Antonia slaps her forehead with the palm of her hand and shouts, "They robbed us!"
>
> This exclamation sets several things in motion simultaneously. Roberto looks up from his work and smiles at the other children at his table. They all catch his eye and smile back, signaling that they know what is about to happen. At the same time, several of the children at the third table look over to Antonia's table and then quickly over to Roberto's. Finally, at Antonia's table Maria jumps up, points to Roberto and shouts: "It was Roberto!" Immediately Antonia, Maria and several other children march over to Roberto's table. Just as they arrive, a girl at the table, Luisa, grabs seven or eight markers (including the one Roberto took) and hides them in her lap under the table. Once at the table Antonia accuses Roberto of stealing the red marker. He denies it, challenging Antonia and the others to find the stolen marker. As Antonia and Maria begin to look for the red marker, Bruna, backed by several other children from the third table, enters the dispute, claiming that Roberto did indeed steal the marker and that Luisa is hiding it. Luisa shouts, "No, it's not true!" But Antonia reaches under the table and grabs the markers that Luisa is hiding. At this point there is a great deal of shouting, gesturing, pushing and shov-

ing and the teachers must once again intervene and settle the dispute.

These children are not squabbling over a red marker; there are more than enough markers to go around. As Corsaro and Rizzo put it, they would simply rather argue than draw. And this seems to go for girls as well as boys in the Italian preschool.

FIGHTING FOR FRIENDSHIP

Though *discussione*—loudly arguing for the fun of it—is enjoyed by both girls and boys in the Italian preschool, American boys and girls are less well matched in their attitudes toward conflict. Boys are far more likely to express and create affiliation by opposition. Teasing is a way that boys show affection to girls by taking an agonistic stance. A common example is the classic scene in which a boy pulls the braids of a girl he likes. I don't know any girls who liked having their braids pulled, but if she likes the boy, a girl might prefer aggression to being ignored. This was the case with a Polish girl, Eva Hoffman, who recalls her childhood companion Marek in her book *Lost in Translation:*

> I'm in love with him. I can't stay away from him, even though sometimes he plays boyishly mean pranks on me: he drops an enormous tome on my head when I pass in front of his window, and once, he tries to stuff me into a hole in the forest, which turns out to have been left there by the Germans, and might still have some mines in it.

Marek's playfulness was potentially lethal. Nonetheless, Hoffman recalls, "We talk to each other ceaselessly, and in games with other kids we're a team." In fact, "in spite of these risky games we play with each other, I have a deep belief that his greater physical strength is there to protect me."

For boys and men, aggression does not preclude friendship. Quite the contrary, it is a good way to start interaction and create involvement. A woman told me of her surprise when she was a member of a mixed group of students attending a basketball game at the University of Michigan. Although their tickets had seat assignments, the usual practice among students at this university was for spectators to take any seats they found—first come, first served. Following these unwritten rules, the students took seats in the front row of the balcony. Before long, a group of men from Michigan State University arrived, assuming they were entitled to the seats shown on their tickets. Finding people in their seats, they ordered them out. When the University of Michigan students refused to vacate the seats, a loud argument ensued in which the men of the two groups denounced and threatened each other, and the women sank down in their seats. After a while, the visitors settled for the seats adjoining the disputed ones. Then the men who had just been engaged in an angry verbal fight began a friendly chat about the teams and the schools and the game about to begin. The women were dumbfounded. They would never have engaged in such an argument, but they assumed that if they had it would have made them enemies for life, not friends in the wink of an eye.

The possibility that a fight could be a way of initiating rather than precluding friendship struck me as a revelation when I read the transcripts in Corsaro and Rizzo's study. For me, observing the peer culture of the nursery school boys was like glimpsing a foreign world. Here, for example, is an episode they describe among American preschool boys:

> Two boys (Richard and Denny) have been playing with a Slinky on the stairway leading to the upstairs playhouse in the school. During their play two other boys (Joseph and Martin) enter and stand near the bottom of the stairs.
>
> DENNY: Go!
>
> [Martin now runs off, but Joseph remains and he eventually moves halfway up the stairs.]

JOSEPH: These are big shoes.

RICHARD: **I'll punch him right in the eye.**

JOSEPH: **I'll punch you right in the nose.**

DENNY: **I'll punch him with my big fist.**

JOSEPH: **I'll—I—I—**

RICHARD: **And he'll be bumpety, bumpety and punched out all the way down the stairs.**

JOSEPH: **I—I—I'll—I could poke your eyes out with my gun. I have a gun.**

DENNY: **A gun! I'll—I—I—even if—**

RICHARD: **I have a gun too.**

DENNY: **And I have guns too and it's bigger than yours and it's poo-poo down. That's poo-poo.**

[All three boys laugh at Denny's reference to poo-poo.]

RICHARD: **Now leave.**

JOSEPH: **Un-uh. I gonna tell you to put on—on the gun on your hair and the poop will come right out on his face.**

DENNY: **Well—**

RICHARD: **Slinky will snap right on your face too.**

DENNY: **And my gun will snap right—**

Up to this point, Richard and Denny seem to be engaged in a bitter fight with Joseph, who has tried to disrupt their Slinky game. Denny introduces a humorous tone by mentioning poo-poo, which makes all the boys laugh. But they are still threatening each other. Corsaro and Rizzo describe what happened next:

At this point a girl (Debbie) enters, says she is Batgirl, and asks if they have seen Robin. Joseph says he is Robin, but she says she is looking for a different Robin and then runs off. After Debbie leaves, Denny and Richard move into the playhouse and Joseph follows. From this point to the end of the episode the three boys play together.

After an angry fight in which they threatened to punch and shoot each other and snap the Slinky in each other's faces, the three boys play together amicably. Not only did the altercation not prevent their playing together; it facilitated it. I suspect that picking a fight was Joseph's way of making contact with the other boys, and engaging Joseph in the fight was Denny and Richard's method of easing his way into their play.

MAKING NICE

Also intriguing in this preschool episode is the part played by the girl, Debbie. It is her appearance in the guise of Batgirl that occasions the end of the boys' verbal fight and their shift to playing together peacefully. Debbie seems to swoop down like Batgirl on a peace mission.

If the boys were creating an argument, the girl manages not to say she disagrees even though she really does. When Debbie says she is looking for Robin, and Joseph says he is Robin, she does not reply, "No, you're not!" Instead, she accepts his premise and says she is looking for a different Robin.

The role of the female as peacemaker crops up again and again. In the following scene from the story "Volpone" by Jane Shapiro, a daughter takes the role of peacemaker in a fight between her mother and brother. The fight erupts because of the mother's and son's differing focuses on intimacy and independence in the act of showing concern.

In this story, the narrator is visiting her son, Zack, at college. He has been taking part in a demonstration against the university's investments in South Africa by sleeping in one of a number of shanties the students have built on campus. At dinner with his visiting family (which includes his sister Nora, his father, William, and his grandfather Pep) Zack explains that he's frustrated because, in contrast to the administrators of other universities where students *"routinely* get their heads smashed," the president of his college tolerates and even supports the student protesters, but does not exert pressure on the trustees to divest.

Here is the voice of Zack's mother, who is narrating the story:

> After a pause, I said, "Well, I'm sorry you're not making more of an impression on the trustees, but, speaking as a mother, there are times when I'm really glad you're not at Berkeley, or wherever, getting your head routinely smashed."
> Zack gave me a curious look, and Nora sat back and gave me an amused one. *"As a mother,"* she said. "You usually try not to say that."

By sitting back and reminding her mother that she usually tries not to speak "as a mother," Nora seems to be trying to divert her mother from the conversational path she has embarked on. But the narrator continues, with disastrous results:

> I said, "Well, I mean, I'm torn. Obviously I support you and I'm proud of you, and I think it's important you stand by your convictions, and obviously I *don't* believe in trying to keep my kids from operating independently and doing what they think is right. At the same time there's a part of me that says I really don't want you getting smashed in the head." Although stagy, this sounded so reasonable to me as to be unassailable. William was supportively, absently nodding. "It's a conflict I've not resolved," I said, "and—"
> "It's kind of irrelevant, Mom, whether *you want* to try to keep us from 'operating' in a certain way," Zack said. "We're people. We're already 'operating.' It's nice that you make an effort to frame it in a 'liberal' way. But your idea, Mom, about whether you should *let us* do it is kind of—I don't know, not exactly germane."

William then moves in to discipline his son in his wife's defense, and father and son are both angered. Nora steps in to defuse the anger and make everyone friends again:

> Nora leaned and set her hand on Pep's forearm. She said, "Come on, guys."

There was a silence, in which Nora reached across to Zack's plate and picked up his last curled shrimp and said to him in a warm voice, "You want this?" He moved his head back and forth. Nora held the shrimp up in her fingers before popping it in her mouth and said, "This is undeniably a Vermont shrimp." She grinned at Pep. She said, "This shrimp regrets everything."

When joking doesn't do the trick, Nora tries a direct appeal, softened with the use of a nickname that calls on her bond with Zack: "Come on, Z."

Zack's angry reaction comes as a surprise to his mother. She thinks she is showing concern for him in the spirit of connection and caring, but he interprets her comments in the spirit of status and control: If she is allowing him to act on his own, then his autonomy is not real, but granted by her. Picking up on the superiority implied by protection, Zack reacts to his mother's framing him as her child. His father tried to settle this conflict by a show of power, reinforcing Zack's lower status: He tells the boy not to talk to his mother that way. But the daughter takes the role of peacemaker, trying to nuzzle Zack out of his anger by a show of bonding.

"DON'T YOU AGREE?"

The role of peacemaker reflects the general tendency among women to seek agreement. When Marge tells John something she thought of or a comment someone else made, John often responds by pointing out a weakness in the position or an alternative perspective. This makes Marge vaguely uncomfortable. One day she repeated someone's comment that echoed a point of view John himself had argued only a few days before. She was sure he would say, "Oh, yes. That's right." In fact, her main reason for repeating the remark was to please John by offering support for his position. But, to Marge's surprise and distress, John pointed out the other side. Even when she was sure she was sowing agreement, she reaped a harvest of disagreement. To John, raising a different point of view is a more interesting contribution to make than agreeing. But Marge finds his disagreeing disagreeable, because it introduces a note of contentiousness into the conversation.

For Marge, disagreement carries a metamessage of threat to intimacy. John does not see disagreement as a threat. Quite the opposite, he regards being able to express disagreement as a sign of intimacy. One man explained to me that he feels it is his duty, when someone expresses a view, to point out the other side; if someone complains of another's behavior, he feels he should explain what that person's motives might be. When someone takes a position, he feels he ought to help explore it by trying to poke holes in it, and playing devil's advocate for the opposing view. In all this, he feels he is being supportive, and in a way he is, but it is support modeled on an adversarial stance—a stance that is more expected and appreciated by men than by women.

ENTER THE CHALLENGER

This difference in approach to agreement versus challenge comes up in educational settings too. A colleague had the students in his linguistics class read my book *That's Not What I Meant!* as a course text. He then set them the assignment of composing questions for me and sent me a dozen to answer. Of the twelve students whose questions I received, ten were women and two were men. All ten women's questions were supportive or exploring, asking for clarification, explanation, or personal information. For example, they asked: "Can you explain further . . . ? "Can you give another example?" "Are differences biological or social?" "Where do you get your examples?" "How will society change if everyone accepts your ideas?" "Why did you marry your husband?" The two questions from men were challenging. One asked, in essence, "Your book deals a lot with psychology;

why did you reject the way a psychologist interrogated you at your seminar?" The other asked, "Doesn't much of the material in your book fall more easily into the realm of rhetoric and communication than linguistics?"

The women's questions seemed charming to me, but the men's seemed cheeky. I remarked on the pattern to my husband. "Well, it was a setup," he commented. "How so?" I asked. "Well," he said, "their professor told them, 'Here's your chance—here's the expert.' It's a setup to challenge you." So there it was again: He too thought it natural to challenge an expert. I, like the women in this class, think that access to an expert is a chance to learn inside information and make personal contact.

What then is the "meaning" of a challenge? I heard the men's questions as attempting to undercut my authority. Both seemed to be saying, "You aren't really a linguist," and one further questioned my interpretation of my own example. I didn't like this. I liked the women's questions better: I felt they reinforced my authority. I didn't even mind the intrusive one about my marriage, which allowed me to be wry and amusing in my response. But challenging can be a form of respect. A male colleague commented that "softball" questions are pointless when there is a serious issue involved. Making a similar point, another male colleague commented, with regard to a somewhat critical book review he had written, "In a way you honor someone by grappling with him (yes, her too)." I was intrigued that both chose adversative metaphors—from sports and combat—to explain why challenging is obviously (to them) constructive in an academic interchange. I doubt I am unusual among women in seeing challenges as somewhat more real than ritual, and to take them personally as attempts to undercut my authority rather than to bolster it by "grappling" with me.

It seems likely to me now that the young men who asked challenging questions were trying to engage me on an intellectual level. But they fell into a "cross-cultural" gap: I do not enjoy "grappling" when I feel personally challenged, though I certainly enjoy intellectual discussion if I feel my authority is respected. I would have valued their questions had they been phrased differently: "Could you explain further why you objected to the behavior of the psychologist in your example?" and "Could you expand on the relationship between your work and the fields of rhetoric and communication?" A way similar questions have been posed to me is "I agree with you, but I have trouble answering people who ask me why what I do is linguistics. How do you answer people like that?" Someone who phrases questions this way elicits the same information but takes the footing of an ally rather than an adversary.

FIGHTING TO BE NICE

Since recognizing these patterns, I have been amazed at how often men invoke the theme of aggression to accomplish affiliative ends. For example, a guest speaker in one of my classes wanted to make the point that seemingly odd behavior could have many different explanations. To illustrate, he said, "Now take this young lady here in the first row. Suppose she suddenly stood up and began strangling this other young lady sitting next to her." In reaching for an example of unexpected behavior, he just happened to think of attack.

Another man was about to begin a workshop for about thirty people in a room that was large enough to hold fifty. The audience had taken seats in the back, leaving a moat of empty rows around the speaker. When his initial request that they move forward produced no response, the speaker resorted to a teasing threat: "If you don't move forward, when you leave, I'll follow you out and kill you."

A hypnotist was trying to help a woman retrieve her knowledge of Japanese, which she had once known well but had forgotten since becoming fluent in Chinese. After inducing a light trance, he suggested, "Imagine that someone is speaking to you in Japanese, trying to push you around. Yell at them in Japanese: 'Get out of here!' " In trying to suggest an emotionally engaging situation, he hit upon one that is pivotal to most men. But I wondered—and doubted—if this would be particularly compelling for the woman. Later, in explaining his approach, he said, "Let's see if we can get the Japanese to arm-wrestle the Chinese and win."

WOLF WORDS
IN SHEEP'S CLOTHING

If boys and men often use opposition to establish connections, girls and women can use apparent cooperation and affiliation to be competitive and critical. Goodwin found, for example, that girls particularly liked a jump-rope rhyme that allowed them to count how many jumps they were making. Gossip too can be competitive, if one vies to be the first to know the news.

Developmental psychologist Linda Hughes shows the subtle balancing of cooperation and competition among fourth- and fifth-grade girls playing a game called foursquare. In this game, each of four children stands in a square drawn on the ground, as they bounce a ball among them. Anyone who misses the ball, hits it out of the square, or bounces it twice is out: She leaves the game and the next child in line comes in. Although in principle the game is played by individuals, in practice these girls played as if they were on teams: They tried to get their friends in and others out.

Hughes explains that the girls played within a complex system that required them to be, in their own terms, "nice" and not "mean." Getting people out was mean, but it wasn't *really* mean if it was done for the purpose of being nice to someone else— getting a friend in. The girls had to be competitive; always being nice and never getting anyone out would be mean to all the children waiting in line who would never get in. But they had to enact competition within a framework of cooperation. So, for example, a girl who was about to hit a ball hard and get someone out might call to her friend, "Sally, I'll get you in!" This announced for all to hear that she was not trying to be mean to the girl she was getting out; she was just being nice to her friend.

The girls referred to this required behavior as being "nice-mean." They told Hughes they didn't like playing with boys, because the boys just tried to get everybody out.

Anthropologist Penelope Brown presents dramatic examples of how Tenejapa women use apparent agreement to disagree. Women in this Mayan Indian community in Mexico do not openly express anger or fight. If they feel angry, they show it by refusing to speak or smile or touch. How, then, do they enact conflict when the situation requires it—for example, in court? Brown filmed a court case that took place following an unusual and scandalous incident in which a young bride abandoned her new husband and married another man. The groom's family sued the runaway bride's family for the return of gifts that they had, in accordance with custom, given the bride.

The two families were represented in court by the mothers of the bride and groom. In presenting their cases, the two women argued angrily—by agreeing with each other in ironic and sarcastic tones. For example, when the groom's mother claimed she had given the bride a belt worth two hundred pesos, the bride's mother responded, "Perhaps it wasn't one hundred or so?" This ironically implied, "It was only worth one hundred pesos." She also denigrated a skirt her daughter had received by saying, "Perhaps it's that it's real wool then, perhaps!"—ironically claiming that the skirt was not made of real wool. The groom's mother countered, "Perhaps it's not that it was expensive then," implying, "It was expensive!" The other retorted, "Really expensive, [it is] itself then, perhaps, eh?"—sarcastically implying, "It was cheap!"

Forbidden to express anger and disagreement directly, these peasant women expressed themselves in the manner that was available to them—the vocabulary of politeness and agreement. This example from an exotic culture may seem extreme, but the pattern is not so different from the ways modern women sometimes accomplish negative ends with apparently positive means. All the verbal ways of being "nice" that are expected of women can be used to hurt as well as to heal.

A common way of hurting someone without seeming to intend to is to repeat a critical remark made by someone else, with the for-your-own-good introduction "I think you should know." For example, Hilda told Annemarie that Annemarie's sister-in-law had regaled a roomful of women with stories about problems Annemarie was having with her teenage son. Annemarie was mortified to learn that her family problems were the topic of public discussion. Since she wouldn't tell her husband not to confide in his sister, and she didn't want to pick a fight with her sister-in-law, she felt there was nothing she could do but stew. Annemarie would not have been hurt had she not been told, so it was her "friend" Hilda who had hurt her, not her sister-in-law.

To make matters worse, every time Annemarie met Hilda thereafter, Hilda gazed at her, brimming with concern, and asked, "How *are* you? How are things working *out*?" This made Annemarie feel like an emotional basket case rather than a normal parent whose children had normal problems. All forms of support can be used to undercut. Showing elaborate concern for others' feelings can frame you as the social worker who has it all together, and them as your patients.

Offering helpful suggestions can also indirectly imply criticism. For example, a woman named Sarah suggested to her friend Phyllis that Phyllis might ease her parents' next visit by having them stay in a hotel instead of in Phyllis's one-bedroom apartment. Instead of appreciating the advice, Phyllis correctly perceived that Sarah thought she was too involved with her parents.

Praise can pack a wallop if it's hiding criticism in its pockets. For example, "Your new beau is fabulous—he's not boring, like the last one" seems to be praising your new beau, yet you walk away smarting from the slap to your old one. Similarly, the compliment "Your presentation was excellent. It was much easier to follow than your last one," leaves you with a vision of your audience scratching their heads over your last presentation.

Another way that criticism can leak out without its author taking responsibility for it is in speculating about others' motives. For example, Patricia was wondering aloud why a man she had met had not called her. Nadine had an idea: "Maybe he thought you were stuck up because you told him you want to be called Patricia instead of Patty." Though Patricia still had no idea about the man's thoughts, she had learned what Nadine thought of her using her full name.

MESSAGES AND METAMESSAGES IN FIGHTS

Though women may be reluctant to fight openly, and men may be inclined to fight playfully, there are many occasions when men and women do engage in conflict—openly, seriously, and with each other. Often such arguments lead to frustration not only about the subject of dissension but also about the other's way of arguing. Once again the difference between messages and metamessages is key.

A man told me about the following conversation, which he felt typified why he found it frustrating to argue with a woman. The encounter began with her waking him up in the middle of the night.

> HE: What's wrong?
> SHE: You were taking up too much of the bed.
> HE: I'm sorry.
> SHE: You're always doing that.
> HE: What?
> SHE: Taking advantage of me.
> HE: Wait a minute. I was asleep. How can you hold me responsible for what I do when I'm asleep?
> SHE: Well, what about the time . . .

She then took him to task for past offenses.

It was hard for this couple to find a meeting ground in their dispute because they were moving on different levels. He was talking on the message level: He took up too much of the bed.

174

But she was focused on the metamessage level: The way he was sleeping showed that he took advantage of her generally, took up "too much space" in their relationship. She took the opportunity of this concrete offense to discuss the pattern of behavior that it represented. He felt it was unfair to pull a string of past events out of the hat of this inadvertent transgression, like so many colored handkerchiefs in a magician's trick.

Exactly the same points of view, similarly allotted, characterize a conversation in Anne Tyler's novel *The Accidental Tourist*. Macon and Muriel have been living together, but Macon is still legally married to someone else. Macon makes a casual remark about Alexander, Muriel's son:

> "I don't think Alexander's getting a proper education," he said to her one evening.
> "Oh, he's okay."
> "I asked him to figure what change they'd give back when we bought the milk today, and he didn't have the faintest idea. He didn't even know he'd have to subtract."
> "Well, he's only in second grade," Muriel said.
> "I think he ought to switch to a private school."
> "Private schools cost money."
> "So? I'll pay."
> She stopped flipping the bacon and looked over at him. "What are you saying?" she said.
> "Pardon?"
> "What are you saying, Macon? Are you saying you're committed?"

Muriel goes on to tell Macon that he must make up his mind whether he wants to divorce his wife and marry her: She can't put her son in a new school and then have to pull him out when and if Macon returns to his wife. The conversation ends with Macon saying, incredulously, "But I just want him to learn to subtract!"

Like the man and woman who were arguing in the middle of the night, Macon is concerned with the message, the simple matter of Alexander's learning math. But Muriel is concerned with the metamessage: What would it say about their relationship if he began paying for her son's education?

An argument that arose between a real-life husband and wife shows the same pattern. In this argument, which was recorded and analyzed (from a different point of view) by Jane Frank, a husband returned home and called his wife to arms: "How would you like to eat humble crow?" She had said it would be impossible to find a painting of a particular size and type that he wanted; now he had found one and he wanted her to admit that she had been wrong. Instead, the wife claimed that she had said it would be difficult, not impossible, to find. She proposed a compromise: She hadn't meant her remark as he interpreted it. But he would have none of that. She had said it; he had proved her wrong; she should admit defeat. Their argument, which became very heated, could not be resolved, because he never wavered from the message level—the literal accuracy of what she had said—but she soon moved on to what seemed far more important to her, the metamessage that his position sent about their relationship: "Why do you always want to prove me wrong and rank me out?"

"THAT REMINDS ME OF A STORY"

These different world views shape every aspect of our ways of talking. One aspect that has been studied by linguists and anthropologists is storytelling—the accounts of personal experiences that people exchange in conversation. And the stories we hear and tell in conversation shape our views. Through hearing people tell what happened to others, we form assumptions about the right way to behave. And the ways that women and men talk about events in their lives reflect and create their different worlds.

Each year, students in my classes record ordinary conversations that they happen to take part in, and transcribe a segment where people tell about personal experiences. One year, two students analyzed all the stories transcribed by class members to compare the ones told by women and those told by men. They found differences that fit in with the patterns I have been describing.

The fourteen stories that men had told were all about themselves. Of the twelve stories told by women, only six were about themselves; the others were about incidents that happened to other people. The men, but not the women, had told stories in which there were protagonists and antagonists. For the most part, the stories that men told made them look good. For example, two men told about times when they had won a game for their team by their extraordinary performance. Many of the women told stories that made them look foolish. For example, one woman told of not having realized she had broken her nose until a doctor informed her of the fact years later. Another told of having been so angry at losing her hubcap to a pothole that she stopped the car, searched in vain among a pile of hubcaps that had found a similar fate, and, not wanting to leave empty-handed, took a Mercedes hubcap that was of no use to her.

My students' informal comparison of the men's and women's stories had results similar to those of a study by Barbara Johnstone of fifty-eight conversational narratives recorded by her students. Johnstone found that

> the women's stories tend to be about community, while the men's tend to be about contest. The men tell about human contests—physical contests such as fights as well as social contests in which they use verbal and/or intellectual skill to defend their honor. They tell about contests with nature— hunting and fishing. Stories about contests with people or animals can take the form of tall tales, which are themselves a kind of contest between a teller and his audience. When a male storyteller is not the protagonist in his story, the protagonist is a man; men rarely tell stories involving women.
>
> The women's stories, on the other hand, revolve around the norms of the community, and joint action by groups of people. The women tell about incidents in which they violate social norms and are scared or embarrassed as a result; about

people helping other people out of scrapes; about sightings of apparent ghosts which are then explained by others; about meeting their mates and acquiring their cats. The women tell about peculiar people, dramatizing their abnormal behavior and setting it implicitly in contrast with social norms. They tell stories about themselves, about other women, and about men.

In Johnstone's study, not only did men more often tell about experiences in which they had acted alone, but when men and women told about acting alone, the outcomes tended to be different. The vast majority of men who reported acting alone also reported a happy outcome. The majority of women who reported acting alone portrayed themselves as suffering as a result. Only a very small number of stories told by men (four out of twenty-one) had the protagonist receiving help or advice from someone. In a much larger proportion of the women's stories (eleven of twenty-six), the protagonist received help or advice from others.

Johnstone concludes that men live in a world where they see power as coming from an individual acting in opposition to others and to natural forces. For them, life is a contest in which they are constantly tested and must perform, in order to avoid the risk of failure. For women, Johnstone claims, the community is the source of power. If men see life in terms of contest, a struggle against nature and other men, for women life is a struggle against the danger of being cut off from their community.

MUTUAL MISJUDGMENTS

These patterns provide a new context in which to place Thomas Fox's observations of the men and women in his writing class. Mr. H tried to exert influence on the group. Ms. M tried to avoid standing out and offending. A large part of Mr. H's self-definition revealed his view of the world as an arena for competition and conflict. According to Fox, Mr. H's writing described "competition and conflict with fellow cadets at West Point where he spent a year, with basketball teams and officials, with school-mates, and most importantly, according to Mr. H, with his brother."

If Mr. H appeared confident, his essays reveal the anguish he has experienced as a result of the agonistic world he inhabits. Since he is always in hierarchies, he has suffered badly in situations where he felt one-down: in his brief military experience, where everyone conspired to make entering cadets feel "like shit," and in his family, where he believed that his brother and sister were favored. Fox explains:

> Mr. H's essays are a litany of hierarchies, from the gradations of classmates at West Point, to his description of a basketball game where the official unjustly penalizes the player, to the way he presents his family as a hierarchy of privilege with his parents at the top, followed by his brother, then his sister, and finally Mr. H at the bottom. All of these hierarchies work to Mr. H's disadvantage, and as he states, in a marvelously appropriate misspelling, they "inferiorate" him.

In other words, what emerges as male confidence can be as much the result of past pain as what appears as female insecurity.

Women and men are inclined to understand each other in terms of their own styles because we assume we all live in the same world. Another young man in Fox's writing class noticed that his female peers refused to speak with authority. He imagined the reason to be that they feared being wrong. For him, the point was knowledge, a matter of individual ability. It did not occur to him that what they feared was not being wrong, but being offensive. For them, the point was connection: their relation to the group.

Both Mr. H and Ms. M expressed dissatisfaction with the roles they learned to play. Ms. M traced hers to her father, who cautioned her not to let on how much she knew. Mr. H blamed the agonistic world for casting him in his role:

> I personally used to be an open and very nice and sensitive person: deep down I still am. However, through competition

with my family and relationships at school, I changed my personality, "toughening up" and shutting others out.

Though opposition can be a means to affiliative ends, the hierarchical, competitive world of boys can also cause emotional pain and interfere with establishing connections.

DIFFERENT COMPLEXITIES

In responding to the differences between women and men described in this chapter, people frequently ask or tell me which style is better. Even researchers sometimes make value judgments. In comparing fifth-grade boys and girls—ten- and eleven-year-olds—at play, Janet Lever concludes that the boys' games better prepare them for life in the world of work because boys' games involve more complex rules and roles. But girls' games also involve complexity—in verbally managing interpersonal relations. Penelope Eckert, who observed boys and girls in high school, points out that boys define their social status in a simple and straightforward way—their individual skill and achievement, especially at sports—but girls "must define theirs in a far *more complicated* way, in terms of their overall character."

Lever describes a game the fifth-grade girls played that seemed "monotonous" to her. A large number of girls stood in a circle and together performed prescribed movements and recited a chant called "Doctor Knickerbocker Number Nine." One girl twirled in the center with her eyes closed, stopping with her arm extended. The girl to whom she pointed had to join her in the center, where she then twirled and picked another girl in the same way. When nine girls were in the center, the ninth became the new number one, and the other eight returned to the circle.

Why was this fun? Lever explains: "Shouts of glee were heard from the circle's center when a friend had been chosen to join them. Indeed, a girl could gauge her popularity by the loudness of these shouts." In other words, the game is fun because it manipulates and plays off the commodity that is important to girls—

the strength of their affiliations—just as the boys' games play off their valued commodity—skill. The girls' game is an experiment in shifting alliances. Their game is indeed a contest, but not one of skill; it is, rather, a popularity contest.

Majorie Harness Goodwin and Charles Goodwin describe an elaborate verbal routine that is one of the main preoccupations of the preteen and teenage girls in the working-class black neighborhood where they lived and worked. Called "He-Said-She-Said" by the girls themselves, this verbal routine is "instigated" when one girl tells another that a third was talking about her behind her back. The Goodwins remark that "the males studied had no structure for extended debate of comparable complexity."

So it is not that the boys' behavior is more complex in general. Rather, boys and girls are learning to handle complexity in different arenas—boys in terms of complex rules and activities, girls in terms of complex networks of relationships, and complex ways of using language to mediate those relationships.

WHOSE WAY IS BETTER?

Is it true that boys' games better prepare men for success in the work world? Surely the conviction that they cannot and should not act alone can be a hindrance to women who need to make quick decisions. But the conviction that they *must* act independently, and always find their way without help, is a hindrance to men, for there are times when they do not have all the information needed to make a decision. Furthermore, studies show that women *and men* who have been successful in the traditionally male fields of business and science are *not* very competitive. Rather, they excel in "work competence" or "work mastery." They simply do their jobs extremely well.

Women's inclination to seek agreement may even be an advantage in management. Many people feel that women make better managers because they are more inclined to consult others and involve employees in decision making, and everyone agrees that employees are more likely to implement a policy efficiently if they feel they have played a part in making it. One man described his wife's small business as an open arena in which people called her by first name, felt free to enter her office unannounced, and felt themselves to be a part of a group endeavor rather than underlings. In his own business, he said, his employees addressed him as "Mr." and never entered without knocking—and, he felt, were less satisfied with their work situation.

Though maintaining an atmosphere of community rather than hierarchy may have advantages in some settings, people who are not afraid of conflict have an advantage in innumerable inevitable situations where others try to get their way. Being willing to make a scene can be an effective form of power. Here's a trivial but telling example.

The audience was sparse at a concert in a large concert hall. Many people were seated in the farthest balcony, but entire sections much closer to the stage were empty, so some of those in the last balcony got up and moved into the closer empty seats. An usher came in just as the crowd was resettling and the concert beginning. She chose a couple she saw reseating themselves, shined her flashlight in their faces, and told them to return to their own seats. The woman was ready to do as they were told, but the man began to shout angrily at the usher, who disappeared instantly, the only way she could put an immediate end to the loud disturbance.

In another instance, a salesman boasted to his colleagues that he was one of the most powerful members of the sales staff. When he spoke at meetings, he was rarely crossed. He was proud of this, attributing it to his high status. In fact, no one crossed him because he was well known to have a quick temper and a nasty tongue, and no one wanted to be on the receiving end of his outbursts. The effect of fear is sometimes indistinguishable from the effect of respect.

Women who are incapable of angry outbursts are incapable of wielding power in this way. Far worse, their avoidance of confrontation opens them up to exploitation. In a word, they don't stand up for themselves. Celebrity women are not immune to this pattern. Oprah Winfrey, for example, has said, "My biggest flaw is my inability to confront people. After all the shows I've done, the books I've read, the psychologists I've talked to, I still allow myself to get ripped off to the *n*th degree. It takes me days and days of procrastinating and agonizing before I can work up the nerve to say anything. Sometimes I think I'd rather just run out and get hit by a truck than confront someone who is ripping me off."

This is not Oprah Winfrey's idiosyncratic flaw; it's a problem that innumerable women experience. In fact, it is not so much a flaw as a strength that is not working in oppositional contexts. Successful women may be especially prone to this weakness because they are likely to have achieved success by getting along with people—not by fighting with them. In order to get along with people and be liked, many women learn to avoid confrontation. But it is easier to rip off a person who is trying to avoid confrontation than someone who regards the world from an oppositional stance.

One Sunday I received a telephone call at home from a student who asked me a slew of questions about the dissertation she was writing. After spending a great deal of time answering her questions, I pointed out that she should really be putting these questions to her "mentor," my colleague who had primary responsibility (and got primary credit) for guiding her research. The student replied that she had to have answers to her questions that day, and she didn't want to disturb him at home.

Why was it all right to disturb me at home on Sunday, and not him, even though it was his job she was asking me to do? People find most women more approachable than most men. There are many possible reasons for this. Perhaps women's time does not seem as valuable as men's. Many of us can recall the feeling that our mother's time was at our disposal, but our father's time was reserved for more important pursuits outside the home; we had to wait for him to have time for us—so his time felt more valuable when we got it. But another reason for the greater ap-approachability of women is their avoidance of conflict, which means they are less likely to respond harshly if displeased.

Always taking an adversative stance can result in avoiding situations one might really enjoy. And always accommodating can result in accepting situations one would really rather avoid. One man described to me what he and his former wife called the I-like-chicken-backs phenomenon. When his family ate a chicken for dinner, someone had to eat the back, and in his family it was always his wife, who assured the others, "I like chicken backs." But, as this man commented to me, nobody really likes chicken backs. She had convinced herself that she liked chicken backs—and broken egg yolks and burned toast—to be accommodating. But years of accommodating built up to mounting frustration that they both believed had contributed to their eventual divorce.

Even among couples who do not divorce, accommodation can take a toll. Again, a celebrity provides an example. The actress Jayne Meadows said in an interview that early in their marriage, her husband, comedian Steve Allen, had "manipulated" her into turning down major offers. For example, she said, "Steve kept me from the lead in *Will Success Spoil Rock Hunter?*" When questioned about this on a talk show, Allen said he had simply remarked, "It's a little gamey, that opening scene," and Meadows herself decided to turn the role down. Jayne Meadows apparently inferred—probably correctly—that her husband preferred that she not take the part. But did she have to honor his preference? At the time she felt she did, but looking back she wished she hadn't.

AND NOW FOR SOMETHING COMPLETELY DIFFERENT

For many women, openly opposing the will of others—or what they perceive to be others' will—is unthinkable. Ironically, it may be easier for some to think of leaving. This was the case with a woman I will call Dora, who did not realize, until it was too late, that opposing her husband's will would not bring the house down. But the cumulative frustration of never getting her way did.

A source of frustration for Dora was a series of used automobiles. It was she who drove to work, and she who took the car to the garage, but her husband, Hank, who chose the cars they would buy. Hank always went for cars that were cheap, interesting, and continually in need of repair. After Dora was nearly killed by a run-down Renault with unfixable brakes, they were in the market for yet another used car.

Hank fixed his sights on a fifteen-year-old Alfa Romeo that a mechanic he knew was getting ready to sell. Dora wanted to take advantage of the chance to buy a late-model VW from a friend who was leaving the country. Determined to reach a decision by consensus, she tried every verbal resource she could think of to convince Hank that it made sense to buy the boring but dependable VW rather than the dashing old Alfa Romeo, but he would not be convinced.

If this had happened at any previous time, Dora would have acceded to her husband's wishes and cursed him in her heart each time she drove the Alfa Romeo to work—or to the garage for repair. But this incident occurred when their marriage was already on the rocks. With so little to lose, she bought the VW from her friend and steeled herself for the torrent of anger she was sure she'd incur. To her amazement, Hank never spoke a word of remonstrance. When she told him what she had expected, he told her she had been foolish: She should have just done what she wanted from the start if she felt that strongly about it. He couldn't understand why she felt she had to have his blessing to do what she was certain was right.

The most extreme example I have encountered of the conviction that accommodation is the best way to achieve domestic harmony came from a woman who talked to me about her very early marriage to a man so violent that she had feared for the lives of her children and herself. In explaining to me why she had tolerated his beatings, she said that her husband had had a difficult childhood, deprived of love, and she had felt she could heal his wounds—and those of their relationship—by providing him unconditional love. One time he beat her so badly that she was knocked unconscious. When she came to, he said, "I guess it's over." She replied, "I still love you." What he saw as a blow so vicious that it would surely drive her away, she saw as a chance to prove once and for all that her love was truly unconditional. Even with such provocation, she did not consider defiance or challenge to be an available response.

No matter how dissatisfied people are with the results they are getting, they rarely question their way of trying to get results. When what we are doing is not working, we do not try doing something totally different. Instead, we try harder by doing more of what seems self-evidently the right way to proceed. But when styles differ, more of the same is usually met with more of the same from the other party as well. As a result, far from solving the problem, our efforts only make things worse.

This came out in the account of a couple, Molly and George. Molly can't bear it when George yells. But yelling seems only natural to him, since he grew up in a home where he, his two brothers, and his father were always opposing each other, struggling and tussling and arguing. Occasionally Molly surprises George by shouting back. She hates this, but he likes it. George explained, "When I get angry about something and I attack, I expect resistance. If I don't get resistance, I get frustrated, and then I get really angry."

As this example shows, attempts to avoid conflict can actually spark it with someone for whom conflict is a valued means of involvement. An earnest American exchange student discovered this in conversation with his Spanish host in Seville. The host liked to talk against Catalans, members of an ethnic group living in northeast Spain, and she knew that her American guest did not share her views. Once she tried to provoke him by saying, "The Catalans are sons of bitches." The young American tried to be conciliatory: "Well, you have your opinion and I have mine, so let's not worry about it." Far from avoiding an argument, this refusal to engage in debate infuriated her and sparked an angry attack. They had to talk for an hour before coming to a partial understanding—not about attitudes toward Catalans, but about attitudes toward verbal conflict.

IN SEARCH OF FLEXIBILITY

When one's habitual style is not working, trying harder by doing more of the same will not solve problems. Instead, men and women could both benefit from flexibility. Women who avoid conflict at all costs would be better off if they learned that a little conflict won't kill them. And men who habitually take oppositional stances would be better off if they broke their addiction to conflict.

Because people are different, not only in gender but in cultural background, differences in attitudes toward verbal opposition will persist among friends, lovers, and strangers. But they are particularly likely—and particularly troubling—in long-term relationships, which are by nature affected by issues of control and conflicting desires. Playing the relationship game together is harder if you're playing by different rules—or playing different games. Since the meaning of conflict, and the means that seem natural to deal with it, are fundamentally different for women and men, this is an arena where men's and women's styles are especially likely to come into conflict. Simply realizing that what seems like unfair or irrational behavior may be the result of a different style helps to reduce frustration. Conflicts will still arise, but at least you'll be arguing about real conflicts of interest rather than fighting styles.

SEVEN

Who's Interrupting?
Issues of Dominance
and Control

H ere is a joke that my father likes to tell.

    A woman sues her husband for divorce. When the judge asks her why she wants a divorce, she explains that her husband has not spoken to her in two years. The judge asks the husband, "Why haven't you spoken to your wife in two years?" He replies, "I didn't want to interrupt her."

This joke reflects the commonly held stereotype that women talk too much and interrupt men.

    In direct contradiction of this stereotype, one of the most widely cited findings to emerge from research on gender and language is that men interrupt women. I have never seen a popular article on the subject that does not cite this finding. It is deeply satisfying because it refutes the misogynistic stereotype that accuses women of talking too much, and it accounts for the experience reported by most women, who feel they are often cut off by men.

Both claims—that men interrupt women and that women interrupt men—reflect and bolster the assumption that an interruption is a hostile act, a kind of conversational bullying. The interrupter is seen as a malevolent aggressor, the interrupted an innocent victim. These assumptions are founded on the premise that interruption is an intrusion, a trampling on someone else's right to the floor, an attempt to dominate.

The accusation of interruption is particularly painful in close relationships, where interrupting carries a load of metamessages—that a partner doesn't care enough, doesn't listen, isn't interested. These complaints strike at the core of such a relationship, since that is where most of us seek, above all, to be valued and to be heard. But your feeling interrupted doesn't always mean that someone set out to interrupt you. And being accused of interrupting when you know you didn't intend to is as frustrating as being cut off before you've made your point.

Because the complaint "You interrupt me" is so common in intimate relationships, and because it raises issues of dominance and control that are fundamental to the politics of gender, the relationship between interruption and dominance bears closer inspection. For this, it will be necessary to look more closely at what creates and constitutes interruption in conversation.

DO MEN INTERRUPT WOMEN?

Researchers who report that men interrupt women come to their conclusion by recording conversation and counting instances of interruption. In identifying interruptions, they do not take into account the substance of the conversations they studied: what was being talked about, speakers' intentions, their reactions to each other, and what effect the "interruption" had on the conversation. Instead, mechanical criteria are used to identify interruptions. Experimental researchers who count things need operational criteria for identifying things to count. But ethnographic researchers—those who go out and observe people doing naturally whatever it is the researchers want to understand—are as wary of operational criteria as experimenters are wedded to them. Identifying interruptions by mechanical criteria is a paradigm case of these differences in points of view.

Linguist Adrian Bennett explains that "overlap" is mechanical: Anyone could listen to a conversation, or a tape recording of one, and determine whether or not two voices were going at once. But interruption is inescapably a matter of interpretation regarding individuals' rights and obligations. To determine whether a speaker is violating another speaker's rights, you have to know a lot about both speakers and the situation. For example, what are the speakers saying? How long has each one been talking? What has their past relationship been? How do they feel about being cut off? And, most important, what is the content of the second speaker's comment, relative to the first: Is it a reinforcement, a contradiction, or a change in topic? In other words, what is the second speaker trying to *do*? Apparent support can subtly undercut, and an apparent change of topic can be an indirect means of support—as, for example, when an adolescent boy passes up the opportunity to sympathize with his friend so as not to reinforce the friend's one-down position.

All these and other factors influence whether or not anyone's speaking rights have been violated and, if they have been, how significant the violation is. Sometimes you feel interrupted but you don't mind. At other times, you mind very much. Finally, different speakers have different conversational styles, so a speaker might *feel* interrupted even if the other did not *intend* to interrupt.

Here is an example that was given by Candace West and Don Zimmerman to show a man interrupting a woman. In this case I think the interruption is justified in terms of interactional rights. (The vertical lines show overlap.)

FEMALE: So uh you really can't bitch when you've got all those on the same day (4.2) but I uh asked my physics professor if I couldn't chan|ge that |
MALE: |Don't |touch that
(1.2)
FEMALE: What?
(pause)
MALE: I've got everything jus'how I want it in that note-book, you'll screw it up leafin' through it like that.

West and Zimmerman consider this an interruption because the second speaker began while the first speaker was in the middle of a word (*change*). But considering what was being said, the first speaker's rights may not have been violated. Although there are other aspects of this man's talk that make him seem like a conversational bully, interrupting to ask the woman to stop leafing through his notebook does not in itself violate her right to talk. Many people, seeing someone handling their property in a way that was destroying their painstaking organization of it, would feel justified in asking that person to stop immediately, without allowing further damage to be done while waiting for the appropriate syntactic and rhetorical moment to take the floor.

Sociologist Stephen Murray gives an example of what he regards as a prototypical case of interruption—where someone cuts in to talk about a different topic when the first speaker has not even made a single point. Here is his example:

H: I think |that
W: |Do you want some more salad?

This simple exchange shows how complex conversation can be. Many people feel that a host has the right, if not the obligation, to offer food to guests, whether or not anyone is talking. Offering food, like asking to have salt or other condiments passed, takes priority, because if the host waited until no one was talking to offer food, and guests waited until no one was talking to ask

191

for platters beyond their reach, then the better the conversation, the more likely that many guests would go home hungry.

This is not to say that any time is the right time to interrupt to offer food. If a host *habitually* interrupts to offer food *whenever* a partner begins to say something, or interrupts to offer food just when a speaker reaches the climax of a story or the punchline of a joke, it might seem like a violation of rights or the expression of mischievous motives. But the accusation of interrupting cannot be justified on the basis of a single instance like this one.

Conversational style differences muddy the waters. It may be that one person grew up in a home where conversation was constant and all offers of food overlapped ongoing talk, while another grew up in a home where talk was sparse and food was offered only when there was a lull in the conversation. If two such people live together, it is likely that one will overlap to offer food, expecting the other to go on speaking, but the overlap-aversant partner will feel interrupted and maybe even refuse to resume talking. Both would be right, because interruption is not a mechanical category. It is a matter of individual perceptions of rights and obligations, as they grow out of individual habits and expectations.

INTERRUPTION WITHOUT OVERLAP

In these examples, an overlap—two voices talking at once—is not necessarily an interruption, that is, a violation of someone's speaking rights. There are also instances where speakers do feel that their rights have been infringed on, and may even feel interrupted, when there is no overlap. An example of such an instance appears in Alice Greenwood's analysis of dinner table conversations among her three children (twins Denise and Dennis, twelve, and Stacy, eleven) and their friends. In the following example, Denise and Stacy have performed a verbal routine for the benefit of their brother's dinner guest, Mark, fourteen. This dialogue, which Greenwood calls the Betty routine, is one the sisters often perform together. Before they start, they get Mark's attention: Denise says, "Listen to this. Mark, listen to this." Then Denise and Dennis announce, "It's so funny." But Mark doesn't agree:

DENISE: [In Betty voice] Excuse me, are you Betty?
      . . .
STACY: Oh, yes.
DENISE: [In Betty voice] Betty who?
STACY: [In Betty voice] Bettybitabitabittabuttabut—
     [Dennis, Denise, and Stacy laugh.]
MARK: Whaaaat?
     [Dennis, Denise, and Stacy laugh hysterically.]

Although this routine sparks delighted laughter from the three siblings, and on other occasions also sparked laughter among friends, Mark did not laugh and claimed not to get the joke. Denise and Stacy tried to explain it to him:

DENISE: I said, "Betty who?," like you say "Betty Jones." Then she says, "Bettybitabitabitta—"
→DENNIS: Did anyone eat from this yet?
MARK: No. Actually, what I was going to say was can I try that soup? It looks quite good.
DENISE: Listen, listen, listen, listen.
MARK: Say it in slow motion, okay?
STACY: Betty bought a bit of bitter butter and she said, "This butter's bitter. If I put it in my batter, it will make my batter bitter." So Betty bought a bit of better butter to—
→DENISE: You never heard that before?
MARK: No. Never.
DENISE: Mark, seriously?
MARK: Seriously.
DENISE: It's like the famous to— |
→STACY: |tongue twister.

MARK: No. The famous tongue twister is
Peterpiperpicked— |

→DENISE: |Same thing. It's like that. It's
like that one.

MARK: **You keep interrupting me.**

In this excerpt, Denise and Stacy repeatedly cut each other off, as shown by the arrows and vertical lines, but there is no indication that either resents it. They do seem to mind their brother Dennis's overlapping to ask about the food ("Did anyone eat from this yet?") because he's interrupting their explanation (Denise protests, "Listen, listen, listen, listen"). The girls are supporting each other, talking on the same team.

Most striking is Mark's complaint, "You keep interrupting me." This is intriguing because what Mark was saying when he got interrupted ("No. The famous tongue twister is Peterpiperpicked—") was actually an interruption of the girls' explanation, even though his voice did not overlap theirs. The same is true for the previous time they "interrupted" him: Just as Denise said, "All right. Watch this," Mark began to ask, "Is it as funny as a—" but he didn't get to finish because Dennis laughed and Denise launched the routine, as announced. So Mark's protest seems like a real-life instance of the humorous line "Don't talk while I'm interrupting you."

Mark also took an oppositional stance, even though he was really supporting rather than disagreeing. The girls just said that their tongue twister was "*like* the famous tongue twister." If Mark had simply offered "the famous tongue twister" (Peter Piper picked a peck of pickled peppers), then his interruption would have been supportive, furnishing the end of Denise's explanation. Instead, he began by saying "No," as if they had been claiming that theirs *was* the famous tongue twister.

In this conversation, the girls were trying to include Mark in their friendly banter. Greenwood found, in studying her children's conversations with their friends, that the more interruptions a conversation contained, the more comfortable the children felt in it and the more they enjoyed it. But Mark refused to be part of their fun by insisting on his right to hold the floor without interruption. Perhaps his being a few years older was a factor. Perhaps he did not like being cast in the role of audience. Perhaps he felt he was being put down when Denise asked, "You never heard that before? . . . Mark, seriously?" Whatever the reason, Denise, Stacy, and Dennis were doing rapport-talk, and Mark wanted to do something more like report-talk. It is not surprising that Denise later told her mother that she didn't like Mark.

Although Denise did "interrupt" Mark to tell him he had the idea ("Same thing. It's like that"), there is no evidence that she was trying to dominate him. Furthermore, though Denise and Stacy interrupted each other, there is no evidence that they were trying to dominate each other. There is, however, some evidence that Mark might have been trying to dominate Stacy and Denise, for example by refusing to laugh at their jokes and rejecting their explanation of their verbal routine, even though he did not overlap their speech. So it is not the interruption that constitutes dominance but what speakers are trying to do when they talk to each other.

OVERLAP WITHOUT INTERRUPTION

Claiming that an interruption is a sign of dominance assumes that conversation is an activity in which one speaker speaks at a time, but this reflects ideology more than practice. Most Americans *believe* one speaker *ought* to speak at a time, regardless of what they actually do. I have recorded conversations in which many voices were heard at once and it was clear that everyone was having a good time. When I asked people afterward their impressions of the conversation, they told me that they had enjoyed themselves. But when I played the tape back for them, and they heard that people had been talking all together, they were embarrassed and made comments like "Oh, God, do we really do that?" as if they had been caught with their verbal pants down.

In a book entitled *Conversational Style,* I analyzed two and a half hours of dinner table conversation among six friends. Looking back on the conversation, some of the friends told me they had felt that others had "dominated" the conversation—and when I first listened to the tape, I too thought that it looked that way. But the accused pleaded innocent: They claimed they had not intended to dominate; in fact, they wondered why the others had been so reticent. Only by comparing different parts of the conversation to each other was I able to solve the puzzle.

The inadvertent interruptions—and the impression of domination—came about because the friends had different conversational styles. I call these styles "high considerateness" and "high involvement," because the former gave priority to being considerate of others by not imposing, and the latter gave priority to showing enthusiastic involvement. Some apparent interruptions occurred because high-considerateness speakers expected longer pauses between speaking turns. While they were waiting for the proper pause, the high-involvement speakers got the impression they had nothing to say and filled in to avoid an uncomfortable silence.

Other unintended interruptions resulted when high-involvement speakers chimed in to show support and participation: High-considerateness speakers misinterpreted the choral support as attempts to yank the floor away from them, and they stopped, to avoid what to them would have been a cacophony of two voices at once. Ironically, these interruptions were not only the interpretations of the apparent victims—they were their creations. When high-involvement speakers used exactly the same techniques with each other, the effect was positive rather than negative: Chiming in with speakers didn't stop anybody from talking. It greased the conversational wheels and enlivened spirits.

Here are two examples from my study that illustrate these two contrasting situations, and the different effects of overlap on conversation. The first example shows overlapping that had a positive effect, in a segment of conversation among three high-involvement speakers. The second shows overlapping between high-involvement and high-considerateness speakers that disrupted the conversation. Though gender is not a factor in the overlap patterns in these conversations, understanding how overlap can work—or fail to work—is fundamental to making sense of the relationship between gender and interruption.

SUCCESSFUL COOPERATIVE OVERLAPPING

The first example took place in the context of a discussion about the impact of television on children. Only three of the six friends were talking here, the three high-involvement speakers: Steve (the host), Peter (Steve's brother, who was a guest), and Deborah (the author, who was also a guest). Steve made the statement that television has been bad for children, and I responded by asking whether Steve and Peter had grown up with television. It might not be a coincidence that I, the woman, shifted the focus from an abstract, impersonal statement to a personal one.

> STEVE: I think it's basically done damage to children. That what good it's done is outweighed by the damage.|
> →DEBORAH: |Did you two grow up with television?
> PETER: Very little. We had a TV in the Quonset—|
> →DEBORAH: |How old were you when your parents got it?|
> →STEVE: |We had a TV, but we didn't watch it all the time. We were very young. I was four when my parents got a TV.|
> →DEBORAH; |You were four?
> PETER: I even remember that. |I don't remember /??/
> →STEVE: |I remember they got a TV before we moved out of the Quonset huts. In 1954.

→PETER: I remember we got it in the Quonset huts.

DEBORAH: [Chuckle] You lived in Quonset huts? When you were how old?

STEVE: You know my father's dentist said to him, "What's a Quonset hut?" And he said, "God, you must be younger than my children." He was. Younger than both of us.

As indicated by vertical lines and arrows, this conversation includes many overlaps and "latchings"—instances where a second speaker begins speaking without leaving any perceptible pause. Yet the speakers show no evidence of discomfort or annoyance. All three speakers take turns that latch onto or intrude into others' turns. In this conversation, Peter and Steve, who are brothers, operate as a duet, much as Denise and Stacy did in the earlier example.

This example contains a clue to why high-involvement speakers don't mind being overlapped. These speakers yield to an intrusion if they feel like it, but if they don't feel like it, they put off responding, or ignore the intrusion completely. For example, when Peter is saying, "We had a TV in the Quonset [huts]," I interrupt to ask, "How old were you when your parents got it?" Steve doesn't answer my question right away. Instead, he first finishes Peter's statement: "We had a TV, but we didn't watch it all the time." Only then does he turn to answering my question: "We were very young. I was four when my parents got a TV." At another point, Steve ignores my question. I ask, "You lived in Quonset huts? When you were how old?" Without even acknowledging my question, Steve simply offers a vignette about his father that the topic of Quonset huts called to his mind. Part of the reason Steve does not find my questions intrusive is that he does not feel compelled to answer them—exactly the assumption that frees me to toss them out exuberantly. Another reason that the overlaps are cooperative is that they do not change the topic but elaborate on it.

UNSUCCESSFUL COOPERATIVE OVERLAPPING

The success of this brief conversation had nothing to do with whether or not speakers overlapped or interrupted; it was successful because the speakers had similar habits and attitudes about overlapping speech. The next example shows a segment of the same dinner table conversation that was not successful. Peter and I appear again here, but, instead of Steve, we are talking to David, who has a high-considerateness style.

David, an American Sign Language interpreter, is telling us about ASL. As listeners, Peter and I use overlap and latching to ask supportive questions, just as I asked supportive, overlapping questions of Peter and Steve in the previous example. Here too our questions show interest in what the speaker is saying rather than shifting focus. But the effect is very different:

DAVID: So, and this is the one that's Berkeley. This is the Berkeley sign for |Christmas.

→DEBORAH: |Do you figure out those, those, um, correspondences? Or do—

DAVID: | /?/ |

when you learn the signs, does somebody tell you?

DAVID: Oh, you mean |watching it? Like—

→DEBORAH: |'Cause I can imagine knowing that sign, and not figuring out that it had anything to do with the decorations.

DAVID: No. Y-you know that it has to do with the decorations. |

→DEBORAH: |'Cause somebody tells you? Or you figure |it out? |

→DAVID: |No. |Oh. You, you talking about me?

199

DEBORAH: Yeah.

DAVID: Or a deaf person?

→DEBORAH: You. You.

DAVID: Me? Uh, someone tells me, usually. But a lot of them I can tell. I mean they're obvious. The better I get, the more I can tell. The longer I do it the more I can tell what they're talking about. Without knowing what the

→DEBORAH: Huh That's interesting.

DAVID: sign is.

→PETER: But how do you learn a new sign?

DAVID: How do I learn a new sign?

PETER: Yeah. I mean supposing Victor's talking and all of a sudden he uses a sign for Thanksgiving, and you've never seen it before.

All Peter's and my comments are latched or overlapped on David's, as the arrows show. But only two of David's seven comments overlap ours. Furthermore, these two utterances—one that was inaudible (shown by a question mark in slashes) and one in which David said, "No"—are probably both attempts to answer the first parts of my double-barreled questions ("Do you figure out those—those, um, correspondences?" and " 'Cause somebody tells you?"). David shows evidence of discomfort in his pauses, hesitations, repetitions, and circumlocutions. When I played the segment back for him, he told me that the fast pace of the conversation in general and the questions in particular had caught him off guard and made him feel borne in upon.

It is difficult for me to regard this conversation in merciless print, because it makes me look overbearing. Yet I recall my goodwill toward David (who remains one of my closest friends) and my puzzlement at the vagueness of his answers. Comparing this effect on David to the effect of my "machine-gun questions" on Steve and Peter, I was relieved to see that "machine-gun questions" had exactly the effect I had intended when used with other high-involvement speakers: They were taken as a show of interest and rapport; they encouraged and reinforced the speaker. But when such questions were used with high-considerateness speakers, they created disruptions and interruptions. It was not the overlapping or fast pacing that created the interruption and discomfort *but the style difference*. Style differences are the very basis of such terms as *fast pacing* and *pausing*. Characteristics such as "fast pacing" are not inherent, but result from the styles of speakers *relative to each other*. I might add that as a result of doing this research, I learned not to use machine-gun questions or cooperative overlapping with people who don't respond well—a tangible benefit of understanding conversational style.

CULTURAL DIFFERENCES

In my study of dinner table conversation, the three high-involvement speakers were New York City natives of Jewish background. Of the three high-considerateness speakers, two were Catholics from southern California and one was from London, England. Although a sample of three does not prove anything, nearly everyone agrees that many (obviously not all) Jewish New Yorkers, many New Yorkers who are not Jewish, and many Jews who are not from New York have high-involvement styles and are often perceived as interrupting *in conversations with speakers from different backgrounds,* such as the Californians in my study. But many Californians expect shorter pauses than many midwesterners or New Englanders, so in conversations between them, the Californians end up interrupting. Just as I was considered extremely polite when I lived in New York but was sometimes perceived as rude in California, a polite Californian I know was shocked and hurt to find herself accused of rudeness when she moved to Vermont.

The cycle is endless. Linguists Ron and Suzanne Scollon show that midwestern Americans, who may find themselves interrupted in conversations with easterners, become aggressive interrupters when they talk to Athabaskan Indians, who expect much longer pauses. Many Americans find themselves interrupting when they talk to Scandinavians, but Swedes and Norwegians are perceived as interrupting by the longer-pausing Finns, who are themselves divided by regional differences with regard to length of pauses and rate of speaking. As a result, Finns from certain parts of the country are stereotyped as fast talking and pushy, and those from other parts of the country are stereotyped as slow talking and stupid, according to Finnish linguists Jaakko Lehtonen and Kari Sajavaara.

Anthropologists have written about many cultures in the world where talking together is valued in casual conversation. This seems to be the norm in more parts of the world than the northern European norm of one-speaker-speaks-at-a-time. Karl Reisman coined the term *contrapuntal conversations* to describe the overlapping style he observed in Antigua. Karen Watson borrowed his term to describe Hawaiian children's verbal routines in which they jointly joke and engage in "talk story." Watson explains that for these children, taking a turn is not a matter of individual performance but "partnership in performance." Michael Moerman makes similar observations about Thai conversation. Reiko Hayashi finds far more simultaneous speech among Japanese speakers in casual conversation than among Americans. Jeffrey Shultz, Susan Florio, and Frederick Erickson found that an Italian-American boy who was considered a serious behavior problem at school was simply chiming in as was appropriate and normal in his home. All of these researchers document overlapping speech that is not destructive, not intended to exercise dominance and violate others' rights. Instead, it is cooperative, a means of showing involvement, participation, connection. In short, simultaneous talk can be rapport-talk.

WOMEN AS COOPERATIVE OVERLAPPERS

Paradoxically (in light of the men-interrupt-women research), and most important for our discussion here, another group that has been found to favor conversations in which more than one person speaks at a time is women. Folklorist Susan Kalčik was one of the first to observe women's use of overlapping talk by taping a women's group. In reviewing studies that compared all-male and all-female interaction, linguists Deborah James and Janice Drakich found that, of those reporting differences, the great majority observed more interruptive talk among the females.

Linguist Carole Edelsky inadvertently uncovered women's preference for overlapping talk when she set out to determine who talked more at a series of faculty committee meetings. She found that men talked more than women if one person was speaking while the others listened silently, but women talked as much as men during periods when more than one voice was heard at the same time. In other words, women were less likely to participate when the situation felt more like report-talk, more likely to do so when it felt like rapport-talk. Cooperative overlapping framed parts of the meeting as rapport-talk.

Following is an example of women in casual conversation overlapping in a highly cooperative and collaborative way. It comes from a conversation recorded at a kitchen table by linguist Janice Hornyak, who was a party to the conversation. Jan and her mother, Peg, who are from a southern state, were visiting relatives in the North, where Jan got to see snow for the first time. Peg and Marge, who are sisters-in-law, reminisce, for Jan's benefit, about the trials of raising small children in a part of the country where it snows. (Jan's mother raised her older children in the North but moved to the South before Jan was born.)

PEG: The part I didn't like was putting everybody's snow pants and boots |and

→MARGE: |Oh yeah, that was the worst part,

PEG: |and scarves

→MARGE: |and get them all bundled up in boots and everything and they're out for half an hour and then they come in and they're all covered with this snow and they get that *shluck* all over |

→PEG: |All that wet stuff and

→JAN: That's why adults don't like snow, huh?

MARGE: That's right.

PEG: Throw all the stuff in the dryer and then they'd come in and sit for half |an hour

MARGE: |And in a little while they'd want to go back out again.

PEG: Then they want to go back out again.

As in the conversation among Steve, Peter, and myself presented above, all three speakers in this example initiate turns that either latch onto or intrude into other speakers' turns. Like Denise and Stacy and like Steve and Peter in earlier examples, Peg and Marge play a conversational duet: They jointly hold one conversational role, overlapping each other without exhibiting (or reporting) resentment at being interrupted.

Hornyak points out the even more intriguing fact that these speakers often end a comment with the conjunction *and*, creating the appearance of interruption when there is none, as when Peg says, "All that wet stuff and." Hornyak claims that this strategy is used by many speakers in her family, and is satisfying and effective when used with each other. She is criticized, however, for using this same strategy among others, who protest that it confuses them. They may even get the impression that someone who ends a sentence with *and* doesn't know whether or not she is finished.

Why would anyone want to create the impression of interruption when there is none? One reason that speakers from some cultural groups leave little or no pause between turns is that they see silence in friendly conversation as a sign of lack of rapport. Overlapping is a way to keep conversation going without risking silence. I should note, though, that Hornyak and the family members she taped do not speak loudly or quickly or all at once. Their overlaps, though frequent, are brief; ending sentences with *and* is a way to achieve the appearance of interruption when there is minimal overlap.

Though Hornyak feels the strategy of creating the appearance of overlap by ending a sentence with *and* is peculiar to her family, others have commented that they know people who do this. At least one man I spoke to said that his mother (to his father's chagrin) regularly ends her comments with *and uh,* and that *her* mother and all her sisters do it too—but her father and brother don't. This man also considered this a family style. Although it clearly does run in families, the style seems to result from a combination of gender and culture.

Gender and culture also dovetail in another example of the false appearance of interruption. William Labov and David Fanshel, in a study of a psychotherapy session between a nineteen-year-old patient called Rhoda and a social worker, show that Rhoda never ended a speaking turn by falling silent. Instead, when she had said all she wanted to say, she began to repeat herself. Her repetitions were an invitation to the therapist to begin speaking by interrupting her. Both client and therapist were New Yorkers, Jewish, and women.

CULTURAL EXPLANATIONS:
A MIXED BLESSING

The realization that people with similar cultural backgrounds have similar ways of talking often comes as a revelation and a relief to people who thought they had personal quirks or even psychological problems. For example, a Greek-American man I interviewed for a study of indirectness in conversation had been told by friends and lovers throughout his life that there was something wrong with him, because he always beat around the bush instead of coming out and saying what was on his mind. He told me that his parents spoke that way, and I told him that I had found that Greeks often tended to be more indirect than Americans, and Greek-Americans were somewhere in the middle. This man was enormously relieved, saying that my explanation rang a bell. He went on to say:

> I see it as either something heroically different or a real impediment. . . . Most of the time I think of it as a problem. And I can't really sort it out from my family and background. . . . I don't know if it's Greek. I just know that it's me. And it feels a little better to know that it's Greek.

Viewing his "family" style as an ethnic style relieved this man of the burden of individual pathology otherwise implied by being different from most of the people he communicated with.

But the tendency of people from similar cultural backgrounds to have habitual ways of speaking that are similar to each other's and different from those of people from other cultural backgrounds, has had unfortunate, even tragic consequences. When people who are identified as culturally different have different conversational styles, their ways of speaking become the basis for negative stereotyping. As I mentioned earlier, anti-Semitism classically attributes loudness, aggressiveness, and "pushiness" to Jewish people—making a leap from ways of speaking to character. For example, in a letter to Henry Miller, Lawrence Durrell described a Jewish fellow writer: "He is undependable, erratic, has bad judgment, loud-mouthed, pushing, vulgar, thoroughly Jewish . . ."

The perception that Jews (or New Yorkers—the categories are often fused in many people's minds) are loud and pushy simply blames the minority group for the effect of their style *in in-*

teraction with others who use a different style. Anthropologist Thomas Kochman shows that a parallel style difference underlies the stereotyping of "community" blacks as inconsiderate, overbearing, and loud. When members of one group have the power to persecute members of the other, the results of such misjudgments are truly tragic.

If cultural differences are likely to cause misjudgment in personal settings, they are certain to do so in international ones. I would wager that the much-publicized antipathy between Nancy Reagan and Raisa Gorbachev resulted from cultural differences in conversational style. According to Nancy Reagan, "From the moment we met, she talked and talked and *talked*—so much that I could barely get a word in, edgewise or otherwise." I suspect that if anyone asked Raisa Gorbachev, she would say she'd been wondering why her American counterpart never said anything and made her do all the conversational work.

Of course not all Russians or Jews or New Yorkers or blacks are high-involvement speakers. Many use the style in some situations but not others. Some have erased, modified, or never used such styles at all. No group is homogeneous; for example, the high-involvement style I describe is more common among East European than German Jewish speakers. But many Jewish speakers do use some variety of high-involvement style in some situations, as do many Italian, Greek, Spanish, South American, Slavic, Armenian, Arab, African, and Cape Verdean speakers—and members of many other groups I have not mentioned.

A WORD OF CAUTION

The juxtaposition of these two lines of inquiry—gender and interruption on the one hand, and ethnicity as conversational style on the other—poses a crucial and troubling dilemma. If it is theoretically wrongheaded, empirically indefensible, and morally insidious to claim that speakers of particular ethnic groups are pushy, dominating, or inconsiderate because they appear to interrupt in conversations with speakers of different, more "mainstream" ethnic backgrounds, can it be valid to embrace research that "proves" that men dominate women because they appear to interrupt them in conversation? If the researchers who have found men interrupting women in conversation were to "analyze" my audiotapes of conversations among New York Jewish and California Christian speakers, they would no doubt conclude that the New Yorkers "interrupted" and "dominated"—the impression of the Californians present. This was not, however, the intention of the New Yorkers, and—crucially—not the result of their behavior alone. Rather, the pattern of apparent interruption resulted from the *difference* in styles. In short, such "research" would do little more than apply the ethnocentric standards of the majority group to the culturally different behavior of the minority group.

In a parallel way, claims that men dominate women because they interrupt them in conversation accept the assumption that conversation is an enterprise in which only one voice should be heard at a time. This erroneous assumption has significant negative consequences for women. Many women, when they talk among themselves in situations that are casual, friendly, and focused on rapport, use cooperative overlapping: Listeners talk along with speakers to show participation and support. It is this practice, when overheard, that has led men to stereotype women as noisily clucking hens. And women who enjoy such conversations when they have them may later feel embarrassed and guilty, because they accept the one-speaker-at-a-time ethic that is more appropriate to men's "public speaking" conversational style, or report-talk, than it is to women's "private speaking" style, which emphasizes rapport-talk.

Juxtaposing research claiming that men interrupt women with my study of dinner table conversation provides a linguistic parallel but a political contrast. Jews are a minority in the United States, as are blacks and members of the other groups that I mentioned as having high-involvement style. Minorities are at a disadvantage. But in the male-female constellation, it is women who

208

are at a social and cultural disadvantage. This transforms the political consequences of blaming one group for dominating the other.

Most people would agree that women as a class are dominated by men as a class in our culture, as in most if not all cultures of the world. Therefore many would claim that viewing gender differences as cross-cultural communication is copping out, covering up real domination with a cloth of cultural difference. Though I am sympathetic to this view, my conscience tells me that we cannot have it both ways. If we accept the research in one paradigm—the men-interrupt-women one—then we are forced into a position that claims that high-involvement speakers, such as blacks and Jews and, in many circumstances, women, are pushy, aggressive, or inconsiderately or foolishly noisy.

The consequences of such a position are particularly dangerous for American women of ethnic or regional backgrounds that favor high-involvement conversational styles. The United States witnessed a dramatic example of just such consequences when Geraldine Ferraro, a New Yorker of Italian extraction, ran for vice president and was labeled a bitch by Barbara Bush, a woman of more "mainstream" background. The view of high-involvement style as dominance, taken from the men-interrupt-women paradigm, yields the repugnant conclusion that many women (including many of us of African, Caribbean, Mediterranean, South American, Levantine, Arab, and East European backgrounds) are dominating, aggressive, and pushy—qualities that are perceived as far more negative in women than in men.

As a woman who has personally experienced the difficulty many women report in making themselves heard in some interactions with men (especially "public" situations), I am tempted to embrace the studies that men interrupt women: It would allow me to explain my experience in a way that blames others. As a high-involvement-style speaker, however, I am offended by the labeling of a feature of my conversational style as loathsome, based on the standards of those who do not share or understand it. As a Jewish woman raised in New York who is not only offended but frightened by the negative stereotyping of New Yorkers and women and Jews, I recoil when scholarly research serves to support the stereotyping of a group of speakers as possessing negative intentions and character. As a linguist and researcher, I know that the workings of conversation are more complex than that. As a human being, I want to understand what is going on.

WHO'S INTERRUPTING?

The key to understanding what is going on, at least in part, is the distinction between rapport-talk and report-talk—the characteristic ways that most women use language to create a community and many men use it to manage contest. As a result, though both women and men complain of being interrupted by each other, the behaviors they are complaining about are different.

In many of the comments I heard from people I interviewed, men felt interrupted by women who overlapped with words of agreement and support and anticipation of how their sentences and thoughts would end. If a woman supported a man's story by elaborating on a point different from the one he had intended, he felt his right to tell his own story was being violated. He interpreted the intrusion as a struggle for control of the conversation.

For example, a man was telling about some volunteer work he had done as a cashier at a charity flea market. At the end of the day, there had been a shortfall in his cash register, which he had to make up from his own pocket. A woman listening to him kept overlapping his story with comments and expressions of sympathy, elaborating on how unfair it was for him to have to pay when he had been volunteering his time. As a matter of fact, the man had not been telling his experience in order to emphasize the injustice of it, and he felt interrupted and "manipulated" by the woman, whom he saw as trying to take over his story. Her offense was an excess (in his view) of rapport-talk.

This brings me back to my father, and why he might take particular relish in telling the joke about the man who didn't talk to his wife because he didn't want to interrupt her. My father believes that only one person should speak at a time. As a result, he often has a hard time getting the floor in conversations involving my mother, my two sisters, and me, since we overlap and do not leave pauses between our comments. He also feels that once he begins to talk, he should be permitted to continue until he is satisfied that he has explained his ideas completely. My mother and sisters and I feel that in a casual conversation among friends or family, it is acceptable to chime in when you think you know what others are getting at; if you're wrong, they are free to correct you, but if you're right, everyone prefers the show of connection and rapport that comes from being understood without having to spell everything out.

My father's view of this situation surfaced some years ago when he was talking and my mother chimed in. He wistfully sighed and said to my mother, "You have an advantage, dear. If I want to say something, I have to wait until no one else is talking. But you can say what you want whenever you think of it." For her part, my mother can't understand why my father needs special privileges to say something—why doesn't he just jump in like the rest of us? And I can recall feeling as a teenager that listening to my father, who is an attorney, explain something to me was like hearing a summation to the jury.

So both the man and the women in my family feel oppressed, at times, by others' ways of talking—he because he is interrupted and doesn't find the pauses he needs to enter the conversation, and we because he forbids and eschews overlaps and won't just take part like everyone else. The women in the family value overlaps and interruptions as shows of involvement in rapport-talk, and the man in the family values not being imposed on in report-talk. And he approaches casual conversations at home more like report-talk than the women do.

Then what is the source of women's complaints that they are interrupted by men? Just as my sisters, my mother, and I expect my father to toss out brief comments like the rest of us, men who approach conversation as a contest in which everyone competes for the floor might be treating women as equals, expecting them to compete for the floor like everyone else. But women are far less likely to do so, since they do not regard conversations as contests and have little experience in fighting for the right to be heard. Quite the opposite, Elizabeth Aries found that women who talked a lot in discussion groups often invited quieter group members to speak.

UNCOOPERATIVE OVERLAPPING

Whereas women's cooperative overlaps frequently annoy men by seeming to co-opt their topic, men frequently annoy women by usurping or switching the topic. An example of this kind of interruption is portrayed in "You're Ugly, Too," a short story by Lorrie Moore. The heroine of this story, a history professor named Zoë, has had an ultrasound scan to identify a growth in her abdomen. Driving home after the test, she looks at herself in the rearview mirror and recalls a joke:

> She thought of the joke about the guy who visits his doctor and the doctor says, "Well, I'm sorry to say, you've got six weeks to live."
> "I want a second opinion," says the guy. . . .
> "You want a second opinion? O.K.," says the doctor. "You're ugly, too." She liked that joke. She thought it was terribly, terribly funny.

Later in the story, at a Halloween party, Zoë is talking to a recently divorced man named Earl whom her sister has fixed her up with. Earl asks, "What's your favorite joke?" This is what happens next:

> "Uh, my favorite joke is probably—O.K., all right. This guy goes into a doctor's office, and—"
> "I think I know this one," interrupted Earl, eagerly. He

wanted to tell it himself. "A guy goes into a doctor's office, and the doctor tells him he's got some good news and some bad news—that one, right?"

"I'm not sure," said Zoë. "This might be a different version."

"So, the guy says, 'Give me the bad news first,' and the doctor says, 'O.K. You've got three weeks to live.' And the guy cries, 'Three weeks to live! Doctor, what is the good news?' And the doctor says, 'Did you see that secretary out front? I finally fucked her.' "

Zoë frowned.

"That's not the one you were thinking of?"

"No." There was accusation in her voice. "Mine was different."

"Oh," said Earl. He looked away and then back again. "What kind of history do you teach?"

When Earl interrupts Zoë, it is not to support her joke but to tell her joke for her. To make matters worse, the joke he tells isn't just different; it's offensive. When he finds out that his joke was not the same as hers, he doesn't ask what hers was. Instead, he raises another topic entirely ("What kind of history do you teach?").

Most people would agree that Earl's interruption violated Zoë's speaking rights, because it came as Zoë was about to tell a joke and usurped the role of joke teller. But Zoë yielded quickly to Earl's bid to tell her joke. As soon as he said "some good news and some bad news," it was obvious that he had a different joke in mind. But instead of answering "No" to his question ". . . that one, right?" Zoë said, "I'm not sure. This might be a different version," supporting his bid and allowing for agreement where there really was disagreement. Someone who viewed conversation as a contest could have taken back the floor at this point, if not before. But Zoë seemed to view conversation as a game requiring each speaker to support the other's words. If they had known each other well enough to argue about this later, Earl might have challenged, "Why didn't you stop me when you saw I was going to tell a different joke, instead of letting me go on and then getting mad?"

Another part of the same story shows that it is not overlap that creates interruption but conversational moves that wrench a topic away from another speaker's course. Zoë feels a pain in her stomach, excuses herself, and disappears into the bathroom. When she returns, Earl asks if she's all right, and she tells him that she has been having medical tests. Rather than asking about her health, Earl gives her some food that was passed around while she was in the bathroom. Chewing, she says, "With my luck it'll be a gallbladder operation." Earl changes the subject: "So your sister's getting married? Tell me, really, what you think about love." Zoë begins to answer:

> "All right. I'll tell you what I think about love. Here is a love story. This friend of mine—"
> "You've got something on your chin," said Earl, and he reached over to touch it.

Like offering food, taking something off someone's face may take priority over talk, but doing so just as Zoë starts to tell a story seems like a sign of lack of interest in her story, and lack of respect for her right to continue it. Furthermore, this is not an isolated incident, but one in a series. Earl did not follow up Zoë's revelation about her health with questions or support, didn't offer advice, and didn't match her revelation with a mutual one about himself. Instead, he shifted the conversation to another topic—love—which he might have felt was more appropriate than a gallbladder operation for initiating a romantic involvement. For the same reason, taking something off her chin may have been too good an opportunity for touching her face to pass up. Indeed, many of his moves seem to be attempts to steer the conversation in the direction of flirting.

WHO'S DRIVING?

Interruption, then, has little to do with beginning to make verbal sounds while someone else is speaking, though it does have to do with issues of dominance, control, and showing interest and caring. Women and men feel interrupted by each other because of the differences in what they are trying to accomplish with talk. Men who approach conversation as a contest are likely to expend effort not to support the other's talk but to lead the conversation in another direction, perhaps one in which they can take center stage by telling a story or joke or displaying knowledge. But in doing so, they expect their conversational partners to mount resistance. Women who yield to these efforts do so not because they are weak or insecure or deferential but because they have little experience in deflecting attempts to grab the conversational wheel. They see steering the conversation in a different direction not as a move in a game, but as a violation of the rules of the game.

Being blamed for interrupting when you know you didn't mean to is as frustrating as feeling interrupted. Nothing is more disappointing in a close relationship than being accused of bad intentions when you know your intentions were good, especially by someone you love who should understand you, if anyone does. Women's effusion of support can be irritating to men who would rather meet with verbal sparring. And a left jab meant in the spirit of sparring can become a knockout if your opponent's fists are not raised to fight.

EIGHT

Damned If You Do

Morton, a psychologist on the staff of a private clinic, has a problem with the clinic director, Roberta. At staff meetings, Roberta generally opens discussion of issues by asking all staff members for their opinions. She invites debate about the pros and cons of proposals, but somehow, when the meeting ends, they always end up deciding—by consensus—to do what Roberta thinks best. The women on the staff are happy with Roberta as a director. They feel she listens to their points of view, and they like the rule by consensus rather than fiat. But Morton feels Roberta is manipulative. If they are going to do what she wants anyway, why does she make them waste their breath expressing opinions? He would prefer she just lay down the law, since she is the boss.

Morton's impression that Roberta does not act like a boss is the result of style differences. She *is* acting like a boss—a woman boss. She prefers to rule by consensus, and the women on her staff like it that way. But he is frustrated by her indirectness; he thinks she should rule by fiat.

Style differences may also be partly responsible for the observation that some women who have achieved high status or positions of authority do not behave in ways appropriate to their positions. But there may be another factor at work too. Since Matina Horner's pioneering research, many psychologists have observed that women seem to fear success. Again, the research on children's play sheds light.

Take Marjorie Harness Goodwin's research on verbal routines by which the preteen and teenage girls in her study criticized each other behind their backs. Significantly, and sadly, the examples Goodwin mentions are based on success: Girls are criticized for appearing better than the others in the group. Of two disputes that Goodwin describes, one girl's offense was to skip a grade in school and get straight A's on her report card; the other girl incurred the wrath of her peers by wearing newer and more expensive clothes than they.

In my own study of videotaped conversations among friends, a similar complaint is lodged by the sixth-grade girls against another girl:

SHANNON: She's gotta wear a Polo every *day.*
 JULIA: I know, well I like *Polo,* but *God!*
SHANNON: Every *day*!?
 JULIA: Really!
SHANNON: Just think how much— and sh-she's putting herself *up.*

Appearing better than others is a violation of the girls' egalitarian ethic: People are supposed to stress their connections and similarity.

In light of these and many other studies of girls' real conversations, it is no wonder that girls fear rejection by their peers if they appear too successful and boys don't. Boys, from the earliest age, learn that they can get what they want—higher status—by displaying superiority. Girls learn that displaying superiority will not get them what they want—affiliation with their peers. For this, they have to appear the same as, not better than, their friends.

The appearance of similarity does not mean actual sameness. Penelope Eckert, who spent several years with high school students in a midwestern city, explains how complex the girls' system of masked status can be. For example, the popular girls are the ones who must determine when to switch from the clothes of one season to the clothes of the next—for example, from winter to spring clothing. If less popular girls show up wearing cotton clothes while the popular girls are still wearing wool, they have committed a gaffe, shown themselves to be outsiders. If they switch after the popular girls have appeared in cotton, they mark themselves as followers, limited to public information. The goal is to dress in unison: If they make the switch on the same day as the popular girls, they are gloriously the same—and have subtly proven that they are in the know.

NEVER BOAST OR BRAG

Another aspect of the pressure on girls not to appear better than their peers is the injunction not to boast. Gender differences in attitudes toward boasting are the cause of much mutual judgment and misjudgment between women and men—and some odd verbal behavior on the part of women.

For example, a college student named Connie was telling her friends that a high school adviser had tried to talk her out of applying to the college they were all now attending. The adviser had felt that Connie's applying would hurt the chances of another girl from the same high school, Sylvia. In explaining the adviser's thinking, Connie said, "Sylvia's grades weren't—I mean—it sounds so pompous of me, but Sylvia's grades weren't as good as mine." Connie could barely bring herself to make a simple factual statement about her grades, because it smacked of boasting.

Margaret and Charles are both successful lawyers. Though they get along perfectly well when alone, they occasionally find themselves arguing after dinner engagements with new acquaintances, especially people who have status and connections in tax law, Charles's specialty. Margaret feels that Charles boasts: He lets it be known how important he is by mentioning recognition he has received, cases he has won, and important people he knows (in Margaret's view, name-dropping). In his eagerness to impress, he sometimes embellishes what he has done and implies that he knows people he has actually met only once or twice. For her part, Margaret tries to hide her success. She deliberately avoids letting on if she knows important people whose names arise in the conversation, and she never alludes to her many accomplishments.

Charles is as frustrated by Margaret's behavior as she is by his. If she will not let on how important she is, he does it for her. This upsets her even more. She feels his boasting for her is as impolite as her doing it herself, and all the alternatives she can imagine are unappealing: She can ignore or disrupt Charles's attempts to speak for her, which seems rude to him and violates what she feels is an obligation to support him; she can let him talk for her, which frames her as a child who cannot speak for herself; or she can participate, and speak in a way she does not want to speak—boasting.

Margaret feels people will not like her if she boasts; she would rather they learn from others how successful she is, and she feels they will approve of her modesty when they do. She also fears people will not like Charles if he boasts, and this is upsetting to her because she is affiliated with Charles, so what people think of him is a reflection on her. Charles, on the other hand, feels that people will not respect him unless he lets them know he merits respect. He also feels they will respect Margaret more if they know that she is an accomplished attorney, not just his wife.

Both Margaret and Charles judge each other's ways of talking in terms of personality characteristics—and each also places moral value on style. Margaret assumes that a good person is modest and self-effacing. Charles considers displaying accomplishments to be a requirement, not a liability, and he regards Margaret's (to him, false) modesty as foolishly self-denigrating, evidence of insecurity. Each one thinks he or she is simply expecting the other to be a good person, but their definitions of a good person vary because of the differing expectations for a good girl and a good boy.

The reluctance of girls and women to boast in certain situations shows up in two strikingly similar examples that I encountered in vastly different contexts. Ingmar Bergman's *Scenes from a Marriage* opens with a couple being interviewed for a magazine by a woman named Mrs. Palm. Marianne and Johan respond very differently to Mrs. Palm's question "How would you describe yourselves in a few words?" This is Johan's answer:

> It might sound conceited if I described myself as extremely intelligent, successful, youthful, well-balanced, and sexy. A man with a world conscience, cultivated, well-read, popular, and a good mixer. Let me see, what else can I think of . . . friendly. Friendly in a nice way even to people who are worse off. I like sports. I'm a good family man. A good son. I have no debts and I pay my taxes. I respect our government whatever it does, and I love our royal family. I've left the state church. Is this enough or do you want more details? I'm a splendid lover. Aren't I, Marianne?

This is Marianne's answer:

> Hmm, what can I say . . . I'm married to Johan and have two daughters.

Even with prodding Marianne doesn't add much information:

> MARIANNE: That's all I can think of for the moment.
> MRS. PALM: There must be something . . .

MARIANNE: I think Johan is rather nice.

JOHAN: Kind of you, I'm sure.

MARIANNE: We've been married for ten years.

JOHAN: I've just renewed the contract.

MARIANNE: I doubt if I have the same natural appreciation of my own excellence as Johan. But to tell the truth, I'm glad I can live the life I do. It's a good life, if you know what I mean. Well, what else can I say . . . Oh dear, this is difficult!

JOHAN: She has a nice figure.

MARIANNE: You're joking. I'm trying to take this thing seriously. I have two daughters, Karin and Eva.

JOHAN: You've already said that.

I was reminded of this fictional conversation when I read the following real-life dialogue in Carol Gilligan's *In a Different Voice*. As part of her research exploring children's moral development, Gilligan interviewed two 11-year-old children named Amy and Jake. Among the questions she asked them was "How would you describe yourself to yourself?" I heard loud echoes of Johan and Marianne in Jake's and Amy's responses. First, here is how Jake answered:

Perfect. That's my conceited side. What do you want—any way that I choose to describe myself? *(Interviewer: If you had to describe the person you are in a way that you yourself would know it was you, what would you say?)* I'd start off with eleven years old. Jake [last name]. I'd have to add that I live in [town], because that is a big part of me, and also that my father is a doctor, because I think that does change me a little bit, and that I don't believe in crime, except for when your name is Heinz [a reference to a previous question Jake was asked]; that I think school is boring, because I think that kind of changes your character a little bit. I don't sort of know how to describe myself, because I don't know how to read my personality. *(If you had to describe the way you actually would describe yourself, what would you say?)* I like corny jokes. I don't really like to get down to work, but I can do all the stuff in school. Every single problem that I have seen in school I have been able to do, except for ones that take knowledge, and after I do the reading, I have been able to do them, but sometimes I don't want to waste my time on easy homework. And also I'm crazy about sports. I think, unlike a lot of people, that the world still has hope . . . Most people that I know I like, and I have the good life, pretty much as good as any I have seen, and I am tall for my age.

This is how the girl, Amy, answered the question:

You mean my character? *(What do you think?)* Well, I don't know. I'd describe myself as, well, what do you mean? *(If you had to describe the person you are in a way that you yourself would know it was you, what would you say?)* Well, I'd say that I was someone who likes school and studying, and that's what I want to do with my life. I want to be some kind of a scientist or something, and I want to do things, and I want to help people. And I think that's what kind of person I am, or what kind of person I try to be. And that's probably how I'd describe myself. And I want to do something to help other people. *(Why is that?)* Well, because I think that this world has a lot of problems, and I think that everybody should try to help somebody else in some way, and the way I'm choosing is through science.

What struck me about these two children's answers to the same question was, first, how much longer Jake's was (and I assume the ellipsis after "hope" indicates even more words were omitted), and how boastful it was—in contrast to Amy's statement, which was not boastful at all. Jake says he's perfect, his father is a doctor, he can solve "every single problem" at school even though he finds school boring, he has the best life he has seen, and he's tall. It is possible that his comment "sometimes I don't want to waste my time on easy homework" might be a defense of less-than-superior achievement at school. In contrast, Amy says she likes school and studying but doesn't say if she does well at it, and that she wants to help people through science.

Both Johan in Bergman's screenplay and Jake in Gilligan's interview are aware that they sound "conceited" and make a joke of it. Indeed, Johan's entire answer seems tongue-in-cheek, like his comments interspersed in Marianne's answer. But Johan and Jake say what they do nonetheless. Though Amy has a bit more to say than Marianne, it isn't that much more. Both Amy and Marianne repeat themselves rather than fulfill the request in a way that might sound like bragging. Marianne does not mention that she is a lawyer. Amy says she plans to be a scientist, but she emphasizes that her purpose will be to help others rather than to achieve money, fame, or status.

Women's feelings that they should not boast come from explicit training as well as peer pressure in childhood. Such training is described in the alumnae newsletter of one of the most academically challenging girls' high schools in the country. In this newsletter a woman wrote an epitaph to her sister, who had been the very top student in her graduating class and who had recently died. A brilliant woman, her sister had had a moderately successful career that did not reflect her spectacular ability. The writer comments that her sister "took too much to heart her mother's admonitions: Stay in the background; never brag; always do your best."

These examples demonstrate that women are expected not to boast in relatively public situations, but it would be misleading to imply that women never boast at all. I return to the couple I dubbed Margaret and Charles for an example of a context in which she boasted but he felt he would not have. In the situation described earlier, Margaret felt Charles should not "show off" to new acquaintances. On another occasion, Charles felt that Margaret was inappropriately boasting. In complaining to close friends that she had not been promoted to partner as quickly as men in her firm who had brought in much less business and had far fewer billable hours, Margaret enumerated her early successes. Charles told her later that he thought this had been insensitive, since one of their listening friends was a young lawyer who was not advancing quickly at all. To Charles, self-aggrandizing information is to be used in public to achieve status, appropriately displayed when first meeting people or with people who have, or seem to be claiming, superior status. But to Margaret, self-aggrandizing information is to be used only in private, appropriately revealed in rapport-talk—conversations with people she knows and trusts, who will not judge her for her pride. When dealing with close friends, she forgets about their relative status—an aspect of relationships that Charles never forgets.

The different lenses of status and connection may once more work against women. Women are reluctant to display their achievements in public in order to be likable, but regarded through the lens of status, they are systematically underestimated, and thought self-deprecating and insecure. It is tempting to recommend that women learn to display their accomplishments in public, to ensure that they receive the respect they have earned. Unfortunately, however, women are judged by the standards of women's behavior.

This was evident, for example, at a faculty meeting devoted to promotions, at which a woman professor's success was described: She was extremely well published and well known in the field. A man commented with approval, "She wears it well." In other words, she was praised for not acting as successful as she was. By implication, if she had acted in a way consonant with her achievement, she would not have been praised—and perhaps would not have been liked.

HIS POLITENESS IS HER POWERLESSNESS

There are many kinds of evidence that women and men are judged differently even if they talk the same way. This tendency makes mischief in discussions of women, men, and power. If a linguistic strategy is used by a woman, it is seen as powerless; if it is done by a man, it is seen as powerful. Often, the labeling of "women's language" as "powerless language" reflects the view of women's behavior through the lens of men's.

Because they are not struggling to be one-up, women often find themselves framed as one-down. Any situation is ripe for misinterpretation, because status and connections are displayed by the same moves. This ambiguity accounts for much misinterpretation, by experts as well as nonexperts, by which women's ways of talking, uttered in a spirit of rapport, are branded powerless. Nowhere is this inherent ambiguity clearer than in a brief comment in a newspaper article in which a couple, both psychologists, were jointly interviewed. The journalist asked them the meaning of "being very polite." The two experts responded simultaneously, giving different answers. The man said, "Subservience." The woman said, "Sensitivity." Both experts were right, but each was describing the view of a different gender.

Experts and nonexperts alike tend to see anything women do as evidence of powerlessness. The same newspaper article quotes another psychologist as saying, "A man might ask a woman, 'Will you please go to the store?' where a woman might say, 'Gee, I really need a few things from the store, but I'm so tired.'" The woman's style is called "covert," a term suggesting negative qualities like being "sneaky" and "underhanded." The reason offered for this is power: The woman doesn't feel she has a right to ask directly.

Granted, women have lower status than men in our society. But this is not necessarily why they prefer not to make outright demands. The explanation for a woman's indirectness could just as well be her seeking connection. If you get your way as a result of having demanded it, the payoff is satisfying in terms of status: You're one-up because others are doing as you told them. But if you get your way because others happened to want the same thing, or because they offered freely, the payoff is in rapport. You're neither one-up nor one-down but happily connected to others whose wants are the same as yours. Furthermore, if indirectness is understood by both parties, then there is nothing covert about it: That a request is being made is clear. Calling an indirect communication covert reflects the view of someone for whom the direct style seems "natural" and "logical"—a view more common among men.

Indirectness itself does not reflect powerlessness. It is easy to think of situations where indirectness is the prerogative of those in power. For example, a wealthy couple who know that their servants will do their bidding need not give direct orders, but can simply state wishes: The woman of the house says, "It's chilly in here," and the servant sets about raising the temperature. The man of the house says, "It's dinner time," and the servant sees about having dinner served. Perhaps the ultimate indirectness is getting someone to do something without saying anything at all: The hostess rings a bell and the maid brings the next course; or a parent enters the room where children are misbehaving and stands with hands on hips, and the children immediately stop what they're doing.

Entire cultures operate on elaborate systems of indirectness. For example, I discovered in a small research project that most Greeks assumed that a wife who asked, "Would you like to go to the party?" was hinting that she wanted to go. They felt that she wouldn't bring it up if she didn't want to go. Furthermore, they felt, she would not state her preference outright because that would sound like a demand. Indirectness was the appropriate means for communicating her preference.

Japanese culture has developed indirectness to a fine art. For example, a Japanese anthropologist, Harumi Befu, explains the delicate exchange of indirectness required by a simple invitation to lunch. When her friend extended the invitation, Befu first had to determine whether it was meant literally or just *pro forma*, much as an American might say, "We'll have to have you over for dinner some time" but would not expect you to turn up at the door. Having decided the invitation was meant literally and having accepted, Befu was then asked what she would like to eat. Following custom, she said anything would do, but her friend, also following custom, pressed her to specify. Host and guest repeated this exchange an appropriate number of times, until Befu deemed it polite to answer the question—politely—by saying that tea over rice would be fine. When she arrived for lunch, she was indeed served tea over rice—as the last course of a sumptuous meal. Befu was not surprised by the feast, because she knew that protocol required it. Had she been given what she had asked for, she would have been insulted. But protocol also required that she make a great show of being surprised.

This account of mutual indirectness in a lunch invitation may strike Americans as excessive. But far more cultures in the world use elaborate systems of indirectness than value directness. Only modern Western societies place a priority on direct communication, and even for us it is more a value than a practice.

Evidence from other cultures also makes it clear that indirectness does not in itself reflect low status. Rather, our assumptions about the status of women compel us to interpret anything they do as reflecting low status. Anthropologist Elinor Keenan, for example, found that in a Malagasy-speaking village on the island of Madagascar, it is women who are direct and men who are indirect. And the villagers see the men's indirect way of speaking, using metaphors and proverbs, as the better way. For them, indirectness, like the men who use it, has high status. They regard women's direct style as clumsy and crude, debasing the beautiful subtlety of men's language. Whether women or men are direct or indirect differs; what remains constant is that the women's style is negatively evaluated—seen as lower in status than the men's.

IT'S DIFFERENT
COMING FROM A MAN

Research from our own culture provides many examples of the same behavior being interpreted differently depending on whether it's done by women or men. Take, for example, the case of "tag questions"—statements with little questions added onto the end, as in "It's a nice day, isn't it?" Linguist Robin Lakoff first pointed out that many women use more tag questions than men. Though studies seeking to test Lakoff's observation have had somewhat mixed results, most support it. Jacqueline Sachs, observing the language of children as young as two to five, found that girls used more than twice as many tag questions as boys. And research has shown that people *expect* women to use tags. Psychologists David and Robert Siegler conducted an experiment asking adults to guess the sex of speakers. Sure enough, the stereotype held: Subjects guessed a woman was speaking when tags were used, a man when they weren't. The stereotype can actually be more compelling than reality: In another experiment, psychologists Nora Newcombe and Diane Arnkoff presented adults with communications in which women and men used equal numbers of tag questions, and found that their subjects thought the women had used more.

Most troubling of all, women and men are judged differently even if they speak the same way. Communications researcher Patricia Hayes Bradley found that when women used tag questions and disclaimers, subjects judged them as less intelligent and knowledgeable *than men who also used them*. When women did not give support for their arguments, they were judged less intelligent and knowledgeable, *but men who advanced arguments without support were not*. In other words, talking in ways that are associated with women causes women to be judged negatively, but talking the same way does not have this effect on men. So it is not the ways of talking that are having the effect so much as people's attitudes toward women and men.

Many other studies have similar results. Psychologists John and Sandra Condry asked subjects to interpret why an infant was crying. If they had been told the baby was a boy, subjects thought he was angry, but if they had been told it was a girl, they thought she was afraid. Anne Macke and Laurel Richardson, with Judith Cook, discovered that when students judged professors, generating more class discussion was taken to be a sign of incompetence—only if the professor was female.

SILENCE IS GOLDEN—OR LEADEN

Research itself has fallen prey to this double standard. In studies claiming that men exert power by talking more than women, women's silence is cited as evidence that they have no power. At the same time, other studies claim that men's use of silence and refusing to speak is a show of their power. A theme running through Mirra Komarovsky's classic study *Blue Collar Marriage* is that many of the wives interviewed said they talked more than their husbands ("He's tongue-tied," one woman said of her husband; "My husband has a great habit of not talking," said another). More of the wives want to talk, and have their husbands talk, about problems. In contrast, more husbands withdraw in the face of troubles ("When I don't feel good, I light out and don't dump my load on them"), emotional stress, or a wife's "demands." Yet there is no question but that these husbands are "dominant" in their marriages. Taciturnity itself can be an instrument of power. Komarovsky quotes a mother who says of her husband, "He doesn't say much but he means what he says and the children mind him."

Jack Sattel believes men use silence to exercise power over women, and he illustrates with the following scene from Erica Jong's novel *Fear of Flying*. The first line of dialogue is spoken by Isadora, the second by her husband, Bennett.

"Why do you always have to do this to me? You make me feel so lonely.

"That comes from you."

"What do you mean it comes from me? Tonight I wanted to be happy. It's Christmas Eve. Why do you turn on me? What did I do?"

Silence.

"What did I do?"

He looks at her as if her not knowing were another injury.

"Look, let's just go to sleep now. Let's just forget it."

"Forget what?"

He says nothing.

"Forget the fact that you turned on me? Forget the fact that you're punishing me for nothing? Forget the fact that I'm lonely and cold, that it's Christmas Eve and again you've ruined it for me? Is that what you want me to forget?"

"I won't discuss it."

"Discuss what? *What* won't you discuss?"

"Shut up! I won't have you screaming in the hotel."

"I don't give a fuck what you won't have me do. I'd like to be treated civilly. I'd like you to at least do me the courtesy of telling me why you're in such a funk. And don't look at me that way . . ."

"What way?"

"As if my not being able to read your mind were my greatest sin. I *can't* read your mind. I *don't* know why you're so mad. I *can't* intuit your every wish. If that's what you want in a wife you don't have it in me."

"I certainly don't."

"Then what is it? Please tell me."

"I shouldn't have to."

"Good God! Do you mean to tell me I'm expected to be a mind reader? Is that the kind of mothering you want?"

"If you had any empathy for me . . ."

"But I *do*. My God, you don't give me a chance."

"You tune out. You don't listen."

"It was something in the movie, wasn't it?"

"What, in the movie?"

"The quiz again. Do you have to quiz me like some kind of criminal? Do you have to *cross-examine* me? . . . It was the funeral scene. . . . The little boy looking at his dead mother. Something got you there. That was when you got depressed."

Silence.

"Well, *wasn't* it?"

Silence.

"Oh come on, Bennett, you're making me *furious*. Please tell me. Please."

(He gives the words singly like little gifts. Like hard little turds.) "What was it about that scene that got me?"

"Don't quiz me. Tell me!" (She puts her arms around him. He pulls away. She falls to the floor holding onto his pajama leg. It looks less like an embrace than like a rescue scene, she sinking, he reluctantly allowing her to cling to his leg for support.)

"Get up!"

(Crying) "Only if you tell me."

(He jerks his leg away.) "I'm going to bed."

This painful scene does seem to support Sattel's claim that Bennett uses silence as a weapon against his wife. Each successive refusal to tell her what's bothering him is like a blow laying her lower and lower—until she is literally on the floor. But would our intepretation change if we reversed the genders in this scene?

With genders reversed, the scene seems impossible. It is hard to imagine a man begging his wife to tell him what he did wrong. What leaped to my mind, when I tried to reverse genders, was a scene in which the man withdraws, disabling her silence as a weapon. What makes Bennett's silence so punishing is Isadora's insistence on making him talk to her. It is the interaction of the two styles—his withdrawal and her insistence that he tell her what she did wrong—that is devastating to both. If Bennett shared Isadora's belief that problems should be talked out, or she shared his practice of withdrawing when problems arise, they would not have found themselves in this devastating scene.

"I'M SORRY, I'M NOT APOLOGIZING"

There are many ways that women talk that make sense and are effective in conversations with women but appear powerless and self-deprecating in conversations with men. One such pattern is that many women seem to apologize all the time. An apology is a move that frames the apologizer as one-down. This might seem obvious. But the following example shows that an apparent apology may not be intended in that spirit at all.

A teacher was having trouble with a student widely known to be incorrigible. Finally, she sent the boy to the principal's office. Later the principal approached her in the teachers' lounge and told her the student had been suspended. The teacher replied, "I'm sorry," and the principal reassured her, "It's not your fault." The teacher was taken aback by the principal's reassurance, because it had not occurred to her that the student's suspension might be her fault until he said it. To her, "I'm sorry" did not mean "I apologize"; it meant "I'm sorry to hear that." "I'm sorry" was intended to establish a connection to the principal by implying, "I know you must feel bad about this; I do too." She was framing herself as connected to him by similar feelings. By interpreting her words of shared feeling as an apology, the principal introduced the notion that she might be at fault, and framed himself as one-up, in a position to absolve her of guilt.

The continuation of this story indicates that these different points of view may be associated with gender. When this teacher told her grown daughter about the incident, the daughter agreed that the principal's reaction had been strange. But when she told her son and husband, they upbraided her for apologizing when she had not been at fault. They too interpreted "I'm sorry" as an apology.

There are several dynamics that make women appear to apologize too much. For one thing, women may be more likely to apologize because they do not instinctively balk at risking a one-down position. This is not to say that they relish it, just that it is less likely to set off automatic alarms in their heads. Yet another factor is that women are heard as apologizing when they do not intend to do so. Women frequently say "I'm sorry" to express sympathy and concern, not apology.

This confusion is rooted in the double meaning of the word *sorry*. This double meaning is highlighted in the following anecdote. A twelve-year-old Japanese girl living in the United States was writing a letter of condolence to her grandmother in Japan because her grandfather had died. The girl was writing in Japanese, but she was more accustomed to English. She began in the appropriate way: "I'm so sorry that Grandfather died." But then she stopped and looked at what she had written. "That doesn't sound right," she said to her mother. "I didn't kill him." Because she was writing in a language that was not second nature to her, this girl realized that an expression most people use automatically had a different meaning when interpreted literally. "I'm sorry," used figuratively to express regret, could be interpreted literally to mean "I apologize."

The difference between ritual and literal uses of language is also at play in the following example. A businesswoman named Beverly returned from an out-of-town trip to find a phone message on her answering machine from her division head. The message explained that he had found an enormous number of errors in a report written by her assistant. He told her that he had indicated the errors, returned the report to the assistant, and arranged for the deadline to be extended while she typed in the corrections. Beverly was surprised, since she had read and approved the report before leaving on vacation, but she said, "I'm sorry"—and was offended when he said, "I'm not blaming anyone." This seemed to imply that he *was* blaming her, since he introduced the idea.

"PLEASE DON'T ACCEPT MY APOLOGY"

Beverly asked her assistant to show her the lengthy corrected report and became angry when she saw that half the pages had "errors" marked, but few were actually errors. Nearly all involved punctuation, and most were matters of stylistic preference, such as adding commas after brief introductory phrases or before the conjunction *and*. In a large number of cases, she felt that her division head had introduced punctuation errors into sentences that were grammatically correct as they stood.

Later that day she encountered the division head at an office party and announced as soon as she saw him that she was angry at him and told him why. She realized by his reaction that she had offended his sensibilities by raising the matter in front of someone else. She immediately apologized for having blurted out her anger rather than expressing it more diplomatically, and she later visited him in his office to apologize again. She was sure that if she apologized for having confronted him in the wrong way at the wrong time, he would counterapologize for having overcorrected the report and for going directly to the assistant instead of through her. Instead, he generously said, "I accept your apology," and affably changed the subject to office politics.

Now accepting an apology is arguably quite rude. From the point of view of connection, an apology should be matched. And from the perspective of status, an apology should be deflected. In this view, a person who apologizes takes a one-down position, and accepting the apology preserves that asymmetry, whereas deflecting the apology restores balance. Although she felt immediately uncomfortable, Beverly did not realize until after she had left the office, all smiles and goodwill, that not only had her division head rudely accepted her apology, but he had not offered a balancing one.

Women's and men's differential awareness of status may have been the cause of Beverly's problem in a more fundamental way too. She felt quite friendly with her division head; she liked him; she had come to think of him as a friend. For her, as for many women, being friends means downplaying if not obliterating status differences. When she blurted out her anger, she was not thinking of herself as upbraiding a superior in front of others. To the extent that he remained aware of the difference in their status despite their friendly relationship, to accept her criticism would have amounted to public humiliation. Had she focused on their status differences rather than their friendship, she would not have approached him as she did. She would not, for example, have taken that tack with the company president.

WOMEN ADAPT TO MEN'S NORMS

In all these examples, the styles more typical of men are generally evaluated more positively and are taken as the norm. In a related and perhaps even more distressing asymmetry, when women and men are in groups together, the very games they play are more likely to be men's games than women's.

In Ursula Le Guin's story "In and Out," a former secretary recalls an all-women meeting:

> Like when the group of secretaries met to plan a meeting to talk about women in the city government, and the meeting had been so terrific, people saying things they didn't even know they thought, and ideas coming up, and nobody pushing anybody around.

By implication, an interchange in which people got to say what they were thinking and nobody was pushing anybody around was not the norm for meetings she had participated in or observed, but a quality that distinguished this meeting, in which only women participated.

A professor commented on how pleasant she found it to work on all-women committees, as compared to the mixed-gender committees she was more used to. But when she made this observation at a mixed-gender dinner party, a man strenuously objected. He said he had noticed no difference between all-male committees and those that included women. This man was surely telling the truth as he experienced it, because when women and men get together they interact according to men's, not women's, norms. So being in a mixed rather than a same-gender meeting makes less difference to men than to women.

Research in a range of disciplines shows that women make more adjustments than men in mixed groups. Elizabeth Aries found, in comparing the body postures of young men and women in all-male, all-female, and mixed discussion groups, that the men sat more or less the same way whether or not there were women present: They sprawled out in "relaxed" positions, taking up a large amount of space around them. The women in her study, however, drew themselves in, assuming "ladylike" postures, when there were men in the group, but relaxed and sprawled out when there weren't. In other words, the men took the same physical positions whether or not there were women present, but the women seemed to feel they were onstage when men were there, backstage when they found themselves with women only.

A similar point emerges from a study by Alice Deakins of the topics that women and men talk about. Deakins did what is called an eavesdropping study: While seated alone in a dining room where bank officers had lunch, she noted what people at adjacent tables were talking about. This was not a situation where the men were executives and the women their wives and secretaries. The men and women in Deakins's study were all bank officers, meeting as equals at work. Deakins found that when there were no women present, the men talked mostly about business and never about people, not even people at work. Their next most often discussed topic was food. Another common topic was sports and recreation. When women talked alone, their most frequent topic was people—not people at work so much as friends, children, and partners in personal relationships. The women discussed business next, and third, health, which included weight control.

When women and men got together, they tended to avoid the topics that each group liked best and settle on topics of interest to both. But in discussing those topics, *they followed the style of the men alone.* They talked about food the way men did, focusing on the food they were eating and about restaurants rather than diet and health. They talked about recreation the way men did, focusing on sports and vacations rather than exercising for diet or health, as the women did when they were alone. And they talked about housing in the way men did, focusing on location, property values, and commuting time, rather than the way women did, focusing on the interiors of houses (for example, layout and insulation) and what goes on among people inside houses (for example, finding cleaning help).

In analyzing tape recordings of private conversations among teenagers, Deborah Lange found a similar pattern. When the girls were alone, they talked about problems in their relationships with friends; when boys were alone, they talked about activities and plans, and made comments about friends. When boys and girls were together, they talked about activities and plans, and made comments about friends. In other words, when boys and girls talked together, they talked more or less the way boys talked when there were no girls present. But when girls got together with no boys present, they talked very differently.

All these (and many other) studies show that male-female conversations are more like men's conversations than they are like women's. So when women and men talk to each other, both make adjustments, but the women make more. Women are at a disadvantage in mixed-sex groups, because they have had less practice in conducting conversation the way it is being conducted in these groups. This may help to explain why girls do better at single-sex schools, whereas boys do about the same whether they go to boys' schools or coeducational ones. It may also explain why the women, but not the men, in Aries's study of college discussion groups said they preferred the same-gender group. All of these studies help to answer the question of why women are dissatisfied with communication in their relationships with men, while men who are parties to the same conversations express less dissatisfaction with them.

The talk that takes place at meetings and discussion groups is relatively more public, more like report-talk. Considering their preference for rapport-talk, it is not surprising that many women find it hard to get the floor at meetings, even though many men have a hard time getting the floor in conversations with women who are overlapping to build rapport. One reason many women find it difficult to get and keep the floor at meetings with men is that they won't compete for it. However, this chapter has presented only a few of many studies showing that even when women do behave the same way as men, they get different responses. This raises the question of how much women's difficulty in getting heard at meetings results from their ways of talking, and how much from their being women. This question also throws into relief the asymmetry of options available to women and men.

EQUAL DISCRIMINATION

Many women tell of having made a comment at a meeting or conference that is ignored. Later a man makes the same comment and it is picked up, approved or discussed, attributed to him rather than to her. Most women feel that this happens because people are less likely to pay attention to an idea that is raised by a woman, and the studies mentioned above indicate that there is truth to that. But the *way* ideas are raised may be a factor too. The following experience indicates this, but it also indicates that women and men do not have the same options available.

Professor A, a biochemist who teaches at a major university and is well known in his field, told me of the following experience. Having a diffident style, and being timid about speaking in public, he geared up his courage to speak following a public lecture in the biology department. He phrased his observation as a question: "Have you considered this chemical influence on the biological process you just described?" The lecturer responded, in effect, "No, I haven't," and the point was dropped. Soon after, however, another man, Professor B, spoke up. He began, "I would like to return to the point made by my colleague Professor A, because I think it is very important." He then repeated the point in a long-winded way. The idea then became the focus of extended discussion, and everyone who spoke to the issue began by saying, "I'd like to comment further on the important point raised by Professor B."

Had Professor A been a woman, it would have been natural to assume that the idea was first ignored because it was expressed by a woman, and later taken up because it was expressed by a man. But in this case, both speakers were men, so their gender could not have been the cause of the different responses they received. What was different was the way the two men expressed the "same" idea. Perhaps Professor A had not explained his idea in enough detail to allow others to see its importance. More likely, the way he spoke—diffidently, briefly, and phrasing his point as a question—framed his idea as not important, whereas the way Professor B spoke—at length and in a loud, declamatory voice—framed the same idea with a different metamessage: "This is important. Take note!"

This example is important because it sheds light on the role played by *how* people speak, regardless of their gender. But it also shows that women are at a disadvantage, since women are more likely than men to phrase their ideas as questions, take up less time with their questions, and speak at lower volume and higher pitch. The example shows that men who do not use the forceful strategies associated with masculinity are also at a disadvantage. In this sense, Professor A was in the same position as a woman who speaks in the same way.

UNEQUAL REMEDIES

But in another sense, Professor A's position is very different from that of a woman who has a similar conversational style. If Professor A decided to adjust his style to be more like Professor B's, he would find himself commanding more attention in public, if that is what he wants. And in the process, he would better fit the model of masculinity in our culture. But women who attempt to adjust their styles by speaking louder, longer, and with more self-assertion will also better fit the model of masculinity. They may command more attention and be more respected, but they may also be disliked and disparaged as aggressive and unfeminine.

239

Indeed, a woman need not be particularly aggressive to be criticized. A professor who invited a prominent woman researcher to speak to his students was shocked to hear some of his students—both female and male—comment later that they had found her arrogant. He had seen nothing arrogant about her at all. She simply hadn't engaged in any of the womanly behavior they had come to expect, such as continually smiling, qualifying her statements, or cocking her head in a charming way.

Ways of talking associated with masculinity are also associated with leadership and authority. But ways of talking that are considered feminine are not. Whatever a man does to enhance his authority also enhances his masculinity. But if a woman adapts her style to a position of authority that she has achieved or to which she aspires, she risks compromising her femininity, in the eyes of others.

As a woman who has achieved a high level of status in my profession, I grapple with this contradiction daily. When I go to academic conferences, I often meet colleagues from other universities who know me only by my scholarly publications and reputation. Not infrequently, new acquaintances say that they are surprised that I am so nice or so feminine. "You're not what I expected," I have repeatedly been told. "You're not aggressive at all." Others have remarked, "I thought you'd be cold," or "hard," or "competitive." When I press them about why they expected that of me, I am told, "I just figured that any woman who is as successful as you would have to be that way."

Just such assumptions emerge from a study by Harriet Wall and Anita Barry of college students' expectations about male and female professors. The researchers gave students identical materials on prospective professors—information about their academic backgrounds, publications, and letters of recommendation—and asked the students to predict how well the candidates would do if hired, including their chances to win a distinguished teaching award. Some who read the materials under a woman's name predicted that she would not win the award because, as one writer put it, "Too much business, not enough personality."

No one made inferences like this when exactly the same "file" was read under a man's name.

Another reason women professors may be judged more harshly than men, Wall and Barry found, is that students expect more of women. Those who thought they were evaluating a woman expected her to be more nurturing and to devote more time to her students outside of class than those who thought they were evaluating a man. The researchers point out that in evaluating real professors, students might have more praise for a male professor than for a female who actually devotes more time to them, because the woman is, after all, just doing what's expected, while the man is doing more than expected. In reading this study, I was, of course, reminded of the graduate student who had called me at home on Sunday because she didn't want to bother her dissertation director at home.

LANGUAGE KEEPS WOMEN IN THEIR PLACE

Nowhere is the conflict between femininity and authority more crucial than with women in politics. The characteristics of a good man and a good candidate are the same, but a woman has to choose between coming across as a strong leader *or* a good woman. If a man appears forceful, logical, direct, masterful, and powerful, he enhances his value as a man. If a woman appears forceful, logical, direct, masterful, or powerful, she risks undercutting her value as a woman.

As Robin Lakoff shows in *Language and Woman's Place,* language comes at women from two angles: the words they speak, and the words spoken about them. If I wrote, "After delivering the acceptance speech, the candidate fainted," you would know I was talking about a woman. Men do not faint; they pass out. And these terms have vastly different connotations that both reflect and affect our images of women and men. *Fainting* conjures up a frail figure crumpling into a man's rescuing arms, the back of her hand pressed to her forehead—probably for little reason, maybe just for dramatic effect. *Passing out* suggests a straightforward fall to the floor.

An article in *Newsweek* during the 1984 presidential campaign quoted a Reagan aide who called Ferraro "a nasty woman" who would "claw Ronald Reagan's eyes out." Never mind the nastiness of the remark and of the newsmagazine's using it to open its article. Applied to a man, *nasty* would be so tame as to seem harmless. Furthermore, men don't claw; they punch and sock, with correspondingly more forceful results. The verb *claw* both reflects and reinforces the stereotypical metaphor of women as cats. Each time someone uses an expression associated with this metaphor, it reinforces it, suggesting a general "cattiness" in women's character.

Even when seeming to praise Ferraro, the article used terms drenched in gender. She was credited with "a striking gift for tart political rhetoric, needling Ronald Reagan on the fairness issue and twitting the Reagan-Bush campaign for its reluctance to let Bush debate her." If we reversed subject and object, *needling* and *twitting* would not sound like praise for Reagan's verbal ability— or any man's. (I will refrain from commenting on the connotations of *tart,* assuming the word's double meaning was at least consciously unintended.)

In his book *The Language of Politics,* Michael Geis gives several examples of words used to describe Ferraro that undercut her. One headline called her "spunky," another "feisty." As Geis observes, *spunky* and *feisty* are used only for creatures that are small and lacking in real power; they could be said of a Pekingese but not a Great Dane, perhaps of Mickey Rooney but not of John Wayne—in other words, of any average-size woman, but not of an average-size man.

I am sure that the journalists who wrote these descriptions of Ferraro came to praise her, not to bury her. Perhaps they felt they were choosing snappy, eye-catching phrases. But their words bent back and trivialized the vice presidential candidate, highlighting, even if unintentionally, the incongruity between her images as a woman and as a political leader. When we think we are using language, our language is using us.

It's not that journalists, other writers, or everyday speakers are deliberately, or even unintentionally, "sexist" in their use of language. The important point is that gender distinctions are built into language. The words available to us to describe women and men are not the same words. And, most damaging of all, through language, our images and attitudes are buttressed and shaped. Simply by understanding and using the words of our language, we all absorb and pass on different, asymmetrical assumptions about men and women.

BOUND BY BODY LANGUAGE

Body language is eloquent too. Political candidates necessarily circulate photographs of their families. In the typical family photograph, the candidate looks straight out at the camera, while his wife gazes up at him. This leads the viewer's eye to the candidate as the center of interest. In a well-publicized family photograph, Ferraro was looking up at her husband and he was looking straight out. It is an appealing photo, which shows her as a good woman, but makes him the inappropriate center of interest, just as his finances became the center of interest in candidate Ferraro's financial disclosure. Had the family photograph shown Ferraro looking straight out, with her husband gazing adoringly at her, it would not have been an effective campaign photo, because she would have looked like a domineering wife with a namby-pamby for a husband.

Ironically, it is probably more difficult for a woman to hold a position of authority in a relatively egalitarian society like that of the United States than in more hierarchical ones. An American woman who owned and edited an English-language magazine in Athens told me that when Greeks came to the magazine to do business, as soon as they realized that she was the boss, they focused their attention on her. But if her male assistant editor was in the room, Americans were irresistibly drawn to address themselves to him. It seems that Greeks' sensitivity to the publisher's status overrode their awareness of her gender, but Americans, who are less intimidated by status than Greeks, could not rise above their awareness of gender.

Much of this book has shown that women's and men's style differences are symmetrically misleading. Men and women learn to use language in the different worlds of boys and girls, and each group interprets the other's ways of talking in terms of its own. But in many ways, differences between women's and men's styles are not symmetrical. When men and women get together in groups, they are likely to talk in ways more familiar and comfortable to the men. And both women's and men's ways of talking are typically judged by the standards of men's styles, which are regarded as the norm. Most distressing in a society where equality is the agreed-upon goal, and where more and more women are entering high-status positions, women in authority find themselves in a double bind. If they speak in ways expected of women, they are seen as inadequate leaders. If they speak in ways expected of leaders, they are seen as inadequate women. The road to authority is tough for women, and once they get there it's a bed of thorns.

NINE

"Look at Me When I'm Talking to You!": Cross Talk Across the Ages

One source of inspiration for this book was a research project I participated in, dealing with how friends talk to each other at grade levels ranging from second grade to university. Although I had not intended to examine gender differences, when I watched the set of videotapes recorded by Bruce Dorval, I was overwhelmed by the differences that separated the females and males at each age, and the striking similarities that linked the females, on one hand, and the males, on the other, across the vast expanse of age. In many ways, the second-grade girls were more like the twenty-five-year-old women than like the second-grade boys.

The two categories of differences between the male and female speakers in the videotapes that were most striking to me were what the friends talked about and their body language—

how they oriented themselves to each other with their bodies and eyes.

Differences in physical alignment, or body language, leap out at anyone who looks at segments of the videotapes one after another. At every age, the girls and women sit closer to each other and look at each other directly. At every age, the boys and men sit at angles to each other—in one case, almost parallel—and never look directly into each other's faces. I developed the term *anchoring gaze* to describe this visual home base. The girls and women anchor their gaze on each other's faces, occasionally glancing away, while the boys and men anchor their gaze elsewhere in the room, occasionally glancing at each other.

The boys' and men's avoidance of looking directly at each other is especially important because researchers, and conventional wisdom, have emphasized that girls and women tend to be more indirect than boys and men in their speech. Actually, women and men tend to be indirect about different things. In physical alignment, and in verbally expressing personal problems, the men tend to be more indirect.

TEASING AND TELLING STORIES AT SECOND GRADE

The two pairs of second-graders provide the most obvious contrast in physical alignment and in what they talk about. The second-grade boys, Kevin and Jimmy, move so incessantly that it seems the chairs they are sitting on can't contain them. They never look directly at each other. They look around the room, at the ceiling, and at the video camera set up in the room. They squirm, jump out of their chairs, rhythmically kick their feet, make faces at each other and the camera, and point to objects in the room. One boy continually pummels the arms of his chair. They sing, make motor sounds by trilling their lips, and utter nonsense syllables.

And what are the boys talking about amid all this hubbub? They make a show of misbehaving by mugging for the camera, saying dirty words, laughing, and then clamping their hands over their giggles and shushing each other up. They tease: Jimmy tells Kevin over and over, "Your hair is standing up! Your hair always sticks up!" and Jimmy tries to smooth his hair, since he has no mirror to see that it looks just fine. They jump from topic to topic, as they try to find "something to do."

"WHAT GAMES DOES HE HAVE?"

For the second-grade boys, "something to do" is "games to play." For example, they look around the room in which they have been placed (Professor Dorval's university office), in search of games:

JIMMY: Look. You know what the game— what the game is over there? We play— we had that in first grade.

JIMMY: What games do we— does he have?
KEVIN: I don't know.
JIMMY: Probably only that. That's a dumb game, isn't it?
KEVIN: Looks pretty good though.

JIMMY: I can't wait until we play games.

Since they can't find any games to play (or don't feel they can help themselves to games they see in the room), they try to think of other things they can do:

JIMMY: Well, if you have something to do, do it.
KEVIN: Here he comes back in. What would you like to do?
JIMMY: Play football.

Though he obviously can't do it right now, Jimmy has no trouble thinking of what he would like to do: play football. He'd like to be outside, running around with a group of boys, not sitting in a chair talking to one friend. Since they can't be physically active now, they talk about being so in the future; Kevin says, "You want to come over to my house one day? Ride my bike?"

The boys do find "something to do," though it is not their first choice. In a tone that shows mock impatience, Jimmy demands that Kevin find something to do and Kevin obliges, making a suggestion that the boys take up:

JIMMY: Would *you* find something to *do*?
KEVIN: Patty cake.
JIMMY: [Laugh] Look. Patty cake. Come on, let's do patty cake. Come on.

All these excerpts give the impression of young children with a lot of energy—much like any young children, I might have thought, until I viewed the videotape of two girls of the same age. The picture the second-grade girls present seems truly to be of another world. Jane and Ellen sit very still, practically nose to nose for much of the time. One or the other or both sit at the edge of their chairs, and they look directly into each other's faces. They calmly look elsewhere in the room only when they are thinking of what to say next. They do not cast about for something to do; they seem satisfied that they are already doing something: talking to each other.

Looking at the two transcripts side by side shows how different these conversations are: Whereas the second-grade boys' transcript is a mass of short spurts of speech, each boy's turn rarely taking more than a line, the transcript of the second-grade girls' conversation shows big blocks of talk, so that a single page of transcript might have one or two turns. This is because the girls are telling each other stories about things that have happened to them and other people. But these are not just any stories. They are about accidents and mishaps, illnesses and hospital visits.

"THAT'S SERIOUS!"

Telling stories about misfortunes seemed to me a rather strange thing to do, until I realized that the girls were strictly following the orders they had been given. Dorval had instructed them, as he did the boys and all the other pairs of friends in his study, to consult with each other and find something serious to talk about. So when he left the room, the girls huddled and whispered and then separated, faced each other, and began to exchange stories about things they considered serious. The stories in the following excerpt are rather short, but otherwise they are typical of the second-grade girls' conversation.

> ELLEN: Remember? What— when I told you about my uncle? He went up the ladder after my grandpa? And he fell and, um, cracked his head open? He's— and you know what? It still hasn't healed.
>
> JANE: One time, my uncle, he was, uh, he has like this bull ranch? In Millworth? And the bull's horns went right through his head.
>
> ELLEN: That's serious.

The way Ellen shows approval of Jane's story, "That's serious," shows that telling stories about disasters was meant to comply with the instructions they had been given.

Comparing the boys and girls of the same age, I had the feeling I was looking at two different species. The request to talk to each other about something serious seemed to make sense to the girls; they were asked to do something they often do by choice: sit together and talk. But the same request was a different one for boys, who are far less likely just to sit together and talk to each other in the course of their play. They are more used to *doing* things together—running around outside or playing games inside.

249

Looking at the tapes from the perspective of status and connection, or of oppositional versus supportive frameworks, I could see the patterns clearly. The boys, who have identified each other as best friends, show their affection for each other in an oppositional framework. Jimmy's repeated teasing, making Kevin think his hair is standing up when it's not, is one example. Jimmy also pretends to shoot Kevin, saying, "You're under arrest." And he says something intentionally mean: "I know William doesn't like you at all." Both boys play-fight, taking harmless swipes at each other.

FLOUTING AUTHORITY

The boys continually show their awareness of the authority figure who has placed them in this situation, as in the brief example above, where Kevin says, "Here he comes back in." They seek to undercut the experimenter's authority by resisting doing what they have been told (to talk about something serious) and by playful defiance. For example, they jump up and make faces at the camera, then giggle and shush each other, pretending momentarily to look like good little boys. They invoke the experimenter to flout his authority when he is nowhere in sight, as when Jimmy says, ". . . and then made a fart—here he comes!" Here, as elsewhere, their "misbehavior" seems aimed at the adult who has told them what to do.

Since they were instructed to talk about something serious, what better way to avoid compliance than to tell jokes? This the boys do:

KEVIN: Knock knock.
JIMMY: Who's there?
KEVIN: Fruit.
JIMMY: Fruit who?
KEVIN: Fruit bar.
JIMMY: What do you call a sleeping bull?

KEVIN: Bull chase. What?

JIMMY: Well? Well?

KEVIN: I don't know.

JIMMY: Bulldozer. You get it? Bulldozer.

Sometimes the jokes are scatological, and it is clear that they are breaking the rules of decorum with the adult authority in mind:

KEVIN: Knock knock.

JIMMY: Who's there?

KEVIN: [Jumping in his seat] Knock knock knock knock.

JIMMY: Who's there? [Pause] Tu tu. Tu tu who? You got tu tu in your panties.

KEVIN: I don't either.

JIMMY: I wonder if he hears us—he can—just move your mouth. [Both boys proceed to do so.]

This brief example has it all: Jimmy tells a joke; he teasingly puts Kevin down; he refers to a taboo subject; he shows his preoccupation with the authority figure who might object to their breaking these rules; and he defies and mocks the situation by pretending (and getting Kevin to pretend) to talk without producing sound. If telling a joke is a kind of performance that sets the teller at center stage, Jimmy is so exuberant in telling his tu-tu joke that he hogs the stage for the audience participation part as well, speaking all four lines of the knock-knock dialogue. On the other hand, he may simply be filling in for Kevin, who started the routine with "Knock knock," but didn't seem to have a joke in mind to follow through.

PLAYING "INTERVIEW"

Finding themselves sitting together and talking seems to suggest to these boys the hierarchical situation of being questioned by an adult. Playacting and mocking this framework, Jimmy takes the role of interviewer:

JIMMY: I've got four things to say.
KEVIN: Yeah?
JIMMY: I've got four things to say.
KEVIN: Tell me.
JIMMY: You doing good in your schoolwork, huh?
KEVIN: Yeah.
JIMMY: Um, play soccer good?
KEVIN: Uh huh.
JIMMY: You're nice. What was the last one? How are you?
KEVIN: Fine.
JIMMY: It's your turn.

Kevin's and Jimmy's turns are all very short—just a few words—with only two exceptions: one in which Jimmy explains a video game, and another in which he explains how to play patty cake (even though it was Kevin who proposed playing it). In both, he is taking the role of teacher.

A WORLD OF DIFFERENCE

These are just a few examples of what is pervasive in the twenty-minute videotape: The boys are physically restless; their idea of what to do involves physical activities; they are continually aware of the hierarchical framework they are in, and they do what they can to mock and resist it; and they show their affection for each other in an oppositional format. They directly disagree with each other, but then disagreement is a natural response to the put-downs and mock assaults that are initiated. For example, Kevin protests, "I don't either" when Jimmy tells him he has "tu tu" in his panties, and "No, I'm not" when Jimmy tells him he is under arrest.

The second-grade girls' conversation in the same situation includes nothing that resembles any of the ways of talking just described for the boys. The girls too are aware of the authoritarian framework they are in, but they are complying with it rather than defying or mocking it. And, far from playfully attacking each other, they support each other by agreeing with and adding to what the other says. Rather than colluding to defy authority, they reassure each other that they are successfully complying, as when Ellen tells Jane, "That's serious." In contrast to the teasing by which each boy implies that the other is doing things wrong, the girls offer reassurance that they are doing things right.

The brief stories the girls tell in the excerpt above are also typical of the ways the stories are linked to each other and to the girls' shared experience. By starting out with "Remember?" Ellen reminds Jane that Jane was there or has heard the story before. Already, in second grade, these little girls tell stories with the characteristic rising intonation that makes every phrase sound like a question. Like so many ways of talking that are characteristic of girls and women, when looked at from the perspective of status, this rising intonation could be interpreted as a request for approval and therefore evidence of insecurity. But it could also be seen—and, I think, is more accurately seen—as a way of inviting the listener to participate by saying something like "uh huh," or nodding. Jane also begins many of her stories by saying her friend's name—another mark of involvement.

The short example above is also typical of the longer conversation in that Jane follows Ellen's story with a similar story. Jane's story matches Ellen's not only in being about an accident, but also in being about an uncle and a head wound.

The second-grade girls, like the boys, talk about future activities, but what they propose is different from what the boys propose. Whereas Kevin invites Jimmy to come over and ride his bike, Jane tells Ellen that she has just read a Bible story that she liked a lot. She says Ellen can come over to her house so that Jane can read it to her—or she can read it herself. Not only does Ellen propose a talking activity, in contrast to Kevin's suggestion of a physical activity, but Jane also avoids framing Ellen as lower in status by assuring her that she can read the story herself rather than being read to, if she prefers.

Before the investigator entered the room and reminded them

to talk about something serious, the girls were exchanging different kinds of stories. Like women who tell troubles as a kind of rapport-talk, these second-grade girls were exchanging matching complaints. For example, Jane complained that her little brother kept asking her to read stories to him but wouldn't let her finish any of them; he kept bringing out new books for her to start reading. Ellen responded with a matching story about reading to *her* brother, only her problem was that he had chosen a long book, and each time she finished a chapter and thought she was done reading to him, he'd insist on hearing one more. Here they were, in second grade, establishing rapport by complaining about others who were close to them and by matching and supporting each other's stories.

Men and women to whom I showed these videotapes had very different reactions to these second-graders. My reaction was typical of women's: I thought Jane and Ellen were sweet little girls, and I smiled to see them. I was touched by their eagerness to fulfill the experimenter's request. My heart went out to them. But the little boys made me nervous. I wished they'd *sit still*! I thought their joking silly, and I didn't like their teasing and mock attacks. I felt sorry for poor Kevin, who kept trying to smooth down his hair and was told that another little boy didn't like him.

But men I showed the tapes to reacted very differently. They thought the boys cute, and they found their energy and glee touching. They were sympathetic to the boys' impulse to poke fun at the situation and defy the experimenter's authority. The girls seemed to them like a pair of Goody Two Shoes. Some men commented that they didn't trust the girls' behavior; they felt that little children couldn't really enjoy sitting so still—they must be on their best behavior to kiss up to the experimenter.

So there it is: Boys and girls grow up in different worlds, but we think we're in the same one, so we judge each other's behavior by the standards of our own.

LIFE IMITATES EXPERIMENT

Nowhere are the consequences of these differences more striking than in elementary school, where teachers expect children to sit quietly and do as they're told, like the girls in the videotapes I examined, and not to fidget and jump around and tease each other and resist orders, like the boys. While reading a study of teaching style in a kindergarten class, I came across real-life support for the pattern I had noticed and described, as well as a dramatic illustration of the consequences of that pattern. Ethnographer Jane White studied what she calls the "relentless politeness" of primary-school teachers. She begins an article with an excerpt from a lesson in which a kindergarten teacher, Mrs. Bedford, is introducing a social studies lesson. Mrs. Bedford says:

> Oh my, what a nice-looking group of kindergartners. Oh, it makes Mrs. Bedford so *happy* to see such smiling faces. Now, are we all sitting comfortably? [*Pause*] Let's see who is here. Looks like everybody's here. Our line leader for today is Mark W. [*Students talking among themselves*] Oh, I like the way Tammy and Barbara are sitting down. They're so *ready* for first grade. Oh, and Corrie and Heather, how nice . . . and Colleen and Sherrie, you look terrific. Joey, could you turn around so I can see your face? Steven T., would you come sit up here by me? Bobby, find yourself a place there. Stephen S., right there is a good place for you. Is everybody comfortable? Are we ready?

White was not concerned with gender differences in her study; her purpose in presenting this excerpt was to show that the teacher used "polite" ways of speaking, like praising good behavior rather than censuring bad, and phrasing directives as questions. But in reading this wonderfully graphic and familiar example, I noticed that all the children who were being praised for sitting quietly were girls, and all the children who were being (indirectly) criticized for not sitting still were boys.

The same impression leaped out at me from another article as well. To show that elementary-school teachers regard boys and girls as separate social groups, sociologist Barrie Thorne quotes a teacher who said, "The girls are ready and the boys aren't." Both these examples from real classrooms dramatize that school requires behavior that is more "natural" for girls than boys.

In the previously mentioned study by Alice Greenwood of her preteen son and daughters talking to their friends over dinner, I encountered another example of real-life support for the patterns I observed in the videotapes of friends talking. Just as the second-grade girls reassured each other, "That's serious," when the girls in Greenwood's study talked to their friends, a funny story was often supported by the reassurance "That's really funny." Even more, the girls would begin to laugh appreciatively *before* a story was told, as soon as another girl announced her intention to tell a story by saying, "This is so funny." In contrast, the boy said a good conversation was one "where we make jokes and crack on each other"—exactly what the second-grade boys chose to do.

These real-life examples reassured me that the two videotapes I had studied were typical, not exceptional. But my findings are also supported by a battery of research on little girls and boys at play, which has documented the greater physical activity and aggressiveness of little boys, their greater tendency to end up in parallel rather than coordinated play, and their greater tendency to take oppositional stances. Developmental psychologist Campbell Leaper, for example, found that five-year-old girls elaborate on each other's ideas in a "mutually positive" manner, whereas little boys of the same age exhibit "negative reciprocity" by which one boy tries to control and the other withdraws. In her study of three- and four-year-olds in a day-care center, Amy Sheldon found that even when the girls and boys both engaged in individual activities with same-sex threesomes, the girls—unlike the boys— kept each other connected by calling out what they were doing and responding to the others' comments.

If it is fascinating to see the source of adult patterns in second-graders, it boggles the mind to see them in three-year-olds. No wonder it is hard for men and women to understand each other's point of view: We have been looking at the view from different vantage points for as long as we have been looking.

TROUBLE WITH PEOPLE AND THINGS IN SIXTH GRADE

The sixth-grade boys and girls present as stark a contrast as the second-graders. Walt, sitting in a high-backed wooden chair with arms, is also physically restless, but he shows it by squirming rather than jumping up and down and in and out of his seat. Walt twists all over his chair. At one point, he leans to the side and reaches one arm way down the side of the chair as if he were Rubber Man. The other boy, Tom, is physically fairly still, but he doesn't look comfortable either. He stretches his legs out in front of him, and much of the time he has one arm draped over the back of his upholstered chair. He is more stiff than still.

These boys don't look at each other either. Walt rubs his eyes continually, creating a physical barrier to looking at Tom. He plays with his fingers, spending more time looking at them than at Tom. Tom too sits aligned with his chair, at an angle to Walt. They frequently look around, apparently searching for things to talk about and often finding them. For example, they comment on the decorations ("That's a funny-looking picture," and later, "Dang, this is quite a picture"); they notice a sprinkler in the ceiling and one boy explains to the other, "It's in case something catches on fire." Spotting his bag, Walt pulls out a new pair of shoes, which they both look at, handle, and talk about.

Turning to the sixth-grade girls, we are looking at a different scene altogether. Rather than aligning themselves with their chairs, the girls sit across the chairs in order to face each other directly. Shannon sits quite still, at the edge of the wooden chair, with her arms resting on the arms of the chair. Julia sits in the upholstered chair without arms, but rather than spreading out from it like Tom, she draws her legs and arms up onto the chair. She puts her left ankle on her right knee, holds her foot, and plays with her shoelaces. She frequently glances at her foot, but her gaze is anchored on her friend's face, in contrast to Walt, whose gaze is anchored on his fingers.

Julia and Shannon change positions several times during their talk, but the changes are neither abrupt nor frequent, and the girls are always tightly and directly aligned with each other in gaze and posture. The boys at this age exude a sense of energy held in check. Walt's squirming and Tom's motionlessness both seem caused by discomfort. The girls seem comfortable with the level of movement allowed them, but the boys seem to be restraining themselves, as if they have learned that the level of energy they feel should not be expressed. Perhaps this contrast holds a clue to the stony quality of many men's stillness.

What the boys and girls talk about is also as different as can be. In the twenty minutes of conversation, Tom and Walt touch on fifty-five topics. They talk about school, homework, cable TV, sports, sex and violence on TV (they don't approve of it), things in the room, things they want (a motorbike, a computer, a shotgun), other boys at school, Walt's shoes, a rock group they play in, inflation, Nancy Reagan's buying a dress for three thousand dollars (they don't approve), girls, guns, videos, and their friendship. None of these topics is pursued for more than a few turns, and each turn is short.

Like the second-grade boys' conversation, the sixth-grade boys' includes only two extended turns, and they are both report-talk, framing the boys as differently placed in a hierarchy: Tom sings a song he recently composed for their rock group, framing himself as the performer and Walt as his audience, and he tells about a bicycle accident he was in.

"IT *HURTS* WHEN YOU LOSE YOUR BEST FRIEND"

Again, moving from the sixth-grade boys to the girls of the same age is like moving to another planet. The girls spend almost all their time talking about Julia's falling out with a third friend, Mary. Julia says how bad she feels about losing a friend ("It *hurts* when you lose your best friend, a really close friend"). The girls agree that the breakup was Mary's fault. Their talk reveals how central their friendships are to their world. Julia says, "I like getting a friend and keeping it *forever*," and "I couldn't live without a friend." Shannon agrees: "I don't think anybody could live without a friend, either." Julia declares to Shannon that they will "be friends practically *forever*."

Over and over, the sixth-grade girls express their fear that anger disrupts friendships. Julia explains that her friendship with Mary ended because Mary got mad, and was therefore "mean." In contrast, she maintains that she herself does not get mad at people, even when she doesn't like what they do:

SHANNON: Too bad you and Mary are not good friends anymore.

JULIA: I know. God, it's— she's so *mean* sometimes. . . . And then— what was so sad, she just— gets *mad* at you all of a sudden. And like if she does something *I* don't like, I mean, I just— I don't *like* it, I mean, I don't get *mad* at her!

JULIA: My mom does things that I don't like a lot, and— I just— I mean, I don't get *mad* at her.

Julia feels—and fears—that when people get mad, they fight, and fighting can lead to separation. At one point she introduces what seems like a new and unrelated topic—her worry that her parents

259

might get divorced. But it is really the same topic: She's afraid her parents will get divorced because she sometimes hears them fight, and she believes that one of the reasons Mary is such a difficult person is that her parents are divorced.

Here again I came across independent corroboration for these patterns in real-life dialogue among children of roughly the same age. The issue of "getting mad" turns up in a conversation between teenage girls taped by Deborah Lange. In that conversation, one girl tells about a problem: She would like to get all her friends together, but she can't, because they don't all like each other. As she keeps repeating that she's not mad, she sounds a lot like Julia:

> I'm not mad at Deena or anything. I'm not mad at Millicent or Rita. But I . . . I always . . . It's so hard to make plans with all of them at once.

Instead of being mad at her friends, she makes efforts to placate them all:

> . . . because Rita gets in fights with Millicent and Deena thinks that Millicent's being a bitcher, and it's so mean because it's not fair because, um, I try to, um, I try to, um, I try to make it so I can make plans with all of them but I-I'd rather just that all of them got along than trying to be, um, than trying to, um, you know I mean I myself have to change.

Not only does this excerpt show sixth-grade girls sharing troubles talk about their relationships with friends, but it also shows that they want to avoid conflict and preserve harmony.

"I KNOW"

In the videotape of sixth-grade girls, Shannon and Julia, like the second-grade girls, reinforce each other's feelings. For example, Shannon repeatedly agrees with Julia about Mary. Here is what they say right after the excerpt in which Julia says that Mary gets mad, whereas she doesn't:

SHANNON: She tries to upset people.
JULIA: She *does*. And she just sees me *cry*ing and everything. She just lets me *suf*fer.
SHANNON: And she loves it.
JULIA: I know. She enjoys the *whole thing*.

Shannon supports Julia's complaint about Mary by offering similar observations, and Julia incorporates Shannon's additions into her complaints.

THE SAME TOPIC—WITH A DIFFERENCE

Even when the sixth-grade boys and girls talk about the same thing, what they talk about is different. For example, both pairs of friends begin by reporting what happened the night before, but Julia tells about a problem with her father, while Tom tells about a problem with the television. First, the boys:

TOM: Man, yesterday? We were sitting and watching cable? Some big old jet came flying by, sounded like he was going to land.
WALT: [Laugh]
TOM: And then our cable went out yesterday.
WALT: Ours too.

And that was that. Now, the girls:

JULIA: Um, guess what happened last night.
SHANNON: What?
JULIA: Um, I went, um, okay. Last night, um, my brother, um, by b— Okay, my dad said, "Julia, you gotta pick up, by yourself." And /?/ I said, "Well, if my brother doesn't have to," and so me and my dad got into a big fight and everything, you know? And um, oh God. And I bit him. I couldn't *be-lieve* it. Oh God.

SHANNON: Oh my gosh. Did he get mad?
JULIA: Yeah, but not— not right now, just— I went in my room. I locked the door.

Julia told about interacting with a person, her father, and Tom told about interacting with an object, the television. Her story is also longer than any turn produced by the boys at the same age. And it is talk about a fight, a primary female concern, because fights threaten intimacy.

Another aspect of Julia's story that is typical of girls and women is that she recreates the drama of what happened between people by acting out what they said, in dialogue. She takes on her father's voice—"Julia, you gotta pick up, by yourself"— and enacts her protest—"Well, if my brother doesn't have to." Because girls and women are concerned with conveying the emotional impact of what happened between people, they use dialogue to dramatize events more than boys and men do.

"WHEN IT'S TIME *TO* TALK, YOU CAN'T TALK"

Like the second-grade girls, the sixth-grade girls appear completely comfortable sitting and talking. But the sixth-grade boys seem to be struggling—struggling to sit in their chairs, and to find something to talk about. They say as much:

TOM: I tried to think of what to say 'cause we were on film. It's different.
WALT: I know.
TOM: When you're outside you can—
WALT: I know, I can scream but not in an apartment.
TOM: Or you can talk up a storm.
WALT: Uh-huh.
TOM: When it's time *to* talk, you can't talk.

Walt seems to take Tom's mention of being "outside" as a reference to the benefits of playing outside rather than inside, and he supports that idea with the example that it's okay to scream outside. But Tom seems to be referring to the world outside this artificial situation, commenting on the difficulty they are having in finding things to talk about when they are told to talk.

These remarks show that Tom is aware that they are in a situation where they have been told what to do, and he suggests that this is part of the reason they are having trouble finding things to talk about. Though it is not as obvious and pervasive as with the second-grade boys, Tom also mocks the situation with a joke: "Smile, you're on *Candid Camera*." Even more dramatically, when Dorval leaves the boys alone following his brief reminder, Tom salutes—first subtly, and apparently automatically, then in an exaggerated way, apparently mocking his own automatic sign of subordination.

In response to the discomfort of being in the experimental situation, the second-grade boys talk about the games they would like to play. The sixth-grade boys imagine being out of this situation when they're grown up. The following example also shows the way they use the room to shift topics suddenly—something the girls never do.

TOM: Man, I can't wait till I'm grown up.

WALT: Yeah, I know what you mean.

TOM: Get out of college, go to the marines. Get out of the marines, go to the air force. Get out of the air force, get married.

WALT: Yeah, I can't wait till I'm sixteen to get my car.

TOM: I can't wait till I'm seventeen to get married.

WALT: Yeah, me too. **Look at that *thing* over there!**

It is touching to see how the boys yearn to be grown up, even though they are a bit confused about what adult behavior they will undertake, at what age. Nothing like this is said by any of the girls in the videotapes. I interpret it as an expression of the boys' discomfort at being children who can be told what to do, and I suspect it comes up here as a fantasy about a way to escape situations like this one. Although more briefly, a similar impulse is expressed by Kevin, one of the second-graders, in an interchange about their ages. Though he isn't sure exactly what age he is and what that means ("I am almost ten but I'm not eight yet"), Kevin reassures himself, "I'm catching up with big people." The boys show more eagerness to be grown up, so they can get out from under in the hierarchy.

CONTRASTING CONCEPTS OF FRIENDSHIP

Despite the striking differences between the boys' and girls' conversations, it would be misleading to imply that there are no similarities in their styles and concerns. The differences are not absolute, but of degree. For example, all these children are concerned with preserving their friendships. Here is what the sixth-grade boys say about it:

> TOM: Seems like me and you do everything together.
>
> WALT: Yeah, we're going hunting this Sunday, right?
>
> TOM: Seems like, if we have something to do, if there's a fight, one of us would be on the same side, or if we have an idea, me and you are automatically in it. And everyone else wants to go against you and everything. It's hard to agree without someone saying something to you.
>
> WALT: I know.
>
> TOM: 'Cause there's *one* group and then there's another. The *good* group is the one who always gets picked on.

Though the boys, like the girls, comment on what good friends they are, there are differences in how they express it. First of all, the boys' discussion of their friendship is brief, and the topic doesn't come up again, whereas the girls' talk about their friendship goes on at length and repeatedly recurs. Tom's remark that he and Walt are good friends focuses on their doing things together ("Seems like me and you do everything together"). And fighting is central to their notion of friendship. Agreement between Walt and him, Tom says, automatically sparks opposition from others. His is an agonistic world, in which friendship is a matter of banding together against others.

In contrast, Julia's claim that she and Shannon are good friends is based on mutual understanding and longevity:

JULIA: At least me and you have been knowing each other since kindergarten, and we know how each other *are*.

and on not fighting with each other:

JULIA: Me and you *never* get in fights hardly.

and on communicating:

JULIA: I mean like if I try to talk to you, you'll say, "Talk to *me!*" And if you try to talk to me, I'll *talk* to you.

Comparing the conversations of these boys and girls in sixth grade, one can see the root of women's and men's complaints about communication in their relationships with each other. The boys do say a bit about their friendships and about other people, but most of their talk is about things and activities and opinions about social issues. The only object the girls handle and discuss is one that symbolizes their friendship. Julia asks Shannon if she has given her a friendship pin, and Shannon says yes. Julia then says she read that if you're really good friends, you give two; she then reaches into her bag and gives Shannon a second friendship pin. All the girls' talk is about friends, friendship, and feelings; they orchestrate this talk at a level of subtlety and complexity that is not seen in the sixth-grade boys' talk.

MERGED AND PARALLEL CONVERSATIONS IN TENTH GRADE

Moving on to tenth grade, we come to a videotape that has been essential to my understanding of men's communication. The girls at this grade level are very much like the sixth-grade girls. They sit drawn up into their chairs, they look straight at each other, and they talk about the problems one of the girls has with her mother and her boyfriend. The tenth-grade boys, however, are different not only from the girls but from the younger boys. Their postures are the most extreme on the videotapes: They are sprawled out, almost reclining against the chairs they are supposed to be sitting in. Richard, like Tom in the sixth grade, is almost motionless, and he looks steadfastly ahead, as if he had been forbidden to look at his friend Todd, as Orpheus was forbidden to look back at Eurydice. Todd uses his feet to drag a swivel chair into place as a footstool and pushes it around with his feet as he looks ahead or around the room, only occasionally glancing at Richard. Someone viewing this tape commented that these boys look like they are riding in a car: Their bodies are parallel rather than facing each other, and they are both looking steadily ahead, one only occasionally glancing as his friend and the other almost never doing so.

But turn up the sound, and this scene is transformed. The boys are not talking about impersonal topics. Far from it. These are the boys whose conversation was presented and discussed in Chapter Two. They are exchanging the most intimate talk that I heard in any of Dorval's videotapes. Whereas the girls talked about problems they had with other people—absent parties—these boys are confronting their relationship to each other, and one is revealing deep feelings of loss and hurt and longing.

"I KNOW WHAT'S BUGGING ME"

As we saw earlier, Todd is feeling alienated: He feels left out at parties; he has no date for an upcoming dance and doesn't want to ask anyone he knows; he doesn't feel right with girls who like him, and he doesn't feel right with his buddies either. He pines for the past when he and Richard spent time alone together and talked more. Todd's complaint can be seen in the following excerpt. To convey the halting quality of the conversation, numbers in parentheses are used to indicate seconds of pause.

TODD: What the hell we supposed to talk about? I mean, I know what's bugging me.

RICHARD: What's bugging you?

TODD: [Snicker] That we don't talk.

RICHARD: Who don't talk?

. . .

TODD: We're doing it again.

RICHARD: What?

TODD: Not talking.

RICHARD: I know. Well, go.

TODD: We're not even making small talk anymore. [Laugh]

RICHARD: Right, okay. (3.4) I mean, you know. What can I say? (3.6) I mean, if you meant everything you said last weekend, and *I* meant everything *I* said. (1.0)

TODD: Well, of course I did. But I mean, I don't know. I guess we're growing up. I mean, I don't know. I guess I live in the past or something. I really enjoyed those times when we used to stay up all night long and just, you know, spend the nights over someone else's house just to talk all night.

RICHARD: Mhm.

TODD: They were kinda fun.

RICHARD: Yeah, that *was* fun. (2.2)

TODD: But now we're lucky if we say anything to each other in the hall.

RICHARD: [With a mock-challenging intonation] Oh, all right!

TODD: I'm serious. I remember walking in the hall and I'd say "Hi" to you and you'd say "Hi there" or sometimes you'll push me in the locker, if I'm lucky. [Laugh] (1.4)

RICHARD: [Protesting] We talk.
    TODD: Not the same way anymore.
        (4.8)
RICHARD: I never *knew* you wanted to *talk*.

Although most men for whom I have played this conversation comment that it is unusual, it nonetheless happened. What is most striking is the stark contrast, almost contradiction, between these boys' words and their body language. Though their words speak of intense involvement, their bodies are in careless, lounging positions.

ARE MEN DISENGAGED?

I told a family therapist about my observation that the girls looked directly at each other and aligned their bodies facing each other, whereas the boys looked anywhere but into each other's faces and positioned themselves at angles to each other. She commented, "That always happens with the families I see. The men won't look at me, and they won't look at their wives. The men are always disengaged." But this pair of tenth-grade boys who are not looking at each other are nothing if not engaged. They are superengaged, even when displaying disengagement nonverbally. For example, Richard stretches and rubs his face in an elaborate yawn when he says, "I never *knew* you wanted to *talk*."

Considering these videotapes of boys and girls at different ages, and the situation described by the family therapist, I was struck by a massive imbalance: When a woman looks at her therapist and her partner, she is simply doing what she has always done, what feels natural and normal and right. But when a man is asked to look directly at his therapist and his wife, he is being asked to do something different—something he has little practice doing, something that might even seem wrong to do. Proclaiming men "disengaged" on the basis of their body language seems premature and unfair. They are being judged by the standards of a different culture. This is not to say that the men might not be disengaged, nor that it might not be beneficial for them to try looking straight at their wives and therapists when they talk to them, just that the interpretation of disengagement is not warranted solely on the basis of indirect physical and visual alignment.

Within the bounds of their own culture, there is plenty of evidence of engagement in the body language of the tenth-grade boys, ample evidence that they are attending and attuning to each other. Their motions are finely coordinated. They make similar movements, in similar directions, at the same time. They are acting in concert, creating ensemble (to borrow a term from Ron Scollon), or (to borrow a concept from A. L. Becker) like two geese preening their feathers, seeming to ignore each other but mirroring each other's movements in coordinated rhythm.

Why would men and boys look outward, away from each other, and around the room, rather than directly at each other? A likely explanation is that looking directly at another man would seem like a hostile action, a display of threat. And looking directly at a woman might seem sexual, a display of flirting. One colleague who made a comment to this effect joined me where I was sitting. Finding a chair facing mine, he pulled the chair farther away and turned it at an angle, so he did not sit facing me directly. We both laughed because this instinctive gesture enabled him to sit at an angle to me—just like the boys and men in the videotapes I had shown him.

Judged by the standards of women, who look at each other when they talk together, men's looking away is a barrier to intimacy, a means of avoiding connection. But if boys and men avoid looking directly at each other to avoid combativeness, then for them it is a way of achieving friendly connection rather than compromising it.

The tenth-grade boys' and girls' physical alignments can be interpreted as different ways of reaching the same goal—involvement—rather than as evidence that the girls are involved and the boys aren't. This symmetry parallels their different ways of accomplishing troubles talk. As we saw in Chapter Two, Nancy and Sally spend most of their time discussing Nancy's problems with her mother and boyfriend, and Sally responds to Nancy's complaints by reinforcing them. In contrast, Richard and Todd both tell of troubles, but they respond to each other's problems by downplaying and dismissing them.

Though different from the girls' ways of responding to each other's problems, the boys' style of reassuring each other has its own logic. Like their postures, the boys' conversation positions them on parallel tracks. Each talks about his own concerns, while the other belittles them or even changes the subject. By women's standards, this shows a lack of caring about the other and his problems. But it can be a way to make the other feel better. Talking about a problem over and over might be a way of expressing concern, but it also might make the problem seem more serious. For example, if Nancy felt bad because she had to leave the party, Sally's telling her that everyone was stunned when she left might make her feel worse. But from another viewpoint, Sally is giving Nancy proof that the girls in the group care about her and missed her when she left.

The tenth-grade girls and boys present a vision of similar goals accomplished in different ways. Both show signs of discomfort with the situation and mock the instructions. (Sally says, "Talk about Jerry. That's serious and/or intimate," and Todd remarks, "Now we have to get intimate.") Both pairs do soon settle down and do just what they were told—though the girls' resistance, expressed as giggling and joking lasts longer than the boys'. In fact, it continues for the first five minutes of the tape, at which point Dorval reminds them of their task. During this time, they tease one another, but a teasing put-down is rescinded as soon as it is uttered: Sally says, laughing, "Dizzy! No, you're not dizzy."

If boys and girls are so different at second, sixth, and tenth grade, what of the men and women in the twenty-four- to twenty-seven-year-old range?

ADULT FRIENDS' CONVERSATION

The videotapes of adult friends talking show a natural develop-ment of the young people's styles. Gone is the pressure cooker of emotions concerning themselves and their alliances. Gone is the preoccupation with parents and their authority. But palpably present are the differences in ways of aligning themselves to each other with their bodies and their talk.

Let's look at the twenty-five-year-old women. Although they seem comfortable with the experimental situation, they seem frustrated by their conversation. Their struggle arises because one friend feels the other has pushed the code of agreement too far.

"I KNOW WE'VE HAD ARGUMENTS BEFORE"

The strain of negotiating agreement and similarity is felt through-out the women's dialogue. Intriguingly, traces of a similar strain are found in the sixth-grade girls' conversation too. In her eager-ness to espouse harmony and eschew conflict, Julia stresses to Shannon that they never fight. Shannon briefly disagrees, point-ing out that they do.

JULIA: Me and you *never* get in fights hardly.
SHANNON: |/?/ to me long
JULIA |Till we get in arg— We get in *arguments*, but not *fights*. Sometimes we do.
SHANNON: Like when we're playing hopscotch, we get in ar-guments and fight and—
JULIA: Right. |But we don't get in *fights!*
SHANNON: |But it's— [shrugs]

271

Not all Shannon's words are entirely audible, but it is clear that when Julia says that she and Shannon do not fight, Shannon subtly disagrees. She says, "Like when we're playing hopscotch, we get in arguments and fight." But Julia insists that although they may have arguments, which are trivial, they do not have fights, which are serious, and Shannon quickly gives up the disagreement.

This germ of dissent grows into a recurrent and controlling theme in the conversation between Pam and Marsha, the adult women in Dorval's videotapes. Pam begins the conversation by saying that one thing she likes about Marsha is that Marsha always agrees with her. Pam seems to intend this as a compliment, a statement about why they are friends. Perhaps she is trying to justify why she selected Marsha to join her in the experiment. But Marsha seems to take the remark as a put-down, an implication that she has no mind of her own. As the conversation proceeds, Marsha repeatedly claims that she disagrees with Pam, and Pam tries to dismiss the disagreement, with the result that the conversation becomes an extended disagreement.

> MARSHA: Um, God, Pam, I know we've had arguments before.
>
> MARSHA: We disagree on a lot of things, though. Um, school for instance. And since you've got such a, you have such a positive—
> PAM: |Positive? You saw me a few minutes ago.
> MARSHA: |Um yeah, well no, you've got such— you've got such a positive attitude.
> PAM: No, I don't.
>
> MARSHA: See, that's one thing that we do disagree on. Maybe I'm not a very confident person, I guess, and you've got my share.
> PAM: Well, I— well, what do you think of my computer science attitude right now?

ONEDOWNMANSHIP

One of the ways Marsha tries to prove that she and Pam disagree or are different is to point out that Pam is a better student and has more self-confidence. This sparks an intriguing display of onedownmanship. Pam claims not to be self-confident, and not to be as good a student as Marsha says. On the other hand, she accuses Marsha of being a better student than she admits:

MARSHA: See, that's another thing. You're always, I mean I'm just so bad about this. I get into a class and the highest that I can really hope to get is may— a B, if I can get a B, out of a course, I guess it's just been so long since I have gotten an A.

PAM: That you don't think about it?

MARSHA: Yeah, well, I don't think that it's attainable.

PAM: I don't either.

MARSHA: But Pam, every, you know, every semester when we start school, it's like you talk about it though, that you've got to get an A in this course.

PAM: A's? I get B's. I try but I never get A's. I always get B's. Well, maybe except in my psychology courses, maybe. But not all of 'em.

In this excerpt, Pam reinforces connection by offering Marsha the conclusion of her sentence:

MARSHA: I guess it's just been so long since I have gotten an A.

PAM: That you don't think about it?

And she tries to play "I'm the same":

MARSHA: Yeah, well, I don't think that it's attainable.

PAM: I don't either.

But Marsha does not want to grant Pam this sameness:

> MARSHA: But Pam, every, you know, every semester when we start school, it's like you talk about it though, that you've got to get an A in this course.

Pam, however, sticks to her claim, saying that she doesn't really get A's, and if she does, it isn't often:

> PAM: A's? I get B's. I try but I never get A's. I always get B's. Well, maybe except in my psychology courses, maybe. But not all of 'em.

Lack of achievement, like similarity and agreement, seems to be the commodity with which Pam is trying to barter for symmetrical connection to Marsha.

As with Marsha's suggestion that Pam is confident, Pam seems to take Marsha's suggestion that she gets good grades as an accusation to be resisted rather than as a compliment to be accepted. As if in counterattack, Pam points out that Marsha did well in a religion class: "You do well on the tests, fifteen out of fifteen," whereas "I hadn't even read those chapters." Symmetrically, Marsha disclaims merit: "It's a lot of common sense." In this regard too, the sixth-grade girls' conversation contains the germs of this verbal game. Early in their conversation, they trade observations about how bad they are at ice skating.

For the women and girls, agreeing and being the same are ways to create rapport. Excelling, being different, and fighting are threats to rapport. The boys are buying rapport too, but they buy it with a different currency: They don't fear disagreement, and they don't seem to need to declare themselves the same. But any strategy can be taken too far, and Marsha seems to resent Pam's assertion that she always agrees.

The game of onedownmanship that these women play is reminiscent of a pattern in Iranian interaction that William Beeman calls getting the lower hand. But this game, Beeman explains, is intensely hierarchical in nature. By portraying himself as lower in status, an Iranian puts himself at the mercy of someone more powerful, who is thereby obligated to do things for him: It invokes a protector schema. Though women may at times take a one-down position so men will take care of them, the game that the women in this videotape play seems to have a very different goal: to reinforce symmetry rather than asymmetry, to keep the scales even by lowering one's own side.

MARRIAGE—
"A SERIOUS ENOUGH TOPIC"

The twenty-five-year-old men present a very different picture. They sit at angles to each other, looking starched or frozen stiff. Timothy almost never looks at Winston. Though Winston looks at Timothy when he's listening, he often looks away, and when he is speaking, he never looks at Timothy at all. The men show a great deal of discomfort and strain in choosing a topic to talk about. They are very earnest about the injunction to talk about something serious, and to them *serious* seems to mean something important in the world, about which they can make a substantive contribution. Here's what they settle on:

> WINSTON: How about marriage?
> TIMOTHY: That's a serious enough topic.
> WINSTON: Serious topic, and it doesn't receive a lot of attention.

In discussing marriage, a potentially personal topic, they speak mainly in the abstract, making general statements without revealing anything personal:

> TIMOTHY: Why do you think, uh, so many marriages ain't making it? That's, uh, you know, a broad question.
> WINSTON: I think most people rush into it, for one thing. (6.0) Just can't wait to get married.

TIMOTHY: I think, uh, I think people, a lot of people, and I'm not saying I *do* but a lot of people don't have an adequate or a mature, you know, definition in their lives of what love is. You know, uh, I don't know, 'cause a lot of the strife, you know, in my opinion, in marriages and relationships is because the person has the, uh, you know, selfish attitude.

There are ways in which these men's conversation conforms to what has been predicted for men, but in other ways it doesn't. According to the stereotype, and the findings of some research, women's talk is more hesitant. But Timothy hesitates and uses fillers like *you know, uh,* and *in my opinion,* giving the impression of insecurity or not being sure of what he is saying. It seems that the situation is making him uncomfortable. Yet by speaking abstractly rather than personally, he conforms to expectations of men's as compared to women's speech.

Later in the conversation, Timothy talks about his relationship with a woman he is dating. He says that he is considering marriage but has gotten no further than that: He is cautious because marriage is forever, and he is wary because women often try to rush men into marriage.

Timothy then says, "You know I don't just want to talk about my situation." After a pause, Winston responds: "Well, mine's with school, and school is just the epitome of being an unsettled person." Winston seems to be implying that he does not have a girl friend because he's a student and therefore his life is unsettled. But he expresses this indirectly, as a general statement about the situation he is in: "mine's with school." Timothy asked him the question indirectly, by making a statement ("I don't just want to talk about my situation") rather than asking directly, "What about you?" In other contexts, for example when trying to negotiate mutual preferences and decisions, women are often more indirect than men. But when it comes to talking about their personal relationships and feelings, many men are more indirect.

"A Pretty Shy Attitude"

A poignant example of indirectness occurs when Winston says that sometimes men become cautious about relationships because they have been hurt, or, in his words, "torched":

> I think a lot of people start off like maybe when they're young they might have the attitude of what they think is a hundred percent give and then they get torched. Or what they think is torched. And it's liable to just, you know, give them, you know, a pretty shy attitude towards it for a long time.

Winston seems to be implying he has been hurt and that is why he is not in a relationship now. But if this is what he means, he does not say it directly. He does not say anything about any relationships of his own.

Follow the Leader

Comparing the videotapes of girls and boys and women and men talking to their friends in this experimental setting provides evidence for the gender differences pattern. These conversations show girls and women working hard to create a community of connection, bonding through talking about troubles in their personal relationships, and struggling to maintain their individuality in the face of pressure to agree. The boys and men are working hard to preserve their independence in a hierarchical world, to achieve intimacy within oppositional frameworks. But it would be misleading to imply that the girls' friendships are entirely egalitarian. An important aspect of these videotapes is the asymmetry in the alignments taken up by the two friends in each conversation.

Among the second-grade boys, Jimmy is clearly a leader: He

has the only extended turns, he gives orders and instructions, he teases, and he initiates most of the conversational moves. Of the sixth-grade boys, Tom is a leader who raises most of the topics, is the main speaker, and takes the performer role in the two instances of report-talk. Of the fifty-five topics covered in their interaction, Tom raises forty. Walt, who generally takes a contributing and supporting role, raises fifteen topics, of which six involve calling attention to objects in the room.

The situation presented by the girls is more complicated. The second-grade girls are the only ones in whom there are no apparent asymmetries in the footings they assume. The alignments taken up by the sixth- and tenth-grade girls are strikingly asymmetrical, even though much of what they say seems intended to achieve the appearance of agreement, support, and connection. Of the sixth-graders, Julia seems to be the leader. Of fourteen topics discussed, she raises twelve. Most of the discussion centers around her relationship with Mary, her concerns about keeping friends, and her anxiety about separation and loss. When the experimenter briefly enters the room at the five-minute mark, Julia is the one who talks to him. Yet it is Shannon who "chooses" the topic of Julia's relationship with Mary by saying, "Too bad you and Mary are not good friends anymore."

Similarly, most of the tenth-grade girls' conversation is about Nancy, but it is Sally who suggests that they talk about Nancy's problems. In response to Nancy's question "Well, what do you want to talk about?" Sally says, "Your mama. Did you talk to your mama?" In terms of the number of topics raised, the girls seem fairly balanced: Sally raises nine topics, Nancy seven. However, all but one of the topics Sally raises are questions focused on Nancy. Much previous research on "topic control" assumes that raising a topic is a sign of dominance in a conversation. From this point of view, Sally "controls" the conversation when she raises topics, although even this is subject to Nancy's collaboration in making it a topic by picking it up. Can she really be said to "dominate," though, if the topics she raises concern Sally?

In some ways, the tenth-grade boys' conversation is more symmetrical than the girls': Nancy and Sally talk entirely about

Nancy's problems, but Richard and Todd both tell about their own troubles, and both respond by dismissing or downplaying the other's. Among the adult men and women, Pam is a kind of leader: She tends to set the themes to which Marsha reacts. Yet the recurrent question of whether or not they disagree becomes a theme because of Marsha's response to Pam's opening observation that Marsha always agrees with her. The adult men present a similar paradox: The topic of marriage is suggested by Winston, and he is the one who talks to Dorval when he comes in. But six of the seven subtopics by which they actually discuss marriage are chosen by Timothy.

Does talking more about her problems put a girl in a higher-status position, since she's taking up more conversational space, or does it put her in a lower one, since she's being portrayed as the one with problems? No one would suggest that the patient has more status or power in a psychotherapy session, even though he or she does most of the talking and raises all the topics. Does raising the topic imply "dominance" in the sense of "controlling" the conversation, if the topic raised is of primary concern to the other girl? I don't know the answers to these questions, but I would know more if I knew whether these girls habitually apportion the roles of troubles teller and supporter in these ways, or if they reverse roles in different conversations. At any rate, it is clear that issues of dominance and control are far more complex than can be captured in surface descriptions such as who raises topics. And although the girls and women are focused on connection, and the boys and men on status, there are nonetheless asymmetries among the women and girls, and symmetries among the men and boys.

In all their complexity, these videotapes show that from the earliest ages through adulthood, boys and girls create different worlds, which men and women go on living in. It is no surprise that women and men who are trying to do things right in relationships with each other so often find their partners wanting, and themselves criticized. We try to talk to each other honestly, but it seems at times that we are speaking different languages— or at least different genderlects.

TEN

Living with Asymmetry: Opening Lines of Communication

An American woman set out for a vacation cruise and landed in a Turkish prison. Reading her book *Never Pass This Way Again,* I could see that Gene LePere's ordeal was an extreme example of the disastrous consequences that can result from cross-cultural differences in what I term conversational style—ways of framing how you mean what you say, and what you think you are doing when you say it. LePere's experience also illustrates, in an unusually dramatic way, the dangers of trying to avoid conflict and say no in a polite way.

LePere left her cruise ship for a brief tour of ancient ruins in Turkey. At an archeological site, she fell behind her group as she became absorbed in admiring the ruins. Suddenly, her path was blocked by a man selling artifacts she had no interest in buying.

Yet she found herself holding a stone head, and when she told him politely that she did not want it, he would not take it back. Instead, he thrust forward another one, which she also automatically accepted. Since the man would not take either head back, the only path to escape she could envision was offering to buy them. She cut his price in half and hoped he'd refuse so she could move on. Instead, he agreed to drop the price, and she dropped the two heads into her tote. But as she handed him the money, he handed her a third head. Once more she insisted she did not want it, but he just stepped back to avoid repossessing it. Seeing no alternative, she paid for the third head and stalked off—shaken and angry. When LePere tried to reboard her cruise ship, she showed her purchases to customs officials, who had her arrested and thrown into jail for trying to smuggle out a national treasure. The third head was a genuine antiquity.

Having lived in Greece and observed the verbal art of bargaining, I could see that talking to the vendor and saying she did not want the artifacts would mean to him that she might want them if the price were lower. If she really had no intention of buying, she would not have talked to him at all. She would have pushed her way past him and walked on, never establishing eye contact—and surely not taking possession of any heads, no matter how insistently he proffered them. Each time she accepted a head, he received evidence of her interest and encouragement to offer another. Each step in his increasingly aggressive sales pitch was a response to what likely appeared to him as her bargaining maneuvers. Refusing to look at or talk to him, or, as a last resort, placing the heads on the ground—these were unthinkable alternatives for a polite American woman.

LePere paid dearly for this fleeting breakdown in communication across cultures. Though cross-cultural communication between women and men generally has less drastic consequences, the process of incremental misunderstanding by which it occurs is similar. And in a way, male-female miscommunication is more dangerous, because it is more pervasive in our lives, and we are less prepared for it. We expect differences when we talk to people who come from different countries; we have ways to think about such differences, like "customs" and "cultural assumptions." But we don't expect family, friends, co-workers, and romantic partners who grew up in "the same culture" and speak "the same language" to understand words differently and have different views of the world. But often they do.

WHY THINGS GET WORSE

Gene LePere's experience illustrates the process that Gregory Bateson identified and named complementary schismogenesis—a mutually aggravating spiral by which each person's response to the other's behavior provokes more exaggerated forms of the divergent behavior. LePere's mounting frustration with the vendor's hard-sell practices resulted in behavior that encouraged him to step them up. For example, she offered a low price for the two heads because she had no interest in buying them, but from his point of view this was a show of interest and willingness to participate in the bargaining process. So what she did to escape the situation only further embroiled her in it.

Complementary schismogenesis commonly sets in when women and men have divergent sensitivities and hypersensitivities. For example, a man who fears losing freedom pulls away at the first sign he interprets as an attempt to "control" him, but pulling away is just the signal that sets off alarms for the woman who fears losing intimacy. Her attempts to get closer will aggravate his fear, and his reaction—pulling further away—will aggravate hers, and so on, in an ever-widening spiral. Understanding each other's styles, and the motives behind them, is a first move in breaking this destructive circuit.

INEQUALITY BEGINS
AT HOME

Another reason that gender differences are so much more troubling than other cross-cultural differences is that they occur where the home and hearth are. We all sense that stepping into a vastly foreign culture involves risk; that's why there's a thrill of adventure associated with foreign travel. But we expect to be safe in our own homes. And there we expect to be equal.

Sociologist Erving Goffman points out that inequality due to differences in race and ethnicity disappears when people of the same race or ethnic background close the doors to their own homes. But in private, personal places that we cherish as havens from the outside world, inequality based on gender comes into its own. Not only do we not escape such discrimination in our most intimate relationships, but we can hardly conceive of them apart from gender-based alignments that are inherently asymmetrical—implying differences in status. We cannot take a step without taking stances that are prescribed by society and gender specific. We enact and create our gender, and our inequality, with every move we make.

PHYSICAL CONSTELLATIONS

A woman and a man showing mutual affection cannot do it in the same way. When a man and a woman walk down the street embracing, his arm is around her shoulders, and her arm rests on his waist. If their stance is more casual, his hand may rest in his pocket as she holds on to his arm. These stances are not symmetrical. If a woman walks with her arm around a man's shoulders and his arm around her waist, passersby look back in a double take. If a woman keeps her hands in her pockets while a male hooks his hand onto her arm, or she has her arm on the shoulder of a male who has his hands in his pockets, chances are the woman is a mother and the male is her child..

Some people point out that men put their arms on women's shoulders, not the reverse, because the man is usually taller, so it would be uncomfortable if not impossible for the woman and man to reverse positions. But these rituals are observed even if the man is not taller and must stretch to maintain the protective position. If he is too short to put his arm around the woman's shoulders, they will not reverse positions but settle for holding hands. Moreover, our society expects the man to be taller (and older and richer and smarter) precisely because this frames him as protective—and higher in status.

The asymmetry of women's and men's alignments is epitomized in the positions they take. Even the most intimate moments cannot be imagined without reference to gender. When a woman and man lie down on a blanket or in bed, he typically lies on his back, flat and straight, while she lies on her side with her body curved and nestled against his. Her head rests on his shoulder; his arm is around her. Daily, men and women take these positions automatically, and their ritualized nature is a source of comfort; it feels right and good, partly because it is personally familiar, and partly because it mirrors a configuration we have seen countless times in pictures and in life. But reenacting the ritual also reinforces the asymmetry of the relationship, as he is solid, firm, protecting, and she is off-balance, off-center, protected.

A poet, Cheryl Romney-Brown, created a poem around the recurrent image of a woman burying her face in the crook of a man's neck. She shows that this gesture recurs throughout a woman's life:

IN THE CROOK OF HIS NECK

Fine hairs on his shoulders gleam
like epaulets, reminding me of silk

mulberry threads Penelope used
for tapestries spun waiting
for her hero to come home.
We, women, always long for men
to step out of a myth or a Marlboro ad.

It begins all over again as he
caresses my back. I inhale the scent,
begin to relax. Once more I become
a defenseless girl wanting only
to close my eyes, bury my head
in the crook of his neck.

How old was I the first time,
possibly three? It happened
when Daddy came home. "Please
hold me, protect me, werewolves
are out, their eyes burning hot.
If you don't I know I will die."
I closed my eyes, buried
my head in the crook of his neck.

When I was sixteen, ripe but pure,
down by the arbor on a hot summer night,
my first beau's lips brushed mine. "My hero,
your Juliet's here." Pink tulle bound
my heart. I closed my eyes, buried
my head in the crook of his neck.

I am a grown woman, mother of men.
Experience fades; memory stills.
If only for a moment, I am saved.
My hero is here for maybe an hour,
willing to do battle, kill all my foes.
Illusions, myths, whatever is true.
I close my eyes, bury my head
in the crook of his neck.

Romney-Brown's poem captures the childlike nature of the asymmetrical embrace by which a woman places her head on a man's shoulder, nestling against him, and its protective meaning. The poet traces this delicious feeling of being protected to her relationship to her father when she was a child. Presumably, a little boy might also have nestled against his father or mother, seeking solace and protection. But as an adult, the woman is still taking the child's position in the constellation, while the man has moved into the position taken by the parent.

This poem also captures the automatic way a woman moves into the protected position with men who are not literally protecting her. The standard tableau is immutably in place, ready for the young girl to take her position in it on her first date, and still there, half a lifetime later, for her to step into after divorce. The woman's role in this ritual configuration is resumed even when she has long since proven her ability to protect others, as the "mother of men."

The rigidity of these ritual constellations is portrayed in a pivotal scene in the film *The Accidental Tourist*. The hero, Macon, appears, disheveled and distraught, at the home of Muriel, a woman who has shown a romantic interest in him. Macon tells Muriel the dreadful story of his son's death, and confesses that he has been unable to recover from it. Touched by his confession, Muriel leads Macon to bed, to comfort him for his devastating loss. In bed, Macon lies on his back and lifts his arm to place it around Muriel, who snuggles against him. In choreographing this scene, the director apparently felt that the demands of convention, which require the man to take the physical position of protector and comforter, were stronger than the demands of the immediate scene in which Muriel is comforting Macon.

The physical alignment that women and men take up to each other when they lie down together is just one of a network of asymmetries that enact our genders and simultaneously reinforce status differences between men and women. Goffman is eloquent in describing these asymmetries:

In our society in all classes the tenderest expression of affection involves displays that are politically questionable, the place taken up in them by the female being differentiated from and reciprocal to the place taken up by the male. Cross-sex affectional gestures choreograph protector and protected, embracer and embraced, comforter and comforted, supporter and supported, extender of affection and recipient thereof; and it is defined as only natural that the male encompass and the female be encompassed. And this can only remind us that male domination is a very special kind, a domination that can be carried right into the gentlest, most loving moment without apparently causing strain—indeed, these moments can hardly be conceived of apart from these asymmetries.

Gender is a category that will not go away. As Goffman put it, it is "one of the most deeply seated traits of man"(!). We create masculinity and femininity in our ways of behaving, all the while believing we are simply acting "naturally." But our sense of what is natural is different for women and men. And what we regard as naturally male and female is based on asymmetrical alignments.

In Goffman's terms, gender relations are patterned on the parent-child complex. In other words, the ways we enact our genders as we try to be good women and men take on meaning by analogy with parents and children. Goffman points out that men are to women as adults are to children: loving protectors who will hold open doors, offer the first portion of sweets, reach high shelves, and lift heavy loads. But along with the privileges of childhood come liabilities: Children's activities are interruptible, their time and territory expendable. Along with the privilege of being protected comes the loss of rights, and not being respected and treated like a full-fledged person. Being the protector frames someone as competent, capable, and deserving of respect. Being protected frames one as incompetent, incapable, and deserving of indulgence.

ASYMMETRIES IN CONVERSATION: "I ONLY DID IT FOR YOU"

In talking to couples about communication in their relationships, I was surprised by how often men referred to their role as protectors of women in explaining why they spoke as they did. For example, one couple told me of a recent argument. The woman had noticed that her husband was favoring one arm and asked why. He said that his arm hurt. She asked how long it had been hurting him, and he said, "Oh, a few weeks." To his surprise, she reacted with hurt and anger: "Go ahead, treat me like a stranger!"

To her, intimacy meant telling what's on your mind, including what hurts. By not telling her that his arm hurt, her husband was pushing her away, distancing her with his silence. I instinctively understood this woman's point of view. But I did not immediately understand the man's. In explaining his side of the story, he said, "I guess men learn from the beginning to protect women." This puzzled me. I asked what protection had to do with not telling his wife that his arm hurt. "I was protecting her," he explained. "Why should I worry her by telling her about my pain, since it might be nothing and go away anyway?"

Deciding what to tell his wife reflects this man's perceived role as her protector. But it also grows out of and reinforces the alignment by which he is in a superior position. He is stronger than she, and he has power to cause her worry by the information he imparts. This man does not feel, as his wife perceives, that he is trying to curtail their intimacy. Intimacy is simply not at issue for him. In her world, the imparting of personal information is the fundamental material of intimacy, so withholding such information deprives her of the closeness that is her lifeblood. Their different interpretations of the same information simply reflect their different preoccupations. They are tuned to different frequencies.

288

It may be that this man was also protecting his autonomy, staving off his wife's excessive show of concern. But this was not the reason he offered in explaining his motives. In his explanatory system, his role as protector was primary. The same was true for another husband whose wife complained about a very different type of behavior.

The wife, whom I will call Michele, objected to the habit her husband, Gary, had of answering her questions by providing information other than what she had requested. Here are two typical exchanges that she recounted:

MICHELE: What time is the concert?
GARY: You have to be ready by seven-thirty.

MICHELE: How many people are coming to dinner?
GARY: Don't worry. There'll be enough food.

Michele gets frustrated because she feels that by withholding information, Gary is holding tight to the reins of power in the relationship. But he maintains that he is "watching out for her" by getting to the real point of her questions. Both points of view are plausible. The cause of their different interpretations of the same conversation resides in the ambiguity inherent in protecting. He sees his attention to her concerns as protective; she sees that the protective stance frames him as one-up in competence and control.

Another man reported similar conversations with his wife. In this case, however, the roles are reversed: It is the wife, Valerie, who gives what she thinks is the relevant information rather than answering the question asked, and it is the husband, Ned, who objects to her doing so. Here are two examples of their dialogues:

NED: Are you leaving now?
VALERIE: You can take a nap if you want.

NED: Are you just about finished?
VALERIE: Do you want to have supper now?

In defending herself against Ned's complaints, Valerie gives an explanation very different from the one given by the husband in the previous example. She says that she is anticipating Ned's desires and concerns.

This man and woman give different explanations for behaving in the same way; they truly seem to think of themselves as doing the same thing for different reasons. Being the protector is central to him; being helpful is central to her.

If women and men sometimes have (or give) different motivations when they behave in similar ways, there are also situations where their different motivations lead them to behave differently. Each individual works out a unique way of balancing status differences and connection to others. But if we think of these motivations as two ends of a continuum, women and men tend to cluster at opposite ends. Because of these differences in points of view, a man and a woman may perceive the same scene in different ways and misinterpret each other's motives. Understanding the differences can deflect the misinterpretation, and make sense where there seemed to be no sense.

SOLVING PUZZLES

A man told me with puzzlement about his most rebellious childhood friend, Henry. Henry flouted authority at every turn: in the way he wore his hair (sticking straight out in all directions), the way he dressed (flamboyantly, absurdly), the things he did (making crank phone calls, publicly ridiculing teachers), the way he planned his future (he refused to go to college; instead, he left the country). But several years later, Henry returned to the United States—transformed into a traditionalist. For example, he insisted that friends who visited him must bring their wives, because wives were supposed to accompany their husbands everywhere. And his political views became more and more conservative.

The rebellious youth who turns into an authoritarian adult is a commonly observed paradox. I recall being surprised at first to hear Charlotte Linde's observation that policemen whose conversations she had studied talked frequently about what "bad boys" they had been, trading stories about their youthful escapades and how cleverly they had broken the law in their wild days. This seeming puzzle returned to me, the pieces now fitting together, as I came to understand the view of the world as a hierarchical social order. "Born rebels" who defy authority are not oblivious of it, but oversensitive to it. Defying authority is a way of asserting themselves and refusing to accept the subordinate position. When they are old enough, or established enough, to take the dominant position, reinforcing authority becomes the way to assert themselves, since the hierarchy is now operating to their advantage.

Another puzzle solved for me was my similarities to and differences from my father. For example, my father passed on to me his love of reading and of words. "What book are you reading?" he regularly asked me when I was a child. But I was disappointed when, as a young adult, I recommended to him some of the novels I loved, and he couldn't get through them. "It's so boring," he'd say. "Nothing ever happens." And he could never get me to read some of the books he loved when he was a child (for example, *The Three Musketeers*) and as an adult (for example, *The Maltese Falcon*). Like most men, my father is interested in action. And this is also why he disappoints my mother when she tells him she doesn't feel well and he offers to take her to the doctor. He is focused on what he can do, whereas she wants sympathy.

TWO PATHS TO INVOLVEMENT

Offering sympathy and offering to do something can be different ways of achieving the same goal—involvement with others. All conversations serve the universal human need for involvement as well as the simultaneous but conflicting need for independence. And just as women and men often have contrasting senses of intimacy, so also do they often have contrasting senses of independence. Those who see relationships as fundamentally hierarchical will feel that to be independent they must be dominant rather than subordinate. But another view is possible. It is possible to avoid being dependent on or subordinate to others, but not dominate them either. In other words, there is a symmetrical rather than asymmetrical independence.

That these two views reflect characteristically male and female views of independence is supported by Philip Blumstein and Pepper Schwartz's study *American Couples*. A husband they quote as typical said he needs to be independent *and to have others dependent on him*. This is an outgrowth of the protector stance that is built into our society's sense of what it means to be masculine. The difference between men's and women's assumptions about independence also emerges in their attitudes toward money. Blumstein and Schwartz found that for men, having money provides a sense of power, but for women, it provides security and autonomy—simply the ability not to be dependent. An intriguing result of their comparison of heterosexual and homosexual couples is that only among lesbian couples did earning more money not establish a partner as relatively more powerful in the relationship. Lesbians, they found, use money to avoid dependence but not to dominate. And only among gay male couples did one partner feel more successful if the other partner's income was lower.

WHEN STRENGTHS BECOME LIABILITIES

These differing understandings of independence grow out of the distinct kinds of relations women and men learn and practice as boys and girls growing up. And these disparate worlds exert distinct pressures on each gender. The pressure to maintain connections with others while appearing skillful and knowledgeable, and while negotiating relative rank, can become a burden for boys and men. The pressure to achieve status while avoiding conflict and appearing no better than anyone else can become a burden for girls and women.

Women sometimes suffer from an overabundance of rapport. For example, their expectation that an expression of troubles should be met with matching troubles can be felt as a stringent requirement to have matching troubles to tell. One woman said of a friend, "Marian tries to rope me into her neuroses, implying I have the same problems she does. I don't like it because I don't have the same problems." A similar frustration was expressed by another woman, Jill, who told me about her friend Elizabeth, who always includes her in her statements: "We have trouble with this," or "That's a problem for us." When Elizabeth issues an inclusive statement, she expects Jill to come up with a matching experience. If Jill says, "That's not a problem for me," Elizabeth feels rejected and accuses Jill of putting her down. "Some women don't let you be different," Jill said. "They don't let you have any individuality."

If women are not always perfectly satisfied by their friendships with women, neither are all men perfectly happy with their friendships with men. Many men told me that they prefer women as friends because they find it harder to talk to men. One man told me it took him two years in a new city to find two men who were willing to talk about how they felt, to admit problems and listen to his, men he did not feel were competitive with him. Men's need to be strong and independent all the time can be felt as a stringent requirement not to have troubles. This was the view expressed to Catherine Kohler Riessman by a divorced man who said, "I think everybody hates to have anybody know that they have problems. . . . You always try and keep your problems to yourself. . . ."

Several men commented to me that it is American men in particular who make friendly conversation into a contest. One British man told me that back home his best friends had been men, but since he emigrated to the United States, most of his friends have been women. On a visit home, he spent time with an old friend who was male. "We yielded to one another," he said, explaining to me what the difference was. "We didn't try to one-up or prevail all the time." An American man expressed a similar opinion. He said he finds European men easier to talk to. "Talking to American men," he commented, "is like a war zone."

And yet, the man who told me it had taken him two years to find men to befriend did find two. And everyone knows women and men who, in some ways, are more "like" the other gender than like their own. This is natural, since individuals develop patterns of behavior based on innumerable influences, such as where they grew up, ethnic background, religious or cultural affiliation, class, and the vast reservoir of personal experience and genetic inheritance that makes each person's life and personality unique. But seeing a pattern against which to evaluate individual differences provides a starting point to develop not only self-understanding but also flexibility—the freedom to try doing things differently if automatic ways of doing them aren't having entirely successful results.

Both women and men could benefit from learning each other's styles. Many women could learn from men to accept some conflict and difference without seeing it as a threat to intimacy, and many men could learn from women to accept interdependence without seeing it as a threat to their freedom.

Women's inclination to preserve intimacy by avoiding conflict also explains the initially surprising finding of Blumstein and Schwartz that women want more time away from their partners than men do. I think there are two reasons for this. First, many women have a kind of communication with their women friends that they don't have with their partners, and that is not possible if their partners are present. Second, when women are with partners, they make more adjustments and accommodations, buying harmony at the cost of their own preferences. Therefore, being with partners is more of a strain on them than it is on men, who are less inclined to accommodate.

If accommodating automatically is a strain, so is automatically resisting others' will. Sometimes it is more effective to take the footing of an ally. The "best" style is a flexible one. The freest person is the one who can choose which strategies to use, not the one who must slavishly replay the same script over and over—as we all tend to do. There is nothing inherently wrong with automatic behavior. If we did not do most things automatically, it would take massive concentration and energy to do anything. But by becoming aware of our ways of talking and how effective they are, we can override our automatic impulses and adapt our habitual styles when they are not serving us well.

IT ALL DEPENDS

In trying to develop such awareness of ways of talking, people often ask me what a particular expression or conversational habit "really means." I always answer that no phrase or device has only one meaning. Like the practice of overlapping—beginning to talk when someone else is already speaking—what looks on the surface like the same way of talking can have varied meanings and effects. A listener may talk along with a speaker to provide support, or to change the topic. Even changing the topic can have a range of meanings. It can show lack of interest, it can be an attempt to dominate the conversation, or it can be a kind of "mutual revelation device"—matching the speaker's experience with the listener's. Even mutual revelation can be done with different motives: either in a spirit of connection, to establish rapport and emphasize sameness, or in a spirit of competition, to top a story and frame oneself as more important.

Evidence that the same behavior can have very different meanings emerges in an article by Lee Cronk comparing gift giving in different cultures. Citing an African example, Cronk describes the custom called *hxaro,* in the words of a !Kung man named !Xoma: "Hxaro is when I take a thing of value and give it to you. Later, much later, when you find some good thing, you give it back to me. When I find something good I will give it to you, and so we will pass the years together." Asked what would count as a fair exchange (for example, how many strings of beads would you have to give if your friend gave you a spear?), !Xoma wouldn't answer. He explained that any return would be acceptable because "we don't trade with things, we trade with people."

In contrast, a New Guinea society has a custom called *moka* by which gifts are given to gain prestige and shame rivals. One legendary *moka* gift given in the 1970s included several hundred pigs, some cows and wild birds, a truck, a motorbike, and thousands of dollars in cash. The person who gave all this is said to have told the person he gave it to, "I have won. I have knocked you down by giving so much."

In these two cultural rituals, the same act—giving gifts—has very different meanings. *Hxaro,* done among friends, is cooperative, whereas *moka,* done among rivals, is competitive. The key difference between these two practices is symmetry versus asymmetry. In *hxaro,* the exchange of gifts is symmetrical, each friend reciprocating with a matching gift. But in *moka,* it is asymmetrical, each rival trying to top the other's gifts so he can come out on top.

Since any statement or action can grow out of widely divergent motives and intentions, it is not safe to trust our instincts about what a comment or action "means." A !Kung person might have a very different instinctive reaction to a gift than a member of the New Guinea tribe that practices *moka*. This awareness can be a key to improving conversations and relationships among women and men. We would all do well to distrust our automatic responses to what others say, especially if our automatic responses are negative. Instead, we should try to see things from the other person's perspective. Once they know that men and women often have different assumptions about the world and about ways of talking, people are very creative about figuring out how this rift is affecting their own relationships.

OPENING LINES OF COMMUNICATION

Many experts tell us we are doing things wrong and should change our behavior—which usually sounds easier than it turns out to be. Sensitivity training judges men by women's standards, trying to get them to talk more like women. Assertiveness training judges women by men's standards and tries to get them to talk more like men. No doubt, many people can be helped by learning to be more sensitive or more assertive. But few people are helped by being told they are doing everything all wrong. And there may be little wrong with what people are doing, even if they are winding up in arguments. The problem may be that each partner is operating within a different system, speaking a different genderlect.

An obvious question is, Can genderlect be taught? Can people change their conversational styles? If they want to, yes, they can—to an extent. But those who ask this question rarely want to change their own styles. Usually, what they have in mind is sending their partners for repair: They'd like to get him or her to change. Changing one's own style is far less appealing, because it is not just how you act but who you feel yourself to be. Therefore a more realistic approach is to learn how to interpret each other's messages and explain your own in a way your partner can understand and accept.

Understanding genderlects makes it possible to change—to try speaking differently—when you want to. But even if no one changes, understanding genderlect improves relationships. Once people realize that their partners have different conversational styles, they are inclined to accept differences without blaming themselves, their partners, or their relationships. The biggest mistake is believing there is one right way to listen, to talk, to have a conversation—or a relationship. Nothing hurts more than being told your intentions are bad when you know they are good, or being told you are doing something wrong when you know you're just doing it your way.

Not seeing style differences for what they are, people draw conclusions about personality ("you're illogical," "you're insecure," "you're self-centered") or intentions ("you don't listen," "you put me down"). Understanding style differences for what they are takes the sting out of them. Believing that "you're not interested in me," "you don't care about me as much as I care about you," or "you want to take away my freedom" feels awful. Believing that "you have a different way of showing you're listening" or "showing you care" allows for no-fault negotiation: You can ask for or make adjustments without casting or taking blame.

If you understand gender differences in what I call conversational style, you may not be able to prevent disagreements from arising, but you stand a better chance of preventing them from spiraling out of control. When sincere attempts to communicate end in stalemate, and a beloved partner seems irrational and obstinate, the different languages men and women speak can shake the foundation of our lives. Understanding the other's ways of talking is a giant leap across the communication gap between women and men, and a giant step toward opening lines of communication.

NOTES

Bibliographical information on research cited below is listed in the References section. If more than one article or book by the same author or authors is included in the References, a note indicates which source is referred to. Bibliographical information for news items and other secondary sources is given in the Notes.

PREFACE

14 My study of indirectness in conversation is "Ethnic Style in Male-Female Conversation."

14 A similar reticence accompanies research on style differences involving minorities. For example, Andrew Hacker ("Affirmative Action: The New Look," *The New York Review of Books,* October 12, 1989, p. 68) discusses an incident in which black organizations demanded the withdrawal of a New York State Department of Education handbook explaining that blacks and whites have different learning styles. Even though the research had been done by a black scholar, Janice Hale-Benson, the protesters branded the findings racist. Hacker explains, "The question, of course, is whether the tendencies Hale-Benson analyzed will be construed not simply as different, but also as inferior." The key word here is *construed.* Readers' reactions may be very different from researchers' intentions.

15 My article "Did You Say What I Just Heard?" appeared in *The Washington Post* on October 12, 1986, p. D3. The *Toronto Star* version appeared (without my knowledge) under the title "Why We Should Also Listen Between the Lines" on November 16, 1986, p. D1. The textbook that includes excerpts from this edited version is *People in Perspective* (second edition), edited by Wayne Sproule (Scarborough, Ontario: Prentice-Hall Canada, 1988). The material appeared as edited by the *Star,* even though I granted permission on condition that the deleted sentence be restored.

16 I have borrowed the metaphor of sweeping things under the

rug from Robin Lakoff. I first heard her use it in her course at the 1973 Linguistic Institute at the University of Michigan.

17 Abby Abinanti, "Lawyer," *Women and Work: Photographs and Personal Writings,* text ed. by Maureen R. Michelson, photographs ed. by Michael R. Dressler and Maureen R. Michelson (Pasadena, CA: NewSage Press 1986), p. 52.

CHAPTER ONE
DIFFERENT WORDS, DIFFERENT WORLDS

25 The term *connection* as a goal motivating women will remind readers of Carol Gilligan's influential work on girls' moral development. I have not cited her in my discussion because, although I may have been unwittingly influenced in my choice of the term, my status-connection framework is a direct outgrowth of the power-solidarity dimension, a fundamental concept in sociolinguistics. This concept was introduced by Roger Brown and Albert Gilman in their 1960 article "The Pronouns of Power and Solidarity," was explored by Paul Friedrich in a 1972 article, "Social Context and Semantic Feature: The Russian Pronominal Usage," and is pervasive in the sociolinguistic literature (see Chapter One, "Address Forms," in Ralph Fasold's *The Sociolinguistics of Language*). The dynamics of this dimension as a motivation for conversation is a theme running through my 1986 book, *That's Not What I Meant!,* which includes a chapter entitled "Power and Solidarity." In this book I use *status* and *connection* in place of the terms *power* and *solidarity* because I realized that the connotations of the latter terms are different for lay readers than for sociolinguists: *Power* in common parlance connotes intentionally wielding power, and *solidarity* has come to suggest Polish politics.

28 The quotation from Tom Whittaker appeared in "A Salute to Everyday Heroes," *Newsweek,* July 10, 1989, p. 46.

33 The term *framing* traces to Gregory Bateson, "A Theory of Play and Fantasy," *Steps to an Ecology of Mind*. Erving Goffman developed the concept in his book *Frame Analysis* and the chapter "Footing" in *Forms of Talk*.

33 Goffman discusses alignment in *Frame Analysis* and "Footing."

40 No page references are given for Riessman because her book was not yet available in print when this book went to press.

41 "The Pros and Cons of an Academic Career: Six Views from Binghamton," *The Chronicle of Higher Education,* January 25, 1989, p. A15.

43 Barrie Thorne has studied extensively the extent to which boys and girls spend their time together and apart. See for example her article "Girls and Boys Together . . . But Mostly Apart: Gender Arrangements in Elementary Schools."

46 The term *positioning* was suggested to me by Bronwyn Davies. See Davies and Harré, "Positioning: Conversation and the Production of Selves."

48 Alice Walker's comment was made in an interview on *The Diane Rehm Show,* WAMU, Washington, DC, August 31, 1989.

CHAPTER TWO
ASYMMETRIES: WOMEN AND MEN TALKING
AT CROSS-PURPOSES

52 The Christophers were discussing their book *Mixed Blessings* on *The Diane Rehm Show,* WAMU, Washington, DC, June 6, 1989.

53 I have borrowed the term *troubles talk* from Gail Jefferson. See, for example, her article "On the Sequential Organization of Troubles-Talk in Ordinary Conversation."

53 The quotation is from "Clobbering Her Ex," a review of Alice Adams's *After You've Gone* in *The New York Times Book Review,* October 8, 1989, p. 27.

54 Bruce Dorval videotaped friends talking at a range of ages. He describes the tapes and how he collected them in a book he edited, *Conversational Coherence and Its Development.* That book includes chapters in which scholars from different disciplines analyze selected videotapes. My analysis of gender differences in the videotapes is included in that collection and is also the basis for Chapter Nine of this book.

54 Excerpts are from transcripts originally prepared by Bruce Dorval and his assistants. I have checked and occasionally refined the transcripts, and made a few changes in punctuation to enhance readability for the nonspecialist reader. In transcripts throughout the book, the following conventions apply: Parentheses indicate parenthetical intonation (pitch and loudness are reduced; intonation is flattened). /?/ indicates that something was said but couldn't be deciphered. A dash following a word indicates that the speaker cut off the word or phrase right there. Usually this represents the slight stumbling of a false start rather than an abrupt self-interruption. *Italics* indicate emphatic stress; CAPITAL LETTERS indicate more emphatic stress. Three spaced periods (. . .) are an ellipsis, showing that several lines have been omitted. Three un-

spaced periods (. . .) indicate a pause. **Boldface** type highlights lines that are crucial for the point I am making about the example.

58 "New Haven," like all the other stories by Alice Mattison that I quote, is in *Great Wits* (New York: William Morrow, 1988). This quotation is from p. 63.

58 Mattison, "New Haven," p. 64.

59 Mattison, "The Knitting," p. 36.

60 The alternative interpretation of the boys' dismissal of each other's concerns was pointed out to me by Ralph Fasold.

72 Mattison, "The Colorful Alphabet," p. 125.

CHAPTER THREE
"PUT DOWN THAT PAPER AND TALK TO ME!": RAPPORT-TALK AND REPORT-TALK

75 Connie Eble (p. 469) cites Gerald Carson (p. 55) for the "cleft stick" reference. In Carson's words, "In East Hampton, New York, cleft sticks were slipped over too-busy tongues. . . ."

Authors who discuss the historical attitude that women talk too much include Dennis Baron, Connie Eble, Alette Hill, and Cheris Kramarae. Deborah James and Janice Drakich have written an article reviewing research that aims to determine who talks more, women or men.

77 The observation that women are thought to talk more if they talk equally has been made by many, including Dale Spender *(Man Made Language)* and Carole Edelsky ("Who's Got the Floor?"). Myra and David Sadker ("Sexism in the Schoolroom of the '80s") report that teachers who were shown a film of classroom discussion overwhelmingly thought the girls were talking more, when in fact the boys were talking three times more.

78 Political scientist Andrew Hacker, reviewing *Husbands and Wives: A Nationwide Survey of Marriage* by Anthony Pietropinto and Jacqueline Simenauer (New York: Times Books, 1979), has also observed that women frequently give lack of communication as a reason for divorce, whereas men who were parties to the same marriages rarely do. (Hacker, "Divorce à la Mode," *The New York Review of Books,* May 3, 1979, p. 24.)

80 Here again I am drawing on Maltz and Borker, who summarize and integrate the research of others, including Marjorie Harness Goodwin, Barrie Thorne, Donna Eder and Maureen Hallinan, Pamela Fishman, and Janet Lever.

80 The observation that men name their wives as their best friends, whereas women name women friends rather than their husbands, is frequently made. See, for example, Robert Sternberg and Susan Grajek, "The Nature of Love."

88 Smeal was a guest on *The Mike Cuthbert Show,* WAMU, Washington DC, January 17, 1989.

88 Rehm's statement is quoted in Patricia Brennan, "Diane Rehm: Making a Foray from Radio to TV," *The Washington Post TV Week,* August 28–September 3, 1988, p. 8.

89 The concept of "backstage" comes from Erving Goffman, *The Presentation of Self in Everyday Life.*

91 Roberts and Jupp presented the findings of their study at the 1985 Linguistic Institute, Georgetown University.

CHAPTER FOUR
GOSSIP

96 Marge Piercy, *Fly Away Home* (New York: Summit, 1984), p. 235.

97 Eudora Welty, *One Writer's Beginnings* (Cambridge, MA: Harvard University Press, 1984), p. 14.

97 Mary Catherine Bateson, p. 193.

98 Mattison, "New Haven," p. 63.

99 Ann Packer, "Mendocino," *The New Yorker,* June 6, 1988, p. 38.

102 Ursula Le Guin, "In and Out," *The New Yorker,* January 16, 1989, p. 30.

104 Edna O'Brien, "The Widow," *The New Yorker,* January 23, 1989, p. 31.

105 Dan Balz, "The Public Politics of Rumor," *The Washington Post,* June 8, 1989, pp. A1, A10.

106 Nora Ephron, *Heartburn* (New York: Pocket Books, 1983), p. 123.

109 Regarding boys' willingness to talk about problems, Penelope Eckert found a difference among the high school students she studied, depending on whether they were "jocks" or "burnouts": The former don't talk; the latter do.

111 Stephens, p. 13.

112 N. R. Kleinfield, "The Whistle Blower's Morning After," *The New York Times,* November 9, 1986, Section 3, p. 1. The discussion of details in this chapter is drawn from my book *Talking Voices: Repetition, Dialogue, and Imagery in Conversational Discourse.*

113 The detail from Russell Baker's book *The Good Times* is taken from "Restless on His Laurels," a review of Baker's book by R. Z. Shepard, *Time,* June 5, 1989, pp. 83–84.

114 Celia Fremlin, *The Jealous One* (Chicago: Academy, 1985), pp. 16–17. Steve Barish called this excerpt to my attention.

116 Mattison, "Sleeping Giant," p. 124.

118 The article about partners Sherry Turner and Linda Rabbitt, written by Randy Reiland, appeared in *The Washingtonian,* June 1988, p. 34.

118 Elizabeth Loftus, "Trials of an Expert Witness," "My Turn" column, *Newsweek,* June 29, 1987, p. 10.

121 The talk show referred to was *Donahue.* I have paraphrased the comments of the audience member and guest, based on my viewing of the show. The transcript of the show is *Donahue* Transcript #031188, available from Multimedia Entertainment, Inc.

121 The study of male and female therapists is reported in *Psychiatry '86,* August 1986, pp. 1, 6.

CHAPTER FIVE
"I'LL EXPLAIN IT TO YOU":
LECTURING AND LISTENING

129 The reference is to Aries (1982).

130 The reference is to Aries (1976).

131 Fox, p. 61.

132 Mr. H's view of female writing reminded me of the comments I encountered by male critics about the novels of a modern Greek writer, Lilika Nakos. Because her novels captured the rhythms of the conversational idiom, some critics mistook Nakos's achievement. For example, one called her masterful prose a "spontaneous outpouring." Another called it "not literature, but conversation." I cite these and other attributions in my book *Lilika Nakos.*

133 Jules Feiffer, *Grown Ups* (New York: Samuel French, 1982), pp. 7–8, 8–9, and 26–27.

139 A. R. Gurney, "Conversation Piece," "My Turn" column, *Newsweek,* June 26, 1989, pp. 10–11.

139 The reference is to Aries (1976).

142 Maltz and Borker did not do the original research, but rather integrated the findings of a number of other researchers. That women ask more questions and give more listening responses is attributed to research by Pamela Fishman and by Lynette Hirschman. That women

respond more positively is also attributed to them, as well as to Fred Strodtbeck and Richard Mann.

145 The reference is to Aries (1976).

146 Frederick Barthelme, "War with Japan," *The New Yorker*, December 12, 1988, pp. 44, 45.

148 The letter, signed Evelyn Aron, Mexico City, Mexico, appeared in *Psychology Today*, May 1988, p. 5.

CHAPTER SIX
COMMUNITY AND CONTEST: STYLES
IN CONFLICT

150 Articles by Amy Sheldon and by Campbell Leaper review the research on gender and conflict.

150 The quotation is from Ong, p. 51.

151 Blumstein and Schwartz, p. 212.

153 Sachs, p. 183.

153 No page references are given for Goodwin because her book was not yet available when this one went to press.

155 Sachs, pp. 180–181.

156 Rodger Kamenetz, "Confessions of a Meddling Dad," *Working Mother*, May 1989, p. 224.

157 The vertical line indicates overlap: Both girls are speaking at once.

157 The observation that boys prefer competitive games is made by Janet Lever (1978) as well as Goodwin.

158 These complaints did often come to light, and direct confrontation did take place, instigated by a third girl who repeated the criticism. The fight then centered not around the original complaint, but the offense of talking behind someone's back. The same pattern is reported by Amy Shuman, who also observed black junior-high-school girls in Philadelphia.

161 Corsaro and Rizzo, p. 63.

162 Eva Hoffman, *Lost in Translation: A Life in a New Language* (New York: E. P. Dutton, 1989), pp. 18–19.

163 Corsaro and Rizzo, p. 34.

166 Jane Shapiro, "Volpone," *The New Yorker*, November 30, 1987, p. 39.

175 Anne Tyler, *The Accidental Tourist* (New York: Alfred A. Knopf, 1985), p. 280.

176 The reference is to Frank (1988).

176 The students who observed gender differences in the class narratives were Elizabeth Nowell and Lalzarliani Malsawma.

177 I have taken the title of this chapter, "Community and Contest," from the title of Johnstone's article.

179 The quotations from Fox are from pp. 62, 65, and 61, respectively.

180 The reference is to Lever (1978).

180 The reference is to Eckert (1990).

180 The quotation is from Lever (1978), p. 478.

181 Walter Ong attributes the finding that successful women excel in "work competence" to Beverly and Otis Duncan.

183 The statement by Oprah Winfrey is from Mary-Ann Bendel, "TV's Super-Women," *Ladies' Home Journal,* March 1988, p. 170.

184 Jayne Meadows's comments are from Richard Meryman, "The Jayne Meadows Story," *Lear's,* June 1989, p. 84. Steve Allen expressed his view in an interview on *The Diane Rehm Show,* WAMU, Washington, DC, October 11, 1989.

CHAPTER SEVEN
WHO'S INTERRUPTING?
ISSUES OF DOMINANCE
AND CONTROL

This chapter is adapted from my article "Interpreting Interruption in Conversation."

189 The researchers most often cited for the finding that men interrupt women are Candace West and Don Zimmerman (for example, West and Zimmerman, 1983, 1985; Zimmerman and West, 1975). However, many others have come to similar conclusions (for example, Eakins and Eakins, Greif). Deborah James and Janice Drakich are currently reviewing the literature on interruption.

190 The point that violation of speaking rights is a matter of degree is made by Stephen Murray.

191 The example comes from West and Zimmerman, 1983, p. 105. The numbers in parentheses show seconds of pause. Vertical lines show overlap: two voices speaking at once.

193 Transcription is based on Greenwood's, with minor adjustments for readability and changes of names. Vertical lines show latching: The second speaker began with no overlap but no perceptible pause either.

197 Analyzing conversations in which the researcher participated

is a common practice among sociolinguists. The conviction is that what is lost in objectivity is counterbalanced by two crucial gains: the abilities to tape and analyze naturally occurring conversation, and to understand more deeply what was going on.

198 I have adopted the term *latching* from the work of Sacks, Schegloff, and Jefferson. Jane Falk coined the term *conversational duet* and described the phenomenon in which two speakers share a single conversational role.

204 Janice Hornyak recorded, transcribed, and analyzed this excerpt in conjunction with my course in discourse analysis at Georgetown University, spring 1989.

206 My study of indirectness in Greek and American conversational style is reported in Tannen (1982).

206 The excerpt from Durrell's letter to Miller is taken from Vivian Gornick, "Masters of Self-congratulation," a review of *The Durrell-Miller Letters,* ed. by Ian S. MacNiven, in *The New York Times Book Review,* November 20, 1988, p. 47.

207 The quote from Nancy Reagan is from her book, *My Turn,* as excerpted in *Newsweek,* October 23, 1989, p. 66.

209 The argument that Maltz and Borker and I are covering up real male domination with the cross-cultural hypothesis is cogently argued in a paper by Nancy Henley and Cheris Kramarae.

212 Lorrie Moore, "You're Ugly, Too," *The New Yorker,* July 3, 1989 pp. 34, 38, 40.

CHAPTER EIGHT
DAMNED IF YOU DO

217 The reference to Matina Horner's research is taken from Carol Gilligan.

218 Other studies of girls' real conversations include those by Penelope Eckert and by Donna Eder.

221 Bergman, pp. 2–4; Gilligan, pp. 33–34.

223 The epitaph, written by Jane Hines Reis about her sister, Joyce Hines, appeared in *AlumNotes: Hunter College High School Alumanae/i Association,* Fall 1988, pp. 3–4.

225 The article "Sexes: Who's Talking?" by Carol Krucoff appeared in *The Washington Post,* November 9, 1981, p. D5.

226 The research project I refer to is described in Tannen (1982).

228 Aries (1987) reviews studies that tested Lakoff's observation about tag questions.

228 Thorne, Kramarae, and Henley, in a chapter reviewing articles

that compared women's and men's speech, cite many studies that show that women and men are judged differently if they speak the same way.

229 The quotations from Komarovsky are taken from pp. 13, 162, 158, 159, 162, and 353.

230 Erica Jong, *Fear of Flying* (New York: Holt, Rinehart and Winston, 1973), pp. 118–119.

235 Ursula Le Guin, "In and Out," *The New Yorker,* January 16, 1989, p. 31.

236 The reference is to Aries (1982).

236 "The Case for Girls' Schools" is summed up by Elisabeth Griffith, *The Washington Post Education Review,* August 6, 1989. M. Elizabeth Tidball reviews her own and others' research testifying to the superior achievement of graduates of women's colleges. Myra and David Sadker's research shows that girls become "spectators" to the educational process in co-educational classrooms: They are called on far less; when they do contribute to class discussion, their contributions are less likely to be evaluated or engaged at length; and teachers are more inclined to do things for them rather than show them how to do things for themselves.

237 The reference is to Aries (1976).

241 "Language Keeps Women in Their Place" was the headline given by the *St. Louis Post-Dispatch* to an op-ed piece I wrote that appeared October 12, 1984. The same piece also appeared under the headline "How the Instilled Gender Sense of Words Handicapped Ferraro," *Baltimore Evening Sun,* November 9, 1984, p. A15. The last two sections of this chapter are based on material from this piece.

242 The *Newsweek* article appeared on August 6, 1989, p. 17.

243 The photograph of Ferarro and family appears in *Newsweek,* August 27, 1984, p. 21.

CHAPTER NINE
"LOOK AT ME WHEN I'M TALKING TO YOU!": CROSS TALK ACROSS THE AGES

245 With support from the Society for Research in Child Development, Bruce Dorval invited me, along with scholars from several disciplines, to analyze his videotapes. As observed in a note to Chapter Two, Dorval provides a description of his research design, sample transcripts, and analyses of the same data by other scholars in his edited volume *Conversational Coherence and Its Development.* This chapter includes material adapted from my contribution to that volume, "Gen-

der Differences in Conversational Coherence: Physical Alignment and Topical Cohesion," as well as similar material presented in "Gender Differences in Topical Coherence: Creating Involvement in Best Friends' Talk."

256 Thorne, p. 170.

256 I later observed other tapes in Dorval's study and confirmed that they fit the pattern described here.

272 What appears to be a false start (Marsha: "You've got such— You've got such a positive attitude") was occasioned by an interruption. In between these two phrases, the investigator entered the room, in accordance with the experimental design, and briefly reminded the speakers of the task at hand.

CHAPTER TEN
LIVING WITH ASYMMETRY:
OPENING LINES OF COMMUNICATION

280 Gene LePere, *Never Pass This Way Again* (Bethesda, MD: Adler and Adler, 1987).

282 For numerous examples of complementary schismogenesis in relationships, see Watzlawick, Beavin, and Jackson.

283 Here and throughout the chapter, reference is to Goffman's essay "Gender Display" in his book *Gender Advertisements*.

284 "In the Crook of His Neck" is from *Circling Home* (Washington, DC: Scripta Humanistica, 1989), pp. 27–28.

287 "Gender Display," pp. 8–9, 7.

292 *American Couples*, pp. 73–76, 163.

295 Cronk cites University of Toronto anthropologist Richard Lee for information about the !Kung of the Kalahari desert. He ascribes the *moka* ritual to the Mount Hagen tribes of New Guinea and gives similar examples from the Kwakiutl of British Columbia, noting that anthropologists generally use the Chinook Indian term *potlatch* to refer to property-giving ceremonies. I am grateful to Ralph Fasold for calling my attention to this article.

REFERENCES

Anderson, Elaine S. 1977. *Learning to Speak with Style*. Ph.D. dissertation, Stanford University.

Aries, Elizabeth. 1976. "Interaction Patterns and Themes of Male, Female, and Mixed Groups." *Small Group Behavior* 7:1.7–18.

Aries, Elizabeth. 1982. "Verbal and Nonverbal Behavior in Single-Sex and Mixed-Sex Groups: Are Traditional Sex Roles Changing?" *Psychological Reports* 51.127–134.

Aries, Elizabeth. 1987. "Gender and Communication." *Sex and Gender*, ed. by Phillip Shaver and Clyde Hendrick, 149–176. Newbury Park, CA: Sage.

Baron, Dennis. 1986. *Grammar and Gender*. New Haven, CT: Yale University Press.

Bateson, Gregory. 1972. *Steps to an Ecology of Mind*. New York: Ballantine.

Bateson, Mary Catherine. 1984. *With a Daughter's Eye: A Memoir of Margaret Mead and Gregory Bateson*. New York: William Morrow.

Becker, A. L. 1988. "Attunement: An Essay in Philology and Logophilia." *On the Ethnography of Communication: The Legacy of Sapir*. Essays in honor of Harry Hoijer, 1984, ed. by Paul V. Kroskrity, 109–146. Los Angeles: UCLA Department of Anthropology.

Beeman, William O. 1986. *Language, Status, and Power in Iran*. Bloomington: Indiana University Press.

Befu, Harumi. 1986 [1974]. "An Ethnography of Dinner Entertainment in Japan." *Japanese Culture and Behavior,* ed. by Takie Sugiyama Lebra and William P. Lebra, 108–120. Honolulu: University of Hawaii Press.

Bennett, Adrian. 1981. "Interruptions and the Interpretation of Conversation." *Discourse Processes* 4:2.171–188.

Blumstein, Philip, and Pepper Schwartz. 1984. *American Couples: Money, Work, Sex*. New York: William Morrow.

Bohn, Emil, and Randall Stutman. 1983. "Sex-Role Differences in the Relational Control Dimension of Dyadic Interaction." *Women's Studies in Communication* 6.96–104.

Bradley, Patricia Hayes. 1981. "The Folk-Linguistics of Women's Speech:

An Empirical Examination." *Communication Monographs* 48.73–90.

Brooks-Gunn, Jeanne, and Wendy Schempp Matthews. 1979. *He & She: How Children Develop Their Sex Role Identity.* Englewood Cliffs, NJ: Prentice-Hall.

Brown, Penelope. 1990. "Gender, Politeness, and Confrontation in Tenejapa." *Discourse Processes* 13:1.

Brown, Roger, and Albert Gilman. 1960. "The Pronouns of Power and Solidarity." *Style in Language,* ed. by Thomas Sebeok, 253–276. Cambridge, MA: M.I.T. Press.

Caraveli, Anna. 1986. "The Bitter Wounding: The Lament as Social Protest in Rural Greece." *Gender and Power in Rural Greece,* ed. by Jill Dubisch, 169–194. Princetown, NJ: Princeton University Press.

Carson, Gerald. 1966. *The Polite Americans: A Wide-Angle View of Our More or Less Good Manners over 300 Years.* New York: William Morrow.

Chafe, Wallace. 1987. "Humor as a Disabling Mechanism." *American Behavioral Scientist* 30:3.16–25.

Cheepen, Christine. 1988. *The Predictability of Informal Conversation.* London: Pinter. New York: Columbia University Press.

Coates, Jennifer. 1986. *Women, Men, and Language.* London: Longman.

Condry, John, and Sandra Condry. 1976. "Sex Differences: A Study of the Eye of the Beholder." *Child Development* 47.812–819.

Conley, John M., William M. O'Barr, and E. Allen Lind. 1979. "The Power of Language: Presentational Style in the Courtroom." *Duke Law Journal,* Vol. 1978, no. 6.

Corsaro, William, and Thomas Rizzo. 1990. "Disputes in the Peer Culture of American and Italian Nursery School Children." *Conflict Talk,* ed. by Allen Grimshaw, 21–66. Cambridge: Cambridge University Press.

Cronk, Lee. 1989. "Strings Attached." *The Sciences,* May/June, 2–4.

Davies, Bronwyn, and Rom Harré. 1990. "Positioning: Conversation and the Production of Selves." *Journal for the Theory of Social Behaviour* 20:1.

Deakins, Alice H. 1989. *Talk at the Top: Topics at Lunch.* Ms., English Department, William Paterson College.

Dorval, Bruce (ed.). 1990. *Conversational Coherence and Its Development.* Norwood, NJ: Ablex.

Dubisch, Jill. 1986. "Culture Enters Through the Kitchen: Women, Food, and Social Boundaries in Rural Greece." *Gender and Power in Rural Greece,* ed. by Jill Dubisch, 195–214. Princeton, NJ: Princeton University Press.

Duncan, Beverly, and Otis Dudley Duncan. 1978. *Sex Typing and Social Roles.* With the collaboration of James A. McRae, Jr. New York: Academic Press.

Eakins, Barbara Westbrook, and R. Gene Eakins. 1978. *Sex Differences in Communication.* Boston: Houghton Mifflin.

Eble, Connie C. 1976. "Etiquette Books as Linguistic Authority." *The Second LACUS Forum 1975,* ed. by Peter A. Reich, 468–475. Columbia, SC: Hornbeam.

Eckert, Penelope. 1989. *Jocks and Burnouts.* New York: Teachers College Press.

Eckert, Penelope. 1990. "Cooperative Competition in Adolescent 'Girl Talk.' " *Discourse Processes* 13:1.

Edelsky, Carole. 1981. "Who's Got the Floor?" *Language in Society* 10.383–421.

Eder, Donna. 1990. "Serious and Playful Disputes: Variation in Conflict Talk Among Female Adolescents." *Conflict Talk,* ed. by Allen Grimshaw, 67–84. Cambridge: Cambridge University Press.

Eder, Donna, and Maureen Hallinan. 1978. "Sex Differences in Children's Friendships." *American Sociological Review* 43.237–250.

Eder, Donna, and Stephanie Sanford. 1986. "The Development and Maintenance of Interactional Norms Among Early Adolescents." *Sociological Studies of Child Development,* Vol. 1, ed. by Patricia A. Adler and Peter Adler, 283–300. Greenwich, CT: JAI Press.

Erickson, Frederick. 1990. "Social Construction of Discourse Coherence in a Family Dinner Table Conversation." *Conversational Coherence and Its Development,* ed. by Bruce Dorval, 207–238. Norwood, NJ: Ablex.

Esposito, Anita. 1979. "Sex Differences in Children's Conversations." *Language and Speech* 22, Pt. 3, 213–220.

Falk, Jane. 1980. "The Conversational Duet." *Proceedings of the Sixth Annual Meeting of the Berkeley Linguistics Society,* 507–514. Berkeley, CA: Department of Linguistics, University of California.

Fasold, Ralph W. 1990. *The Sociolinguistics of Language.* Oxford: Basil Blackwell.

Fishman, Pamela M. 1978. "Interaction: The Work Women Do." *Social Problems* 25:4.397–406. Revised version in *Language, Gender and Society,* ed. by Barrie Thorne, Cheris Kramarae, and Nancy Henley, 89–101. Rowley, MA: Newbury House, 1983.

Fox, Thomas. 1990. "Gender Interests in Reading and Writing." *The Social Uses of Writing: Politics and Pedagogy,* 51–70. Norwood, NJ: Ablex.

Frank, Jane. 1988. "A Comparison of Intimate Conversations: Pragmatic Theory Applied to Examples of Invented and Actual Dialog." *The SECOL Review* 12:3.186–208.

Frank, Jane. 1989. "Communicating 'by Pairs': Agreeing and Disagreeing Among Married Couples." Ms., Georgetown University.

Friedrich, Paul. 1972. "Social Context and Semantic Feature: The Russian Pronominal Usage." *Directions in Sociolinguistics,* ed. by John J. Gumperz and Dell Hymes, 270–300. New York: Holt, Rinehart and Winston. Reprint, Oxford: Basil Blackwell.

Geis, Michael L. 1987. *The Language of Politics.* New York: Springer-Verlag.

Gilligan, Carol. 1982. *In a Different Voice: Psychological Theory and Women's Development.* Cambridge, MA: Harvard University Press.

Gleason, Jean Berko. 1987. "Sex Differences in Parent-Child Interaction." *Language, Gender, and Sex in Comparative Perspective,* ed. by Susan U. Philips, Susan Steele, and Christine Tanz, 189–199. Cambridge: Cambridge University Press.

Gleason, Jean Berko, and Esther Blank Greif. 1983. "Men's Speech to Young Children." *Language, Gender and Society,* ed. by Barrie Thorne, Cheris Kramarae, and Nancy Henley, 140–150. Rowley, MA: Newbury House.

Goffman, Erving. 1959. *The Presentation of Self in Everyday Life.* Garden City, NY: Doubleday.

Goffman, Erving. 1967. *Interaction Ritual.* Garden City, NY: Doubleday.

Goffman, Erving. 1974. *Frame Analysis.* New York: Harper and Row.

Goffman, Erving. 1979. "Gender Display." *Gender Advertisements,* 1–9. New York: Harper and Row.

Goffman, Erving. 1981. "Footing." *Forms of Talk,* 124–159. Philadelphia: University of Pennsylvania Press.

Goodwin, Marjorie Harness. In press. *He-Said-She-Said: Talk as Social Organization Among Black Children.* Bloomington: Indiana University Press.

Goodwin, Marjorie Harness, and Charles Goodwin. 1987. "Children's Arguing." *Language, Gender, and Sex in Comparative Perspective,* ed. by Susan U. Philips, Susan Steele, and Christine Tanz, 200–248. Cambridge: Cambridge University Press.

Greenwood, Alice. 1989. *Discourse Variation and Social Comfort: A Study of Topic Initiation and Interruption Patterns in the Dinner Conversation of Preadolescent Children.* Ph.D. dissertation, City University of New York.

Greif, Esther Blank. 1980. "Sex Differences in Parent-Child Conversations." *Women's Studies International Quarterly* 3:2/3.253–258.

REFERENCES

Hayashi, Reiko. 1988. "Simultaneous Talk—from the Perspective of Floor Management of English and Japanese Speakers." *World Englishes* 7:3.269–288.

Henley, Nancy, and Cheris Kramarae. Forthcoming. "Miscommunication, Gender and Power." *Handbook of Miscommunication and Problematic Talk,* ed. by Nikolas Coupland, John Wiemann, and Howard Giles. Bristol: Multilingual Matters.

Hill, Alette Olin. 1986. *Mother Tongue, Father Time: A Decade of Linguistic Revolt.* Bloomington: Indiana University Press.

Hirschman, Lynette. 1973. "Female-Male Differences in Conversational Interaction." Paper presented at the annual meeting of the Linguistic Society of America, San Diego, CA.

Hoffman, Eva. 1989. *Lost in Translation: A Life in a New Language.* New York: E. P. Dutton.

Horner, Matina S. 1972. "Toward an Understanding of Achievement-Related Conflicts in Women." *Journal of Social Issues* 28.157–175.

Hughes, Linda A. 1988. " 'But That's Not *Really* Mean': Competing in a Cooperative Mode." *Sex Roles* 19:11/12.669–687.

James, Deborah, and Janice Drakich. 1989. "Understanding Gender Differences in Amount of Talk." Ms., Linguistics Department, University of Toronto, Scarborough Campus.

Jefferson, Gail. 1988. "On the Sequential Organization of Troubles-Talk in Ordinary Conversation." *Social Problems* 35:4.418–441.

Johnstone, Barbara. 1989. "Community and Contest: How Women and Men Construct Their Worlds in Conversational Narrative." Paper presented at Women in America: Legacies of Race and Ethnicity, Georgetown University, Washington, DC.

Kalčik, Susan. 1975. " '. . . Like Ann's Gynecologist or the Time I Was Almost Raped': Personal Narratives in Women's Rap Groups." *Journal of American Folklore* 88:3–11. Reprinted in *Women and Folklore,* ed. by Claire R. Farrer. Austin: University of Texas Press.

Keenan, Elinor. 1974. "Norm-makers, Norm-breakers: Uses of Speech by Men and Women in a Malagasy Community." *Explorations in the Ethnography of Speaking,* ed. by Richard Bauman and Joel Sherzer, 125–143. Cambridge: Cambridge University Press.

Keller, Evelyn Fox. 1985. *Reflections on Gender and Science.* New Haven, CT: Yale University Press.

Kennedy, Robinette. 1986. "Women's Friendships on Crete: A Psychological Perspective." *Gender and Power in Rural Greece,* ed. by Jill Dubisch, 121–138. Princeton, NJ: Princeton University Press.

Komarovsky, Mirra. 1962. *Blue-Collar Marriage.* New York: Vintage.

Kramarae, Cheris. 1981. *Women and Men Speaking*. Rowley, MA: Newbury House.

Kuipers, Joel C. 1986. "Talking About Troubles: Gender Differences in Weyewa Speech Use." *American Ethnologist* 13:3.448–462.

Labov, William. 1972. "The Linguistic Consequences of Being a Lame." *Language in the Inner City*, 255–292. Philadelphia: University of Pennsylvania Press.

Labov, William, and David Fanshel. 1977. *Therapeutic Discourse*. New York: Academic Press.

Lakoff, Robin. 1975. *Language and Woman's Place*. New York: Harper and Row.

Lange, Deborah. 1988. "Using *Like* to Introduce Constructed Dialogue: How *Like* Contributes to Discourse Coherence." Master's thesis, Georgetown University.

Leaper, Campbell. 1988. "The Sequencing of Power and Involvement in Girls' and Boys' Talk." Ms. submitted for publication, Psychology Department, University of California, Santa Cruz.

Leet-Pellegrini, H. M. 1980. "Conversational Dominance as a Function of Gender and Expertise." *Language: Social Psychological Perspectives,* ed. by Howard Giles, W. Peter Robinson, and Philip M. Smith, 97–104. Oxford: Pergamon.

Leffler, Ann, D. L. Gillespie, and J. C. Conaty. 1982. "The Effects of Status Differentiation on Nonverbal Behavior." *Social Psychology Quarterly* 45:3.153–161.

Lehtonen, Jaakko, and Kari Sajavaara. 1985. "The Silent Finn." *Perspectives on Silence,* ed. by Deborah Tannen and Muriel Saville-Troike, 193–201. Norwood, NJ: Ablex.

Lever, Janet. 1976. "Sex Differences in the Games Children Play." *Social Problems* 23.478–483.

Lever, Janet. 1978. "Sex Differences in the Complexity of Children's Play and Games." *American Sociological Review* 43.471–483.

Linde, Charlotte. 1988. "The Use of Narrative in the Negotiation of Values: Group Identity in an Airborne Police Agency." Paper presented at the annual meeting of the Linguistic Society of America, New Orleans.

Macke, Anne Statham, and Laurel Walum Richardson, with Judith Cook. 1980. *Sex-Typed Teaching Styles of University Professors and Student Reactions*. Columbus: Ohio State University Research Foundation.

Maltz, Daniel N., and Ruth A. Borker. 1982. "A Cultural Approach to Male-Female Miscommunication." *Language and Social Identity,* ed. by John J. Gumperz, 196–216. Cambridge: Cambridge University Press.

Mitchell, Carol. 1985. "Some Differences in Male and Female Joke-Telling." *Women's Folklore, Women's Culture*, ed. by Rosan A. Jordan and Susan J. Kalčik, 163–186. Philadelphia: University of Pennsylvania Press.

Moerman, Michael. 1987. "Finding Life in Dry Dust." *Talking Culture: Ethnography and Conversation Analysis*, 19–30. Philadelphia: University of Pennsylvania Press.

Murray, Stephen O. 1985. "Toward a Model of Members' Methods for Recognizing Interruptions." *Language in Society* 13.31–41.

Newcombe, Nora, and Diane Arnkoff. 1979. "Effects of Speech Style and Sex of Speaker on Person Perception." *Journal of Personality and Social Psychology* 37.1293–1303.

Newman, Barbara Miller. 1971. *Interpersonal Behavior and Preferences for Exploration in Adolescent Boys: A Small Group Study*. Ph.D. dissertation, University of Michigan.

Ong, Walter J., S. J. 1981. *Fighting for Life: Contest, Sexuality, and Consciousness*. Ithaca, NY: Cornell University Press. Paperback: Amherst, MA: University of Massachusetts Press, 1989.

Philipsen, Gerry. 1975. "Speaking 'Like a Man' in Teamsterville: Culture Patterns of Role Enactment in an Urban Neighborhood." *Quarterly Journal of Speech* 61.13–22.

Reisman, Karl. 1974. "Contrapuntal Conversations in an Antiguan Village." *Explorations in the Ethnography of Speaking*, ed. by Richard Bauman and Joel Sherzer, 110–124. Cambridge: Cambridge University Press.

Riessman, Catherine Kohler. In press. *Divorce Talk: Women and Men Make Sense of Personal Relationships*. New Brunswick, NJ: Rutgers University Press.

Sachs, Jacqueline. 1987. "Young Children's Language Use in Pretend Play." *Language, Gender, and Sex in Comparative Perspective*, ed. by Susan U. Philips, Susan Steele, and Christine Tanz, 178–188. Cambridge: Cambridge University Press.

Sacks, Harvey, Emanuel A Schegloff, and Gail Jefferson. 1974. "A Simplest Systematics for the Organization of Turntaking for Conversation." *Language* 50:4.696–735.

Sadker, Myra, and David Sadker. 1985. "Sexism in the Schoolroom of the '80s." *Psychology Today*, March 1985, 54–57.

Sadker, Myra, and David Sadker. 1986. "Sexism in the Classroom: From Grade School to Graduate School." *Phi Delta Kappan* 67:7.

Sattel, Jack W. 1983. "Men, Inexpressiveness, and Power." *Language, Gender and Society*, ed. by Barrie Thorne, Cheris Kramarae, and Nancy Henley, 119–124. Rowley, MA: Newbury House.

Schiffrin, Deborah. 1984. "Jewish Argument as Sociability." *Language in Society* 13:3.311–335.

Scollon, Ron. 1982. "The Rhythmic Integration of Ordinary Talk." *Analyzing Discourse: Text and Talk. Georgetown University Round Table on Languages and Linguistics 1981,* ed. by Deborah Tannen, 335–349. Washington, DC: Georgetown University Press.

Scollon, Ron, and Suzanne B. K. Scollon. 1981. *Narrative, Literacy and Face in Interethnic Communication.* Norwood, NJ: Ablex.

Sheldon, Amy. 1990. "Pickle Fights: Gendered Talk in Preschool Disputes." *Discourse Processes* 13:1.

Sherzer, Joel. 1987. "A Diversity of Voices: Men's and Women's Speech in Ethnographic Perspective. *Language Gender, and Sex in Comparative Perspective,* ed. by Susan U. Philips, Susan Steele, and Christine Tanz, 95–120. Cambridge: Cambridge University Press.

Shultz, Jeffrey, Susan Florio, and Frederick Erickson. 1982. "Where's the Floor? Aspects of the Cultural Organization of Social Relationships in Communication at Home and at School." *Ethnography and Education: Children in and out of School,* ed. by Perry Gilmore and Alan Glatthorn, 88–123. Washington, DC: Center for Applied Linguistics (distributed by Ablex, Norwood, NJ).

Shuman, Amy. 1986. *Storytelling Rights: The Uses of Oral and Written Texts by Urban Adolescents.* Cambridge: Cambridge University Press.

Siegler, David M., and Robert S. Siegler. 1976. "Stereotypes of Males' and Females' Speech." *Psychological Reports* 39.167–170.

Smith, Frances. 1990. *Gender and the Framing of Exegetical Authority in Sermon Performances.* Ph.D. dissertation, Georgetown University.

Spender, Dale. 1980. *Man Made Language.* London: Routledge and Kegan Paul.

Stephens, Mitchell. 1988. *A History of News: From the Drum to the Satellite.* New York: Viking.

Sternberg, Robert J., and Susan Grajek. 1984. "The Nature of Love." *Journal of Personality and Social Psychology* 47.312–329.

Strodtbeck, Fred L., and Richard D. Mann. 1956. "Sex Role Differentiation in Jury Deliberations." *Sociometry* 19.3–11.

Swacker, Marjorie. 1976. "Women's Verbal Behavior at Learned and Professional Conferences." *The Sociology of the Languages of American Women,* ed. by Betty Lou Dubois and Isabel Crouch, 155–160. San Antonio: Trinity University.

Tannen, Deborah. 1982. "Ethnic Style in Male-Female Conversation." *Language and Social Identity,* ed. by John J. Gumperz, 217–231. Cambridge: Cambridge University Press.

Tannen, Deborah. 1983. *Lilika Nakos*. Boston: G. K. Hall.

Tannen, Deborah. 1984. *Conversational Style: Analyzing Talk Among Friends*. Norwood, NJ: Ablex.

Tannen, Deborah. 1986. *That's Not What I Meant! How Conversational Style Makes or Breaks Your Relations with Others*. New York: William Morrow.

Tannen, Deborah. 1989. "Interpreting Interruption in Conversation." *Papers from the 25th Annual Regional Meeting of the Chicago Linguistic Society. Part Two: Parasession on Language in Context*, ed. by Bradley Music, Randolph Graczyk, and Caroline Wiltshire, 266–287. Chicago: Chicago Linguistic Society.

Tannen, Deborah. 1989. *Talking Voices: Repetition, Dialogue, and Imagery in Conversational Discourse*. Cambridge: Cambridge University Press.

Tannen, Deborah. 1990. "Gender Differences in Conversational Coherence: Physical Alignment and Topical Cohesion." *Conversational Coherence and Its Development*, ed. by Bruce Dorval, 167–206. Norwood, NJ: Ablex.

Tannen, Deborah. 1990. "Gender Differences in Topical Coherence: Creating Involvement in Best Friends' Talk." *Discourse Processes* 13:1.

Thorne, Barrie. 1986. "Girls and Boys Together . . . but Mostly Apart: Gender Arrangements in Elementary Schools." *Relationships and Development*, ed. by Willard W. Hartup and Zick Rubin, 167–184. Hillsdale, NJ: Erlbaum.

Thorne, Barrie, Cheris Kramarae, and Nancy Henley. 1983. "Language, Gender and Society: Opening a Second Decade of Research." *Language, Gender and Society*, ed. by Barrie Thorne, Cheris Kramarae, and Nancy Henley, 7–24. Rowley, MA: Newbury House.

Tidball, M. Elizabeth. 1989. "Women's Colleges: Exceptional Conditions, Not Exceptional Talent, Produce High Achievers." *Educating the Majority: Women Challenge the Tradition*, ed. by Carol S. Pearson, Donna L. Shavlik, and Judith G. Touchton, 157–172. New York: Macmillan.

Wall, Harriet M., and Anita Barry. 1985. "Student Expectations for Male and Female Instructor Behavior." *Women in Higher Education: Traditions, Transitions and Revolutions*, ed. by Roy E. Cheatham, 283–291. Proceedings for Women in Higher Education Conferences. St. Louis: Saint Louis University, Metropolitan College, and SAASS, Inc.

Watson, Karen A. 1975. "Transferable Communicative Routines." *Language in Society* 4.53–72.

REFERENCES

Watzlawick, Paul, Janet Helmick Beavin, and Don D. Jackson. 1967. *The Pragmatics of Human Communication.* New York: Norton.

West, Candace, and Don H. Zimmerman. 1983. "Small Insults: A Study of Interruptions in Cross-Sex Conversations Between Unacquainted Persons." *Language, Gender, and Society,* ed. by Barrie Thorne, Cheris Kramarae, and Nancy Henley, 103–117. Rowley, MA: Newbury House.

West, Candace, and Don H. Zimmerman. 1985. "Gender, Language, and Discourse." *Handbook of Discourse Analysis,* Vol. 4: *Discourse Analysis in Society,* ed. by Teun A. van Dijk, 103–124. London: Academic Press.

White, Jane J. 1989. "The Power of Politeness in the Classroom: Cultural Codes That Create and Constrain Knowledge Construction." *Journal of Curriculum and Supervision* 4:4.298–321.

Yamada, Haru. 1989. *American and Japanese Topic Management Strategies in Business Conversations.* Ph.D. dissertation, Georgetown University.

Zimmerman, Don H., and Candace West. 1975. "Sex Roles, Interruptions and Silences in Conversation." *Language and Sex: Difference and Dominance,* ed. by Barrie Thorne and Nancy Henley, 105–129. Rowley, MA: Newbury House.

INDEX

Deborah Tannen, Ph.D., is professor of linguistics at Georgetown University. She has received grants from the Rockefeller Foundation, the National Endowment for the Humanities, and the National Science Foundation. She has written numerous scholarly books and articles, as well as articles that appeared in *The New York Times Magazine, Vogue, New York Magazine,* and *The Washington Post.* She lives with her husband in Washington, D.C.